BLACK TITAN *W. E. B. DU BOIS*

BLACK TITAN
W. E. B. Du Bois

AN ANTHOLOGY BY
THE EDITORS OF
FREEDOMWAYS

JOHN HENRIK CLARKE
ESTHER JACKSON
ERNEST KAISER
J. H. O'DELL

BEACON PRESS BOSTON

Library of Congress catalog card number: 71–119675
International Standard Book Number: 0–8070–5446–1 (casebound)
0–8070–5447–X (paperback)

Beacon Press books are published under the auspices
of the Unitarian Universalist Association

Published simultaneously in Canada by Saunders of Toronto, Ltd.

Printed in the United States of America

The Editors gratefully acknowledge permission to use the following material in this book:

"W. E. B. Du Bois and the Black Messianic Vision," by Vincent Harding. Used by permission of the author. The writings of W. E. B. Du Bois used with the permission of Bernard Jaffe, legal representative of Shirley Graham Du Bois. "50 Years After," by W. E. B. Du Bois, from the Fawcett Premier Edition of *The Souls of Black Folk* by W. E. B. Du Bois, copyright 1953 by W. E. Burghardt Du Bois. Used with the publisher's permission.

Introduction to the Fawcett Premier Edition by Saunders Redding, copyright © 1961, Fawcett Publications, Inc., used with the publisher's permission. The poem "Nocturne at Bethesda" by Arna Bontemps, copyright 1926 by Arna Bontemps, copyright renewed. Used with permission of Harold Ober Associates, Inc., and Mr. Bontemps.

Contributions first published in *Freedomways* are copyright by Freedomways Associates, Inc., and are reprinted here with their permission.

Contents

PART THREE · W. E. B. DU BOIS AS AN ACTIVIST

PART FOUR · DU BOIS: INTERNATIONAL MAN

PART FIVE · HIS WRITING

Introduction

Above all else he was a teacher, this Black Titan, this most remarkable man of enormous energy and great talent, William Edward Burghardt Du Bois. It was through his teachings that he exerted his leadership upon his people and developed the concept of Pan Africanism. This influence reverberated in Africa, the Caribbean Islands, and other areas of the world where African people are predominant. Later he urged Afro-Americans to move toward socialism as a solution to their problems and for the progress of mankind.

His wisdom and his teachings are a legacy for the ages. More than twenty volumes of major works were published by Du Bois, and now many more additional volumes of his collected articles and letters will be published. In his lifetime he wrote with insight on a wide range of subjects and left behind volumes of work setting forth the most dependable guidelines for the future of his people.

The main thing that this great teacher sought to instruct the Black man in and warn the unheeding about was best expressed by Du Bois when, remarking upon the essence of John Brown's legacy, he said

> [He] taught us that the cheapest price to pay for liberty is its cost today. (page 402)

> The cost of liberty is thus a decreasing cost, while the cost of repression tends to increase . . . (page 395)

The antecedents of the modern-day Black liberation movement go back to the antislavery emancipatory and militant abolitionist movements. The towering figure of the fugitive slave, Frederick Douglass, dominates the whole abolitionist period, certainly the foremost Black historical figure of the nineteenth century. Yet, it is Du Bois who is truly the father of the modern Black liberation movement, the twentieth-century leader of the struggle against racial oppression and discrimination at home and for national liberation from the yoke of colonialism abroad.

Early in his career as a concerned and committed man of color occupying himself with the task of removing all color bars to the progress of his people, Du Bois sought to appeal to advanced American self-interest and an enlightened world public opinion as levers to raise the cause of Black freedom to the level of national and world politics. With undeflectable dedication and discipline he brought into play the wide range of his talents to serve the cause of his people's true emancipation. At one time or another, he taught history, economics, sociology, Greek, Latin, and English literature. He was a journalist without peer, his commentaries and editorials in the *Crisis* magazine addressed the nation and the world on all the vital topics of the times for decades. A pioneer social-historian and the first American to develop a scientific method of sociology, Du Bois was never an ivy-tower researcher but a front-ranks activist who welded learning and culture as weapons of battle in the service of Black liberation.

In his long lifetime, W. E. B. Du Bois involved himself on every level of his people's struggle for survival and basic dignity. He was the prime inspirer, philosopher, and father of organized Afro-American protest movements and a founding member of the NAACP. He was primarily responsible for guiding Black Americans away from accommodation to the system of racial segregation, as advocated by Booker T. Washington, to militant opposition to any system which regarded Black people as less than men and citizens. At a time when some public men of power and national influence were urging Black Americans to forego basic and civil rights in favor of obtaining recognition and advancement through industrial training and the acquisition of property, Dr. Du Bois continued to demand the rights to vote, to civic equality on every level, and to education of youth, according to their ability.

Du Bois saw the interrelatedness and interconnection of social problems and was an internationalist at an early age. He showed the meaning of Africa to the American Negro through his writings and lectures and helped the African peoples to beat the drums of anticolonialism faster and louder. He would say with the great Frederick Douglass, "A blow struck for freedom anywhere is a blow for freedom everywhere." The battle flags of all who rose up against colonialism, militarism and racism were his battle standards as well.

It is best said of Du Bois that he wrote of John Brown,

> He believed in the abilities and worth of the souls of Black folk. He believed in the gifts that they would be able to furnish America and he regarded them as equals to all Americans of any color. He believed that men should labor for what they earned and should not get their income by chance or inheritance. He believed in the freedom of the land and its fruits to be distributed in accord with the labor which was put upon it. Thus he was a pioneer in the fight for human equality and in the uplift of the masses of men. (*John Brown,* page 400)

We are proud that *Freedomways* was a project that engaged the thought and energies of Dr. Du Bois in the year before he left for Africa to edit the *Encyclopedia Africana.* He shared with us his many years of editing experience and launched into the numerous details of preparing the first issue for the printer with zest, humor, and the projection of confident enthusiasm.

This book is an extension of the special W. E. B. Du Bois Memorial issue of *Freedomways* magazine (Vol. 5, No. 1, Winter 1965). This special issue was planned and published before the current interest in the life and works of Dr. Du Bois that has resulted in a large number of his works' being brought back into print.

In this volume have been assembled a collection of writings by a distinguished group of authors and public personalities who plumb the real meaning of the man to his time and to the fate of the cause to which he devoted all the day of his long and prolific life. We have proud confidence that the collective assessment in this book may well become a classic statement on the life and works of this truly great man.

The Editors

PART ONE

TRIBUTES

Letter from Kwame Nkrumah

We in Ghana remember Dr. Du Bois as a brilliant scholar, a great champion in the struggle for the rights of man, and an undaunted fighter against racial inequality, discrimination, and injustice.

I am therefore particularly happy to be able to send a commemorative message on this occasion and to say how dearly we cherish the memory of Dr. Du Bois. He was not only a champion of the oppressed, but also a source of inspiration in our struggle for freedom and the right of the African to govern himself. We are fortunate and honored that Dr. Du Bois chose to spend his last years in Ghana and dedicated those years to laying the foundation for compiling the *Encyclopedia Africana,* a project in which his intellectual life found a fitting consummation.

May his life and work be an inspiration to all who fight for human dignity.

KWAME NKRUMAH

FLAGSTAFF HOUSE
ACCRA
GHANA

Letter from Nnamdi Azikiwe

Dr. Du Bois was a pioneer reformer who dreamt dreams of a free Africa. His efforts from the beginning of this century until his death in 1963 have distinguished him as a hero and prophet of his age.

It was this great leader who predicted that the "Problem of the twentieth century is the problem of the color line." It is significant that this thinker was able to implement his ideas during his lifetime. For example, his founding of the Pan-African Congress in 1919, in Paris, was a signal for the historic struggle by African nationalists which led ultimately to the political emancipation of this continent.

His influence as a writer and reformer will never diminish and the monument to his greatness, vividly apparent in his many published works, will always serve to guide men and women everywhere in the holy crusade for human freedom.

NNAMDI AZIKIWE
President of the Federal
Republic of Nigeria

STATE HOUSE
LAGOS
NIGERIA

Shirley Graham Du Bois

For W. E. B. Du Bois there must be no idle mourning. *He lives* in greater abundance than ever before. *He lives* on both sides of the Atlantic. From the campuses of America's leading universities youth sends his name like a flame across the land. In Africa they pass on the words of "Our Father," sometimes "The Oldest Freedom Fighter," as Pan-Africanism unfolds over the vast continent, and his valiant, noble son, Nkrumah, steadily, undaunted, presses forward, leading Africa ever nearer to strong, united, continental oneness!

He lives in the face of every black child who laughs with joy; he lives in the orange trees he planted in the garden, in the fragrant blooms that climb up to his window. He lives in our deepest convictions, faith, work, and dreams.

"You will never be alone," he promised me. And W. E. B. Du Bois always keeps his promise.

Roy Wilkins

In his long and fruitful life William Edward Burghardt Du Bois was cast in many illustrious roles—scholar, teacher, historian, sociologist, author, and editor. But his greatest and most enduring impact upon his times stemmed from his role as philosopher and leader of the civil rights movement, particularly during the nearly thirty years he served with the National Association for the Advancement of Colored People.

Dr. Du Bois was not only the philosopher and leader but, more importantly, the sire of the modern Negro protest movement. He was an inspirer and a founder of the NAACP. At a time when compulsory racial segregation seemed a fixed and permanent pattern in the South and was creeping throughout the nation, Dr. Du Bois sharply challenged the morality, feasibility, and constitutionality of this racial denial of basic human rights.

A resolution, passed by the NAACP Board of Directors at its quarterly meeting on September 9, 1963, said: "It was Dr. Du Bois who was primarily responsible for guiding the Negro away from accommodation to racial segregation to militant opposition to any system which degraded black people by imposing upon them a restricted status separate and apart from their fellow citizens."

In the early years, only a small band of Negro intellectuals and the remnants of the radical Abolition movement consistently stood with Dr. Du Bois in challenging the destructive power of Jim Crow. He continued to assail this iniquity in searing essays as well as in barbed editorials in *The Crisis,* the NAACP organ, which he founded and edited for a quarter of a century. His brilliant exposition and his unrelenting attacks swelled the ranks of the anti-segregation forces. Fortunately he lived to see constitutional sanction of this infamy stricken down by the United States Supreme Court.

A gifted writer, Dr. Du Bois articulated the aspirations and demands of the Negroes as no one had done before. Steeped in the history of the Negro, he instilled pride of race in young colored people. A crusader for human rights, he was an early foe of colonialism, an uncompromising champion of African nationalism, and an ardent advocate of the spiritual unity of peoples of African descent the world over. A seer, he prophetically warned at the turn of the century: "The problem of the twentieth century is the problem of the color line—the relation of the darker to the lighter races of men in Asia and Africa, in America and the islands of the sea."

Not only his fellow Negro Americans, but the whole of America and the children of Africa wherever they may live have been enriched by the life and work of Dr. Du Bois. He was the inspirer of a new, freer way of life for all of us, white as well as black. His brilliant, vigorous and sustained assault upon the citadel of Jim Crow contributed immeasurably to the present breaching of that sinister barrier. Within twenty-four hours of his passing in faraway Accra, the idea of freedom for black people which he fostered bloomed into its most massive expression as more than 200,000 men, women, and children gathered in Washington, August 28, 1963, to present demands for full equality now.

It is timely and fitting that *Freedomways* published this Du Bois Memorial Issue as a tribute to his illustrious career without which life in the United States may well have been vastly different, and far less hopeful, than it is today. That conditions are not as they were in 1910 and that hope and the prospect of a brighter future are better than ever before may be attributed in large measure to the dedication, talent, and foresight of William Edward Burghardt Du Bois.

Langston Hughes

So many thousands of my generation were uplifted and inspired by the written and spoken words of Dr. W. E. B. Du Bois that for me to say I was so inspired would hardly be unusual. My earliest memories of written words are of those of Du Bois and the Bible. My maternal grandmother in Kansas, the last surviving widow of John Brown's Raid, read to me as a child from both the Bible and *The Crisis*. And one of the first books I read on my own was *The Souls of Black Folk*. Years later, my earliest poems were accepted for publication by *The Crisis* under the editorship of Dr. Du Bois. It seems as if, one way or another, I knew Dr. Du Bois all my life. Through his work, he became a part of my life.

Ruby Dee

My closest association with Dr. Du Bois is through a brief essay he wrote in 1900. In searching over the years for special material to do on platforms, street corners, and stages for brotherhoods, sisterhoods, unions, schools, demonstrations, I came upon the *Credo*. I read it over and over with joy—I had found something to balance selections on frustration and anger—I had found an affirmation, a prayer, a poem, a longing for humanity to fulfill its promise of greatness. For a long time, after the discovery, I felt a program was not complete, no matter what went before, without concluding with the *Credo*.

For reasons I mention now, however, I confess to having altered it a little. In the first paragraph he says, "I believe that all men, black and brown and white, are brothers." I took the liberty of adding "yellow" because I felt he would have approved. In 1904 he had not yet been to China; he had not known the Chinese people. For a while I omitted the second paragraph which begins, "Especially do I believe in the Negro Race. . . ." That statement seemed chauvinistic, exclusive, and too special. Wasn't it inclusion we were struggling for? Later, I came to realize that belief in ourselves had not been allowed; belief had been systematically and ruthlessly beaten down. Belief in self needed attention. The scars on "Negroness" had to be removed . . . Du Bois, the prophet, knew the need; and in that paragraph he reminds us of the soul sweetness, the beauty, and the strength of our people—essential to inclusion. I say it now; I know he understands the slow acceptance.

I have never included the fifth paragraph which begins, "I believe in the devil and his angels." I feel the *Credo* is an affirmation —a holding on to the reality of (the possibility) of mankind's strength. I think the note of aspiration would become clouded. "Devil" may be a reality, but to believe in him at this point changes the emphasis on hope.

If, on occasion, after much repetition, my approach to the *Credo* is less than inspired, I know that soon the paragraph will come in which he sets forth the heart of all our essential yearning. A belief in the possibility of "Life lit by some large vision of beauty and goodness and truth." At this point, the words seem to take wings.

He concludes with his belief in "Patience." At first I thought he meant a patience that I had learned about as a child—a patience of slaves, of black suffering people, a patience from the Bible. Now I know he meant a working patience, a loving, fighting patience, a learning, planning, dedicated patience. A patience near the end of its rope.

It is tremendously satisfying for a performer to have the opportunity to bring from the page beautiful ideas and to try to make them live. At such times, we would like to have more incisive understanding, to be more capable of communication, and to be much better human beings. Shakespeare inspires actors in such a way. W. E. B. Du Bois, philosopher, author, *man,* has this meaning for me even more particularly.

Horace Mann Bond

My father was a charter subscriber to *The Crisis* magazine when it began publication in 1910. This was the year when I had my sixth birthday and, as I note from a letter written by my mother to a friend that year, advanced from the First to the Second Reader.

I was an avid reader of *The Crisis,* from my earliest literate days. We lived in rural Kentucky places and my isolation from the world was the greater because I read omnivorously. Through *The Crisis* Du Bois helped shape my inner world to a degree impossible to imagine in the world of contemporary children, and the flood of various mass media to which they are exposed. I remember the pleasant faces of brown and black children pictured in the magazine; I remember the photographs of decently garbed men and women of color, never seen elsewhere in the publications that came to our home; and I remember, also, the horrifying cartoons depicting "lynch law" that frequently appeared in the magazine. Indeed, I remember a period during which the same frightening nightmare would recur, night after night; I was being pursued by the grisly form of "lynch law," to awaken only at that dreadful moment, when the monster has you immobilized at last and you realize that you cannot escape him.

The cartoons were strong stuff for a child, perhaps, as were the factual accounts of the lynchings through burnings, ending with fragments of fingers and toes for sale as souvenirs for the mob; the lynchings through hangings, the lynchings through gun shot, the mass lynchings through disfranchisement and discrimination and brutalizing oppressions of all sorts. Yet I am glad that through Du Bois I had these vicarious experiences with the real and brutal world of race and color, as with the real world of black men and women clothed in beauty and dignity.

A number of years later—in 1924—Dr. Du Bois published, as editor of *The Crisis,* the first article I had to appear in a nationally circulated journal. Two years later, he provided me with a small grant from the Garland Fund, through which I was able to contribute to a national survey he was then conducting of the education of Negroes. My assignment was Oklahoma. These were small beginnings; but they were truly "seed" grants in inspiring and confirming my bent toward writing and research.

And Africa! For an American child growing up between 1910 and 1920, there was scarcely an antidote anywhere for the poisonous picture of Africa, and of Africans, painted in the school geographies, the newspapers and magazines, and by the movies. *The Crisis* magazine gave me the one antidote available. From the earliest day of *The Crisis,* Africans were revealed as intelligent human beings. I have long counted it as one of my great blessings that I read Du Bois on Africa when I was very young.

The real truth about a brutal social order, however frightening; the beauty and dignity of black people; these learnings were almost impossible to come by, for children of whatever color or race in the United States, when I was a child. This is what I know that Du Bois did for me. I believe he was the teacher, likewise, of a host of other persons in this country, and throughout the world. For me, and for others, he was the Great Revelator.

Henry Arthur Callis

My childhood and youth were spent in western New York state, chiefly in Rochester. This city was still the center of racial liberalism. Frederick Douglass had lived there and in 1895 he was buried near the entrance of Mount Hope Cemetery. In the year of Douglass' death, I was stunned by the racial philosophy proposed at the Atlanta Cotton Exposition by Booker T. Washington.

In 1885 the Supreme Court had declared unconstitutional the Civil Rights Act of 1875. By 1901 the freedman had lost all his rights in the former Confederate States. I was enheartened by the Niagara Conference called in 1905 by Dr. Du Bois and held in July in a hotel on the Canadian side of the Niagara River. No American hotel would receive the twenty-nine men from fourteen states who met together and formulated the Niagara Manifesto—the first demand for full manhood rights of the American Negro after Reconstruction.

In September 1905, I was one of a half dozen of our young men entering Cornell University. We were serious. Dr. Du Bois had inspired us. In 1906 we formed a study group. We were convinced that leadership in the struggle to overcome race prejudice in America depended upon college trained young people. "The talented tenth," Dr. Du Bois had heralded as the hope of the Negro American rather than the humble servitor prescribed by Booker T. Washington's program. In a nation at the crest of uncurbed industrialization, the Washington philosophy had already been outmoded. In December 1906, the study club evolved into a fraternity and was incorporated under New York state laws for the purpose of stimulating education and developing leadership among Negroes in America.

During the spring of 1909, I traveled to the University of Michigan to establish our fifth chapter. A few weeks later Dr. Du Bois was speaking there. He learned of our movement and its purpose. He approved our young organization and gave Alpha Phi Alpha his blessing. He became our first honorary member.

At Cornell University, we took pride in the fact that Professor Walter Wilcox, head of the Department of Sociology, quoted Dr. Du Bois in his lectures. He distinguished him only as Dr. Du

Bois, Professor of Sociology at Atlanta University. Often Professor Wilcox spent his summers with Dr. Du Bois at Atlanta. It was there that Dr. Du Bois prepared the first unbiased studies of the plight of the Negro, published as *The Atlanta University Papers.*

I was privileged to meet Dr. Du Bois for the first time in 1909 during the summer of my graduation from Cornell. It was a great satisfaction to me that he always remembered me whenever we met afterward. From the time of The Niagara Manifesto, William E. B. Du Bois has remained for me a beacon light of freedom in America.

Irene Diggs

One seeks meaning in the life of Du Bois and accepts the death of this vital man at ninety-five years, still intellectually lively, in which an unquenchable flame still burned fiercely, but a man ill, travel stained, weary of fighting and being fought. On the eve of the most triumphant march in protest against what he had spent a lifetime protesting, far from the Valley of the Housatonic of his birth, amid friends, boldly he may have beckoned to Death from the cool cisterns of the midnight harmattan. And Death, her sable skirts all fringed with light came, I hope, hastily and painlessly. Without resistance he lay silent, serene, cold, and still; no more fighting, no more insults, no more humiliation, no more struggle—at peace. May no treachery of fate rob him of the welcomed, the thrice-worked for, the beloved eternal rest "in that upper realm where there is no color nor race, sex, wealth, nor age, but all men stand equal in the sun."

Each of the few who knew him well carries his own image of him. An image characterized by extremes depending upon the relationship. He pricked Negroes; he goaded whites. Little is known of his inner life, he was reticent; seldom did he talk about himself or those whom he loved. In some respects he was a lonely man, a resigned man who carried the self-imposed burden of the nonwhite peoples of the world; a man who recognized the relationship between the oppressed nonwhites and the "poor whites." Much of the man himself is made manifest through his writings in which there is wisdom, prophecy, sorrow, scorching bitterness, resentment, great sensitivity, satire, prayer. Only a few can truthfully write about him in terms of intimacy and affection; most will deal with the incisive brilliance of his perceptive encyclopedic mind, the qualities of his spirit. Du Bois knew the importance of integrity, excellence, documentation, verification, the marshaling of evidence. The nimbleness of his intellect was observable in the question and answer period following a lecture, in his classes, in his repartee with both admirers and detractors.

A nonpayable debt we owe Du Bois for his thoughts and writings which laid the foundation for a revolutionary approach to the problem of color; for much of what the nineteen-sixties have given wings to in the United States and in the world in the areas of freedom, equality, and independence especially for nonwhites.

He is not likely to be remembered as or made a saint—there will not be many myths about Du Bois but history will record him as an extraordinary productive writer, an unrelenting advocate of human dignity, a believer in the primacy of human conscience, a gentle jovial human being with a disarming air of simplicity, tough of purpose, with a biting but warm sense of satirical humor, persistent in his demands, shy but unafraid.

Lorraine Hansberry

I do not remember when I first heard the name Du Bois. For some Negroes it comes into consciousness so early, so persistently that it is like the spirituals or the blues or discussions of oppression; he was a fact of our culture. People spoke of him as they did the church or the nation. He was an institution in our lives, a bulwark of our culture. I believe that his personality and thought have colored generations of Negro intellectuals, far greater, I think than some of those intellectuals know. And, without a doubt, his ideas have influenced a multitude who do not even know his name.

Now he is dead and his legacy is, in my mind, explicit. I think that it is a legacy which insists that American Negroes do not follow their oppressors and the accomplices of their oppressors—anywhere at all. That we look out at the world through our own eyes and have the fiber not to call enemy friend or friend enemy. I think that it tells us to honor thought and thinking; to keep always as our counsel distinguished scholarship and hold sacred strong and purposeful art; such as beautifully crafted and humanly involved writing.

I think that this legacy bid us pay attention to the *genuine* needs of humankind and not to the frivolities which are the playthings of its parasites. I believe with all my heart that the teachings of Du Bois teach us to disavow racism of any nature whatsoever wherever it raises its head—including in the ranks of black folk.

And, tonight, in his memory, I mean to say what I mean and mean what I say: think that certainly Du Bois' legacy teaches us to look toward and work for a socialist organization of society as the next great and dearly won universal condition of mankind.

I think these are the clear aspects of his legacy and I, for one, as one of his pupils, have found no cause to detour from these great notions of the master. However, I think that there is one more point which should be made tonight. That never, *never* again must the Negro people pay the price that they have paid for allowing their oppressors to say who is or is not a fit leader of our cause.

Remarks made at Carnegie Hall at memorial for W. E. B. Du Bois, February 23, 1964. One of last speeches made by Miss Hansberry before her fatal illness.

James E. Jackson

What Emerson said of John Brown can be said with equal justice of W. E. B. Du Bois: "He was the most ideal of men, for he wanted to put all his ideas into action."

This man of letters, this social scientist, this scholar who scaled the highest peaks of academic attainment; this man of great thought was also a man of resolute action. No armchair philosopher, theory for him was a guidelight against the darkness that concealed the path of progress.

His was a place in the vanguard of the torchbearers of history who illuminate the freedomway for the cavalcade of mankind to advance on the future. Dr. Du Bois' great intellect and prodigious labors were directed not merely at *understanding the world* and the relations of man to man in it, they were primarily committed to the task of *changing the world* of men so that man would be to man as a brother and not as a beast.

"What is the meaningful formula to enable black and white men to fathom and to solve the problem of the oppression of man by man?" Through a long life arduously lived, Du Bois was ever the pilgrim in "Quest of the Silver Fleece," of an all-encompassing philosophical conception and guide to the social action of the masses. On November 26, 1961, he announced to the world that he had experienced a personal success in his search. The key to the science of social progress, he said, was already present in a hundred year old body of theory which remains eternally youthful because it recognizes only one absolute and that being *change* itself. That world outlook and guide to the science of society being Marxism-Leninism; the advocacy, theory, and practice of the parties of the communists in most of the countries of the globe.

Du Bois did not limit himself to an affirmation of the philosophy of socialism/communism, this great man who "wanted to put his ideas into action," announced his membership and made public his letter of application for membership in the Communist Party of the United States. Dr. Du Bois was ninety-three when he joined the Communist Party, U.S.A., and because of his age there were those who wish to efface this act from his recorded biography. They would dismiss it as some irascible Shavian act of pique; or the political syndrome of a senile old man. The truth is far from the wishes of such people. To Du Bois, becoming a communist was the consummate act of commitment to the social forces which the people can command to forge and fashion for all of mankind a bright and joyous future. He came to communism only after long study and reflection, after years of experience and experimentation. I recall conversations with Dr. Du Bois going back for better than two decades on questions of Marxist approaches to problems of race and nationality, on the arts of political action, on problems of philosophy and ethics. Over the widest spectrum of subject matter the Du Bois logic was essentially the Marxian dialectical process of reasoning. Yet, the purity of the man's integrity was such that he protested that he was too old to ever earn the right to identify himself as a Marxist. "Most of my books were written before I read deeply of Marxism," he said, "I would have to rework, or append afterthoughts to each of them. I couldn't possibly live so long. No. They will have to judge me with the contemporaries of my generation against the then dominant philosophy—bourgeois democracy." Nevertheless, our dialogue on communist theory and practice continued through the years. When he decided to migrate to Ghana to take up work there on the *Encyclopedia Africana,* he asked me to his home to take up a serious matter.

"I think I've written enough new things and added new explanatory prefaces to a number of old works to take the title of communist in good conscience now," he said. Though he was dubious about delaying an announcement, he agreed that his *Letter of an American Communist* be released after he was well settled in his new home. The Du Bois letter to the American Communist spokesman Gus Hall is a political testament of great power and historic moment. Standing upon the summit of great works performed in a long life of service to the cause of the advancement of humanity, he pointed to communism as the direction in which human history moves toward its golden tomorrow.

"I have been long and slow in coming to this conclusion, but at last my mind is settled," he wrote in this letter which traces the evolution of his beliefs, his judgment against capitalism and his conclusion for socialism. In it he disclosed a very early socialist association:

"At the University of Berlin . . . I attended meetings of the Socialist Party and considered myself a Socialist." Back in America he joined the Socialist Party in 1911, "But still I neither read or heard much of Marxism," he recalled. Soon, he was making a serious study of Marxist works. He hailed the Russian Revolution in 1917. Ten years later he made his first visit to the Soviet Union. He returned to visit at almost ten-year intervals thereafter. This is the concluding section of the *Letter:*

Capitalism cannot reform itself; it is doomed to self-destruction. No universal selfishness can bring social good at all.

Communism—the effort to give all men what they need and to ask of each the best they can contribute—this is the only way of human life. It is a difficult and hard end to reach—it has and will make mistakes, but today it marches triumphantly on in education and science, in home and food, with increased freedom of thought and deliverance from dogma. In the end, Communism will triumph. I want to help bring that day.

The path of the American Communist Party is clear: it will provide the United States with a real Third Party and thus restore democracy to this land.

It will call for:

Public ownership of natural resources and of all capital.

Public control of transportation and communications.

Abolition of poverty and limitation of personal income.

No exploitation of labor.

Social medicine, with hospitalization and care of the old.

Free education for all.

Training for jobs and jobs for all.

Discipline for growth and reform.

Freedom under law.

No dogmatic religion.

These aims are not crimes. They are practiced increasingly over the world. No nation can call itself free which does not allow its citizens to work for these ends.

The twentieth-century struggle for equality and freedom of the American Negroes opened with a thundering declaration from the pen of W. E. B. Du Bois, the *Address to the Country of the Niagara Movement;* it proved to be both guideline and prophecy. In it he wrote then in 1906:

"The morning breaks over the hills. Courage, brother! The battle for humanity is not lost or losing. The Slav is rising in his might, the Yellow minions are testing liberty, the black Africans are writhing toward the light, and everywhere the Laborer is opening the gates of Opportunity and Peace." The great social scientist who began his work some sixty years before with the *Address* concluded it with the *Letter*. History has already made him a prophet in respect to the *Address;* I believe history will also fulfill the *Letter*.

C. L. R. James

It is natural and proper for Africans and people of African descent in the United States and elsewhere, and their friends, to hail Dr. Du Bois as one of the great leaders of colored people and an eminent proof that all men are created equal, equal in potentiality, ability to use opportunity and the right to have it.

But let us beware of confining ourselves to the corner into which we have been driven.

Dr. Du Bois wrote on the American slave trade, on Negro urban life and on the Negro community in the rural South: modern European critics recognize that in American historical scholarship he initiated a method which has profoundly influenced all succeeding American writers on history and sociology.

In founding the NAACP and *The Crisis* he more than any other individual taught the nation and the world that the persecution of a national minority was a national wound and its cure the responsibility of the nation.

To Africa he brought the same social breadth and practical humanity. Far in advance of all the official politicians and publicists of his time, in his Pan-African conferences and his writings, he made the world aware that the emancipation of Africa and the life, liberty and the pursuit of happiness by Africans was an international responsibility. The League of Nations and now the United Nations pursue the paths he charted. Here there is no American whose head reaches near his massive shoulders.

Always the intellectual pioneer, he startled American historians by his audacious revaluation of the historical role of John Brown. His *Black Reconstruction* is one of the finest books of history ever written anywhere. Allow me to say that I doubt if any more pregnant historical writings have ever been published on the American continent than Du Bois' *Black Reconstruction* and Gilberto Freyre's *The Masters and the Slaves*. Why should this be so? The answer goes far beyond the achievements of any single individual, whatever his ability, whatever his role.

Let me, as a citizen of another country, conclude. It seems to me that as mankind lists the innumerable memorabilia of history as it must do, on any list, however select, of the Americans who have pointed new roads for the American nation, it will be impossible to omit the name of W. E. B. Du Bois. He was a leader of his people, yes. But he was more: one of the greatest leaders of a great nation. Essentially a man of ideas, he had the rare capacity of making his ideas accessible to the activity of ordinary men. We need only precision to measure accurately the cubits of this magnificent person. Future generations will write their own history, but they will build on the foundations that we leave. Not only racial justice but history itself demands that we give Du Bois his due. He was a great American but, beginning as professor of classical languages, then of economics, then of sociology, he moved on ceaselessly, taking in his stride the post of Consultant to the United Nations and before he died he had the world, the whole world, in his hands. Without his life, the world would be a poorer place.

Lee Lorch

The legacy of Dr. Du Bois is all around us. Fresh reminders come daily. Before me now is the editorial analysis of the U.S. elections by the *New York Times* (International Edition, November 9). Reminding the Republicans that their party cannot survive unless it repudiates racism, it demands of the winner:

> What is the President now going to do to insure the equality of every citizen before the law in Mississippi as well as in Michigan? What is he going to propose to crack the chronic unemployment problem and to meet the onrush of automation?
>
> The President knows that we cannot string along indefinitely as we have been doing in Vietnam, supporting still another shaky regime with diminishing popular appeal. He knows that we cannot continue indefinitely the sterile battle to keep China out of the U.N., or to ignore diplomatically a nation of 700 million people. He knows that . . . Latin America is exercising a new independence, that the African giant is rising from his sleep.
>
> He knows that the spread of nuclear knowledge carries with it the most dangerous military and political consequences. He knows that all of this ferment throughout the globe may well require of us the courage to readjust our sights and possibly even to revise some of our policies, our programs and our thinking.

Not for a moment do I suggest that the *New York Times* has in mind such fundamental solutions as Dr. Du Bois was accustomed to advocate. What is striking is the nature of the problems listed. Do they not echo what Dr. Du Bois proclaimed early in the century, that the twentieth century would be characterized by the struggle for freedom of colonies abroad, freedom from racism at home?

On whom, too, does poverty lay its heaviest hands? American workers of African ancestry suffer twice the unemployment rate, and face twice the job displacement rate threatened by automation, as do other American workers.

Also long ago, Dr. Du Bois joined to his expectations for this century the general problem of universal social reconstruction, and of peace.

In the battle against nuclear weapons he was one of the first to enlist—for his foresight to be arrested, handcuffed, fingerprinted, prosecuted by the federal authorities at the age of eighty-three (1951).

Others will write—as others have written—of each of the multitudinous contributions from his wide-ranging genius. His works, literary, historical, sociological, editorial, educational, organizational, Africanist, will inspire generations to come, and will be studied with meticulous care.

Biographies will be written, character and personality made the subject of much comment. That he was incorruptibly honest, courageous, indomitable is true to the full. Yet to say this sounds curiously flat, like noting that the ocean is wet. These were such inalienable features of his character that he cannot be imagined without them. I believe that it was never difficult, in a psychological sense, for him to give his honest opinion, nor resist pressure, however heavy, nor develop new views if his older ones did not meet the test of time. It would simply not occur to him to behave differently. But it was often made difficult for him in material ways, as in 1951.

He fought hard in defense of his views and activities, but with monumental calm and objectivity and with every confidence in the ultimate victory his studies and feelings told him that decency would achieve. Never would he bend the knee to reaction or capitulate to hysteria, nor withhold criticism or support out of crass expediency. In June 1953, for example, he gave the graveside address at the interment of Ethel and Julius Rosenberg, in a national atmosphere that beggars description.

I met him first when he was eighty-two, in 1950. The last time I saw him was in September 1962, as he was leaving London with his wife, Shirley Graham, to rest briefly in Switzerland following surgery (at age ninety-four) before returning to Ghana.

In between there were many pleasant visits to their home in Brooklyn and exchanges of letters.

The warm affection and genuine admiration which he and Shirley had for one another imbued their home with a joy and comfort in which it was a great pleasure to share. Normally, I suppose, she did most of the "looking after." But he was quite willing to do his share.

One winter found them bathing in the Caribbean. He had his swim all right, but somehow poor Shirley broke her leg. By the time of my next visit, the fracture was nearly healed and all was cheerful. He had just finished doing the dishes, so Shirley announced, whereupon he produced a paper recording that he had just washed, say, his 1,323rd dish.

Their tasteful home, adorned with prized Africana and Asiana, was no solemn place. It rang with Shirley's irrepressible laughter and his quiet chuckle. Conversation was not frivolous (except for the affectionate banter), but it was easy and laced with humor, on his part likely to carry some of the dry wit of his New England background, never sour or malicious. Warmth there was aplenty, and a vivid interest in the well-being and doings of their friends. In discussing ideas, Dr. Du Bois used his vast erudition and keen mind to illuminate issues, not to overwhelm listeners. Calm objectivity and careful consideration of views characterized the form of conversation. Its substance was always the living world and the future, which was faced with sublime confidence.

The house was no salon, but a literary workshop, at the heart of which were found the carefully assembled library, extensive files and well-planned outlines for future work.

Diligently pursuing his great goals with gigantic talents and stern self-discipline, he sustained himself not with vague hopes but with a deep confidence in the righteousness of his endeavors and the perfectibility of man. In this, he was of course inspired still further by having become witness in his own lifetime to the dreams, struggles, and fruits of his youth.

Born and grown to manhood in a world where color was a badge of oppression, he had lived to see Asia and Africa commanding great respect, Latin America stirring, and Afro-America marching. In the growth of the world of socialism, and in the inability of the war to destroy it, he found additional guarantors of the new day dawning. Of all this he was very conscious, and by it particularly determined to make his study of the past, and lively participation in the present, help shape a worthy future.

On leaving life, we would all like to reflect on ours and find the certainty that we were bequeathing something worth cherishing.

On the eve of the March on Washington, in his home in Accra, far from his native New England hills, but close to his heart, asking his beloved Shirley to forgo preparing supper and just sit with him instead, taking her hand in his, the "philosopher and father of the Negro protest movement, . . . uncompromising foe of colonialism" gently felt life ebb.

George B. Murphy, Jr.

The name William Edward Burghardt Du Bois, stands for an intellectual, a people's giant of twentieth-century United States of America, one of the great men of the world.

I had only a youthful, confused understanding of this when I saw him for the first time in Baltimore, through the eyes of a thirteen-year-old boy.

It was not until many years later, in the 1930's, during the early years of the great American Depression that I was to comprehend the full meaning of his being, his life, in the history and development of our country.

I came to a full realization of this in the course of a conversation I had with him in Harlem, a conversation that lasted only a brief instant in the cycle of time, but for me encompassed all the thoughtful days of my years up to that moment.

In our home of many children in Baltimore, the names of Frederick Douglass and W. E. B. Du Bois were familiar, household words, understood with pride and love, as were the names of scores of others, out of our people's rich history of freedom struggles.

For me, the exciting difference was, Douglass and the others were dead; Du Bois was still alive.

My father did not press upon us the idea of reading books. He simply saw to it that books, magazines, and pictures were constantly at hand. Thus we could weave our own stories about who we were, what our relation to these United States was, how these famous people fitted into the lives of our forebears, into our own lives then and in the future.

My father was a teacher, a public school principal, and a dedicated educator in a Jim Crow school system in the state of Maryland for nearly half a century. He knew, loved, and understood children even as he presented them and us with the picture of a stern schoolmaster.

So, it was something more than suppressed delight that I felt when my mother told me one afternoon that Mrs. Hawkins wanted me and the other members of my high school freshman

Latin club to serve as waiters in her home at a cultural evening when Dr. Du Bois would speak.

To my knowledge, this was the first organization among our people to be named after Dr. Du Bois and now some sixty years old, it is still functioning in the Monumental city.

Although I had read quite a few books for a freshman high school student, there were only two that ran like rivers through my mind, nourishing my thinking, sharpening my youthful understanding, filling me with great pride in the culture and heroism of my people.

Frederick Douglass's autobiography of his life and times and Du Bois' *Souls of Black Folk,* represented for me the staff and shield with which I could do battle in understanding the ghetto world in which I lived.

How happy I was. Here, at last, I would get to meet the man who fired my imagination, carried me to far-off lands, peopled by people like myself, and other peoples too, of all colors and creeds and languages. I followed him avidly in his editorial column in the NAACP's *Crisis* magazine, which was titled: "As the Crow Flies."

Here was the man who sometimes frightened me, even as he evoked my deep admiration and affection, with the searing, stinging logic of his poetic prose that sent me spinning into intellectual orbit around the United States and far out into the realms of Africa, China, and the islands of the seven seas.

He made me feel, even then, my kinship with these peoples, inviting me to see how clearly their lives, their fortunes, their sacred honor, were inextricably bound up with me, my hopes, my aspirations and the hopes and aspirations of my people. And the beauty and rhythm of his words made me want to be a poet, a musician, set them to music and sing them out on the street corner.

I thought about all this as I walked the few blocks to Mrs. Hawkins' home. I wondered how I would greet him. Perhaps I should recite some Latin. It never occurred to me that I should tell him about his great book that I had read. I was too intent on proving to him that I too had "great learning."

Fortune did not smile on me that evening. Another club member got the chance to serve him. And I did not get a chance to hear him either. The crisp, precise English of his finely modulated voice did not flow out into the kitchen where we were eating under Mrs. Hawkins' soft admonition to "clean up everything nicely."

We rushed to finish our work, hoping to hear some of his remarks near the end. But, alas, when we tiptoed to the door of the parlor, watching his distinguished figure, his smooth skin looking like parchment, his almost dandified Vandyke beard, he was looking at his watch.

"I am sorry, ladies," he answered to their insistent plea that he talk longer. "This is my retirement hour and I must leave you. Thank you, and good night."

There was a moment of pained silence before Mrs. Hawkins led him from the room, walking right past us like the Ambassador from out of the "Arabian Nights," up the stairs and out of our sight. I tried to solace myself that all of us might get to see him again under more favorable circumstances.

I was upset too. Couldn't we have had a chance to at least shake hands? And what about the piece of conversation that my long ears heard from one of the ladies: "It was wonderful, but he is so cold and distant, he would not even bend an instant to our polite request."

I was confused. Maybe the lady was right. I had heard many times that he was a remote, scholarly man, who did not make friends easily. I had also heard that he kept a rigid, disciplined schedule of hours for work and rest and leisure. Still, why could he have not stopped to let us greet him; we, the members of the Council Amicitiae—the Council of Friendship—we who hoped he might tell us some word, from "up on high." It was to be many years before I found the answer to these questions.

The deep Depression of the 1930s had a profound effect on the American people, the working people, the artists, the writers, the actors, the trade unionists, the Negro people, the foreign born, the youth, the church, the Government, the courts, the law enforcement agencies, including the FBI. The Depression released the creative energies of the people in every field, shook them to the depths even as they came to grips with the reality that capitalism and the United States did not spell security, freedom from fear, poverty, disease, and death forever and ever, Amen!

In no other urban center of the United States could one better view this in microcosm, raw, firsthand, than in Harlem, the largest Negro community in the world, just a few score blocks from Wall Street, hub of the most powerful capitalist nation on earth.

It was in Harlem, in the late fall, during the early part of the Depression, that I read the handbill announcing the fact that Du Bois was to speak at the George Washington Carver Workers School, housed in a loft building on Lenox Avenue just off 125th Street.

The evening was cold and blustery, the winds swirling the dirt, dust, and city noises down into the mouth of the subway and then vomiting all the feathery mixture from the belly of the city, underground, back into the street filled with people hurrying to and fro.

I had no special appointment. My friend said simply, "You know Dr. Du Bois will be there ahead of time, but that is no guarantee that he will talk with you. I'll simply tell him you want to talk with him for a few moments." I was grateful.

How many years had it been since that evening of long ago in Baltimore? I knew I had to meet this man, get to know him, let him hear my story, how I had followed him through the years, watched the evolution of his thinking, seen the deepening conviction of his socialist philosophy ripen until today he was placing his ideas, his humanism, his great learning, at the disposal of the working people in a lecture at a community school for the people of Harlem.

But I had to do more. I had to rid myself of a secret, which, once shared with him, would enable me to muster the courage to fight doggedly the battle I knew must be fought, if I was to win his attention, his respect, his friendship, and, perhaps, his affection.

I rapped gently on the door. That same modulated voice that I remembered bade me enter.

He was seated in a comfortable chair, under a lamp, holding his papers on his lap, his briefcase on a table near at hand. He looked up, took off his pince-nez with the thin black ribbon and inquired, "Yes?"

"Dr. Du Bois," I began, "my name is"—but the words would not come.

Sensing my emotional confusion, politely ignoring it, he motioned me to sit down. He said he had just a short time, that he knew some members of my family, and he would give me a little time to hear what I had to say.

His quiet, fatherly manner broke the tension in the pit of my stomach, and the words tumbled out, pushed along by my fear that I might not get the chance to say all I had to say during what might be my one and only chance to talk to him for another long period of time.

I told him of that early evening in Baltimore. I spoke of all the sharp, cutting, and unkind things I had heard about him; his coldness, his remoteness, his distant manner that made many people feel that he was not the warm, gracious, and human author of *Souls of Black Folk*.

Then I felt the pain coming up through the pit of my stomach again, but I went on; I knew what I had to do. I told him that although I knew and felt differently, I had not defended him, even though I had read a number of his books, read his essays, wept with him over "The Lost Atlantis."

I wanted to say much more, but I was afraid of the flight of time and with it, my chance to make my declaration.

I asked him to forgive me for being weak before the storm of ignorance, for ever doubting his humanity. With the strength of those released from a heavy burden, I went further; I asked him for the right to be his friend. I asked him for the right to go along with him in the future, even if I had to walk a little behind him until I had proved my friendship.

I let him know that this confession was painful for me, but I had to come, let him know, like the "Member at the Mourner's Bench," that I understood him at last.

He looked at me for a moment, glanced at his watch. He seemed to ponder whether he should break his lifelong habit of punctuality.

"Young man," he began—it would be some time before he permitted himself to call me George—"I don't have much time, but let me say this to you."

"I am happy that you felt you had to come to me and say these things; and I respect your honest feelings in the matter.

"Let me tell you that I am aware of the criticisms that have been made of me from time to time. Most of what I have said and thought over many years, I have put into books, pamphlets, and essays, so you see that it is quite natural for my life to be what you call an 'open book.'

"It is also natural that I should be criticized. It is not the criticisms that are most important, but the convictions that count. Keep your convictions and you will learn how to understand and deal with the criticisms.

"Thank you for coming to see me; I shall be happy to have you for a friend.

"Now, I must leave you; my time is up."

He got up, gathered his papers, shook my hand as I mumbled my thanks, and walked out the room, down the hall to his lecture.

In my joyful confusion I rushed out the door, down the stairs, and out into the street. I hurried along 125th Street, enjoying the friendly jostle of the crowds, the sweet and sour smells of Harlem.

Forgotten was the lecture I was to attend; forgotten the pain of my confession, everything.

He had forgiven my weakness, my unkind thoughts. He had said I could be his friend. Nothing else mattered.

Paul Robeson

Casting my mind back, my first clear memory of Dr. Du Bois was my pride in his recognized scholarship and authority in his many fields of work and writing. In high school and at college our teachers often referred us to standard reference works on sociology, race relations, Africa, and world affairs. I remember feeling great pride when the books and articles proved to be by our Dr. Du Bois, and often loaned these to my fellow students, who were properly impressed by his universally respected and acknowledged authority.

We Negro students joined the NAACP which Dr. Du Bois helped to organize and build; we read religiously *The Crisis,* of which he was editor for so many years, and in which he wrote clearly, constructively, and militantly on the complex problems of the American scene, on the Negro question, on Africa, and on world affairs. He called upon the American people, and particularly upon the whole labor movement, to understand the need for unity in the struggle of the working masses, including the Negro, for a decent standard of living.

We spoke of Dr. Du Bois as Our Professor, The Doctor, The Dean, with great respect, paid close attention to his pronouncements, and many of us followed him proudly marching down New York's Fifth Avenue in a protest parade led by the NAACP for civil rights.

Dr. Du Bois talked and wrote and marched for civil rights. He insisted upon first-class citizenship for all Americans, upon full equality of opportunity, dignity, legal rights for us all. And he directed universal interest and attention to our Negro history and our rich African ancestry, to give us solid background for our struggle.

All this was way back many, many years ago, long before I graduated from college in 1919. Our good doctor, this great man, understood our situation, and our world, and was often a lone but clarion voice pointing out the urgent need for change.

Dr. Du Bois was a distinguished historian as well as a social scientist. We often talked about the wealth and beauty of our folk heritage, particularly about Negro music which he loved and found deeply moving. He often stressed the importance of this special contribution to American culture. We had interesting discussions about the likeness of our Negro folk music to many other folk musics throughout the world.

Our professor was not only a great and recognized scholar, he was also our most distinguished statesman. His knowledge of world affairs, his founding of the Pan-African Congress, his continuing work in many capitals of the world for African independence, made him widely known and respected abroad, and beloved in Africa. His book *The World and Africa* was one of the first important books on modern postwar Africa, and helped to point out and focus attention on the continuing exploitation of Africa by the "free world."

We of the Council on African Affairs were very fortunate and proud when Dr. Du Bois joined our organization as Chairman in 1949. His knowledge, experience, and wisdom, together with our very able and devoted Executive Secretary, Dr. Alphaeus Hunton, helped us to make some meaningful contribution to the struggle of the African people, particularly in South Africa.

Fifteen years ago, when we built the Negro newspaper *Freedom,* under the very fine editorship of our friend and colleague, the late Louis Burnham, Dr. Du Bois was one of our very frequent and most brilliant contributors. His clear, forthright, informative articles on Africa, on the Negro in America, on the changing world situation, added stature to our publication.

Association, discussion, and work with this great man were always richly rewarding.

Probably as a result of his research and work in sociology, his close scientific observance of American history and social scene, his keen and continuing interest in Africa and in international affairs, Dr. Du Bois became a strong supporter of socialism as a way of life. He followed the rise of the Soviet Union with understanding and appreciation, and made friends with the whole socialist world.

He welcomed not only their rejection of racism, but also, as a social scientist, he appreciated their constructive and practical interest in, and effective governmental activity for the welfare of the vast majority of the people. Dr. Du Bois said many times that he believed the 1917 Russian Revolution was the turning point in modern history, and was of first importance in the shaping of a new world with the emergence of many other socialist lands.

So that it was logical and deeply moving when, in 1961—having the whole world picture in focus—Dr. Du Bois became a member of the Communist Party of the United States, and still later became a welcome and honored citizen of Ghana, in his beloved Africa. He followed with deep concern the independence struggles in various parts of Africa, and knew that these struggles must be won, so that Africa and the African people could develop their great potential.

With his brilliant mind, his far-reaching education, his scholarly academic background, Dr. Du Bois was nevertheless a very much down-to-earth human being, with a delightful and ready wit, a keen and mischievous sense of humor, and enjoyed life to the full. I especially remember his gay spontaneous laughter.

And I remember particularly a wonderful Thanksgiving dinner at his home in Grace Court in Brooklyn about ten years ago. He had invited some guests from the United Nations, because he knew they had heard and read about Thanksgiving, but had no personal experience and understanding of this special American holiday. So this was as typical a Thanksgiving dinner and evening as he and his wife Shirley could make it, with the good Doctor a gay and witty host, explaining everything step by step—from turkey and cranberry sauce to pumpkin pie and early American history. After the delicious dinner, over coffee and brandy before the log fire burning in the spacious living room fireplace, he spoke of Frederick Douglass, whose portrait hung over the mantel, and of his place in American history. That day is a happy and cherished memory.

I also remember so well the political campaigning of Dr. Du Bois when he was candidate of the American Labor Party of New York for the U.S. Senate. In the usual free-for-all scramble which American political campaigns involve, Dr. Du Bois always remained calm and dignified. He never descended to shrill attack or name-calling, but discussed the real issues with brilliant speeches in which he combined his keen intelligence and trenchant humor. All of us worried about how he, at the age of eighty-two and seemingly fragile, would withstand the grueling pace of the campaign. But Dr. Du Bois took care of his health as intelligently as he did everything else, and those who planned meetings at which he would speak knew that if he was scheduled for 10 P.M. for half an hour, then no matter what the unpredictable state of the meeting, at ten o'clock precisely Dr. Du Bois would walk onto the platform, speak brilliantly for half an hour, rest a while, then go on his way.

The more Dr. Du Bois observed and understood world events, the more he recognized that peace was a prime issue in this nuclear age. And so, typically, he became associated with peace movements all over the world, and worked actively for peace. In 1949 he became Chairman of the Peace Information Center here in our country, and was later indicted, tried, and acquitted for his leadership in work for peace.

When Dr. Du Bois and Shirley came to London in 1958, we were living in a flat in Maida Vale. Soon after their arrival Eslanda and I went to Moscow for a long visit and turned our flat over to the Du Boises. We were very happy when they told us they had enjoyed their stay there, and we had thus helped to make their London visit comfortable. After they left we felt we should put a plate on the door saying "Dr. Du Bois slept here."

My last memory of Dr. Du Bois is in London, in less happy circumstances, in 1962. The Doctor, then ninety-four years old and very ill, had been brought to London for a very serious operation. He was tired and weak, and we worried about how he could stand the ordeal.

I was ill in a London nursing home at the time, and felt very sad and helpless about the Doctor's condition. So that when my wife, who visited him regularly in the hospital, told me that he wanted very much to see me and had asked especially for me, I got up and went to London University Hospital and we spent some time together. Ill as he was, he told me about his work on the Encyclopedia Africana; we talked about the progress of the Negro revolt at home in America, about the power and influence of the socialist world, about the marvelous coming-of-age of the African people.

I visited him once again in the hospital, and was delighted and greatly relieved to find him miraculously improving. This was in August 1962.

While I remained in the London nursing home, still ill, Dr. Du Bois recovered from his operation, got up, and with Shirley traveled to Switzerland where he rested in the sun, went to Peking where they attended the October Celebration, on to Moscow where they attended the November Celebration, and back again to London in late November, where Dr. Du Bois visited *me* in the nursing home! He gave a fascinating account of his trip and experiences, which he had enjoyed immensely.

That was the last time I saw him. He and Shirley went on to Ghana where a marvelous welcome awaited them.

My cherished memories of Dr. Du Bois are his brilliant and practical mind, his intellectual courage and integrity, his awareness of the world and of our place in it—which helped to make us all also aware. His fine influence on American thinking and on Negro thinking will continue to be incalculable. We admired, respected, appreciated, and followed him because he was clear and forthright, because he was militant with a fighting strength and courage based upon wide knowledge, great wisdom, and experience. I remember too his deep kindness.

Dr. Du Bois was and is in the truest sense an American leader, a Negro leader, a world leader.

Poem by Elma Stuckey

Now the fragrant petals shower downward
That hung suspended in an air of fear
But he is gone and now they fall resplendent
In solemn reverence for that mighty seer

That great exponent of the freedom surge
Who advocated that the black man fight
Whose dreams transcended all our shallow hopes
And set a fuse exploding into light

Our cross lay like a millstone on his heart
We let him bear the burden all alone
Now we come forward eloquent with praise
Our silence broken after he is gone

Too late! But not too late to change our lot
And re-evaluate the Negro's gains
To call together twenty million men
And break the lock that holds us now in chains

For now we see the fierceness of his truth
A history of cruelty to our race
It shall be changed if written with our blood
His name will be a sign to mark the place

Oh, Africa! Be gentle to his mound
For tender is your bosom for your own
Dark are your nights but filled with stars of hope
That we shall reap the harvest he has sown

Richard G. Hatcher

Since Dr. Martin Luther King, Jr., stood before this assembly and inaugurated the W. E. B. Du Bois Centennial, a year that can only be termed as tragic has passed. In that year we have all been diminished personally, as has our nation and our world, with tribulation. There has been some triumph, but however desperately we seek to cheer ourselves, however often we tell ourselves that we passed through a year of gain, another voice tells us that the balance is far from redressed. Another voice tells us that we must not content ourselves with only progress toward our goal, but that the goal must be won conclusively, and it must be won now; and when we seek to pause, to rest, to catch our breath, the insistent voice of Martin Luther King propels us on and it reminds us that we were taken to a mountain top and of what we saw from the crest. It tells us that we may stop, but the current age will not, that we may rest, but the killing of spirit, the assassination of hope, the murder of justice, all these things go on; and we must feel compelled to heed that voice. If we do not, we insult the memory of a man who built not of bricks and mortar but who constructed a more enduring monument from the collective conscience of his fellow man. His legacy to us endures. The long, black line of martyrdom has lengthened and it will lengthen more. And in that line, the arms of Dr. Du Bois, Malcolm X, Medgar Evers, and Dr. King, and all the rest are linked with those of the nameless ones, those who were lynched in fact and those who were lynched in spirit, the dispossessed, the disenchanted, those who came as strangers to the village of America and who found, not democracy, but hypocrisy, who found, not the American dream but the American nightmare, those who found hate instead of love, despair instead of hope, and sorrow instead of happiness. We have a faith to keep with them all. There are few men, I think, we need not wait for history to judge and I think that Dr. Martin Luther King was one of them. He was known to us in his lifetime as a giant and he has not dropped a torch for us to pick up, but he has simply passed it on to us and we must pass it on brighter than it was when we received it.

Excerpt from *The Age of a New Humanity.*

William Edward Burghardt Du Bois was another who was secure in history before it was written. He was a scholar of awesome intellectual depth and range, a poet and prophet, a leader and a teacher. He could have been comfortable, a coddled, colored exception, a parlor Negro in white men's parlors, paid in conscience money from the purses of a self-deluded majority, the same majority that has so often sought to prove its liberality by practicing a basic conservatism, different only in form, not in content, from the antebellum southern thought. When W. E. B. Du Bois chose not to be comfortable in the more traditional sense, he found his only comfort in the only place that he could, and that was in the front lines and, like Martin Luther King, Jr., he spent an adult lifetime fighting in the trenches. His words, written and spoken, he catapulted over the walls of bigotry and ignorance. He laid a long siege to the *fact* of America. He chose not to be pointed at in smug condescension. He knew he was too good for that, too right for that; but he recognized not just his own worth, he recognized the essential genius of being black. He saw black as visceral and noble; he understood black. He wrote magnificent history and irrefutable essays. He wrote poetry that soared and he also wrote in the magazine that he founded for black schoolchildren to offset the white propaganda that they were forced to read and this all as long ago as 1918. He wrote distinguished monographs at Fisk, where he earned his A.B. degree, at Harvard, where he won another, at the University of Berlin, where he did postgraduate work, and at Harvard again, where he won his Ph.D. Out of his enlightened blackness he wrote, "I am the smoke king, I am black, I am darkening with song, I am hearkening to wrong, and I will be black as blackness can, the blacker the mantle, the mightier the man."

With his founding of the NAACP, his fatherhood of the Niagara Movement, his perseverance in the cause of Pan-Africanism, and with much of his writing that corrected both history and the future, he spoke to black men. He spoke to white men, also, and he reminded them of the folly of their arrogance. For those who would let them, Du Bois and King made the corrections. Like black ghosts of Christmas past, they showed this nation the terrible truth of where it had been. Like black ghosts of Christmas present, they showed this nation the terrible truth of where it was; and like black ghosts of Christmas to be, they showed this nation the terrible abyss that it teetered on, the horror of its future if it didn't change its ways drastically, convincingly, and immediately.

They foreshadowed an age of a new humanity as the only acceptable alternative to a heritage of hate that man could not possibly withstand. They trumpeted at the walls, and if the walls did not tumble down, they trembled enough to send all of us on. The walls trembled enough so that at the age of eighty-three, Dr. Du Bois was arrested. Some saw his arrest, his seizure, and his search, his public handcuffing as a tragic thing. It was, but I am certain, not for Dr. Du Bois. I can think of many worse things than, at the age of eighty-three, to be considered such a danger to the opponents of justice, to make them so shudder in fear that they surface to show themselves in all their hopeless, barren brutality. These handcuffs, as they clicked closed on his black wrist, were like a fear-stricken shriek of *"nigger!"* into an empty night. Those who scream "nigger" never define the man that they shout at any more than those handcuffs define Dr. Du Bois as a criminal. The shouters define only themselves and the handcuffs were a judgment only on the keepers of those keys . . . the criminal institutions of a criminal society that thought they could hold captive an *idea* by imprisoning the *man*. An eighty-three-year-old man watched in complete dignity, some sorrow and in considerable outrage, the stupidity of men as they confirm their ignorance with handcuffs. He had called his society brutal and it responded with brutality. He had called his society unthinking, and it did not think. He had called his society inhumane, and it reacted with inhumanity. His society proved his point in every step of the way. Of course, he was not stopped, not even momentarily held up. He probed the raw nerves of the body politic until they twanged in agony, and then he stabbed at them some more. It was as though somehow Dr. Du Bois' lifelong dedication to radical politics was an ointment with which they could rinse the stains of conscience and justice from their hands. Those who fear the truth that was his life try to cancel it by guilty association.

Somehow, they thought his honest arrival at a political stance washed the truth from his study of Reconstruction, sapped his poetry of integrity, weakened his philosophy, and gave the lie to his prophecy. W. E. B. Du Bois remains our great historian, our great teacher, our great philosopher, our great poet, our honest black prince and prophet and we sit yet at his feet to learn, to replenish ourselves and go on in strength.

When the end came for him, some said he was in a kind of exile. I don't believe that. I think that he died at home. It was he, after all, who convened the Pan-African Conferences, who gave that moment its major impetus; and for such a man, home has little to do with national boundaries in any event. In his driving thrust toward Pan-Africanism, he told us something about unity here. He told us something about black power; he told us something about pride and no apology; he told us something about making our own judgments and not concerning ourselves with white approval for our heroes, our martyrs, our beliefs, and our directions.

PART TWO

W. E. B. DU BOIS: SCHOLAR–ACADEMICIAN

'The Souls of Black Folk': Du Bois' masterpiece lives on

SAUNDERS REDDING

The publication of Du Bois' *The Souls of Black Folk* in 1903 was an event of major importance. It not only represented a profound change in its scholar-author's view of what was then called the "Negro Problem," but heralded a new approach to social reform on the part of the American Negro people—an approach of patriotic, nonviolent activism which achieved its first success less than a decade ago. The boycott of the buses in Montgomery, Alabama, had many roots—the example of Gandhi's movement of passive resistance against the British in India, the precedent-making 1954 Supreme Court desegregation decision which showed that the American people as a whole were ready for racial equality, the leadership of a young Negro minister dedicated to peaceful reform—but none more important than this little book of essays published more than a half century ago.

W. E. Burghardt Du Bois graduated from Fisk University in Nashville in 1888. Moving on to Harvard, he spent four years of graduate study in psychology, philosophy, and history under some of the best minds of the age—William James, Josiah Royce, George Santayana, and Albert Bushnell Hart—and there formulated the scholarly ambition of pursuing "knowledge only." Two fruitful years followed at the University of Berlin (1892–94) where, encouraged by the illustrious historian Gustav Schmoller, Du Bois came to believe that the solution to the Negro problem was "a matter of systematic investigation"—that ignorance alone was the cause of race prejudice and that scientific truth could dispel it.

Following this line of thought, Du Bois completed his doctoral dissertation at Harvard, *The Suppression of the African Slave*

This introduction is from the Premier Americana Series, Fawcett World Library.

Trade, which was hailed as the "first scientific historical work" written by a Negro and, because of its quality of scholarship, achieved publication as the first volume of the new Harvard Historical Studies (1896). With characteristic versatility, Du Bois then turned from history to the study of sociology, then in its infancy, and wrote *The Philadelphia Negro: A Social Study,* published in 1899 by the University of Pennsylvania. In the meantime he had accepted an invitation to teach sociology at Atlanta University, where he set up a program of studies of the American Negro which was to be "primarily scientific—a careful search for Truth conducted as thoroughly, broadly, and honestly as the material resources and mental equipment at command will allow." Nevertheless (as hinted in his use of the word "primarily") he was already beginning to suspect that such detached inquiry was not enough—and by 1903, the date of *The Souls of Black Folk,* he was asserting that truth alone did not "encourage [or] help social reform."

To understand this revolution in Du Bois' thinking, one must understand what had happened to the hopes of the American Negro. The Emancipation and the period of the Reconstruction following the Civil War—the period of Du Bois' childhood—had brought dreams of equality and, for a time, some actual power to the Negro. But then the reaction had set in, and by the turn of the century the dreams had been shattered, and what Du Bois saw around him was the steady—and apparently accelerating—deterioration of the position of the Negro in American life. An almost complete disenfranchisement of the Negro had been effected in state constitutional conventions, the delegates to which were elected, as Virginia's Carter Glass declared, "to discriminate . . . with a view to the elimination of every Negro voter who can be gotten rid of, legally, without materially impairing the numerical strength of the white electorate." Anti-Negro demagogues—Tillman of South Carolina, Watson of Georgia, Vardaman of Mississippi—had become rampant, and lynchings averaged one in every three and a half days. Negro schools, where they existed at all, were so poor that attendance made little difference in a Negro's "education;" Negro poverty and crime were increasing everywhere. And the Negro leaders? Booker T. Washington was *the* Negro leader; and he was measuring the statistical indices of these sobering facts with an imperturbability that seemed at times to amount to indifference. This was the situation that Du Bois saw, and—because, finally, Du Bois the scholar was only a graft on Du Bois the Negro—could not tolerate. In the face of the circumstances, he "could not [remain] a calm, cool, and detached scientist."

The Souls of Black Folk is more history-making than historical. It is, among other things, a statement of personal attitudes and principles that have determined the public career of a great man for more than half a century, a career that has profoundly influenced the thoughts and actions of thousands of people, white as well as black, abroad as well as at home.

But *The Souls of Black Folk* is history-making in another sense too. Peter Abrahams, the South African "colored" writer, was not alone when he said, upon first reading this book in 1948, that until then he had had no words with which to voice his Negroness. It had, he wrote, "the impact of a revelation . . . a key to the understanding of my world." Much earlier, the American Negro leader James Weldon Johnson stated that it had "a greater effect upon and within the Negro race in America than any other single book published in this country since *Uncle Tom's Cabin*." Thus *The Souls of Black Folk* may be seen as fixing that moment in history when the American Negro began to reject the idea of the world's belonging to white people only, and to think of himself, in concert, as a potential force in the organization of society. With its publication, Negroes of training and intelligence, who had hitherto pretended to regard the race problem as of strictly personal concern and who sought individual salvation in a creed of detachment and silence, found a bond in their common grievances and a language through which to express them.

In the most famous of the essays, "Of Mr. Booker T. Washington and Others," Du Bois writes, ". . . the time is come when one may speak in all sincerity and utter courtesy of the mistakes and shortcomings of Mr. Washington's career, as well as of his triumphs. . . . So far as Mr. Washington preaches Thrift, Patience, and Industrial Training for the masses, we must hold up his hands and strive with him, rejoicing in his honors and glorying in the strength of this Joshua called of God and of man to lead the headless host. But so far as Mr. Washington apologizes for injustice, North or South, does not rightly value the privilege and duty of voting, belittles the emasculating effects of caste distinctions, and opposes the higher training and ambition of our brighter minds—so far as he, the South, or the Nation, does this—we must unceasingly and firmly oppose them. By every civilized and peaceful method we must strive for the rights which the world accords to men. . . ." Eighteen months after these words were in print, they were confirmed by the formation of the famous Niagara Movement—the forerunner of the NAACP.

Du Bois' words were a counterpoint to Washington's feathery phrases of compromise, and, not surprisingly, were greeted with much Southern criticism. Georgia's *Atlanta Constitution* ran a three-column review which concluded that *The Souls of Black Folk* "is the thought of a Negro of northern education who has lived among his brethren of the South, yet who cannot fully feel the meaning of some things which these brethren know by instinct—and which the southern-bred white knows by a similar instinct—certain things which are by both accepted as facts." The *Nashville Banner* agreed, and added a warning: "This book is dangerous for the Negro to read, for it will only excite discontent and fill his imagination with things that do not exist, or things that should not bear upon his mind."

But the things about which Du Bois wrote did exist—both in attitudes and in historical fact. Some of the essays, notably IV through IX, are based on the sociological studies Du Bois developed at Atlanta University. They are at once vigorous statements of the Negro's case against the prevailing white attitudes that relegated him to noncitizen status, and commendably objective analyses of that status, with postulates so sound that they are still assumed by scholars and social commentators concerned with the South. Perhaps the most "scientific" of the essays is "Of the Dawn of Freedom" which, despite its oracular and somewhat misleading beginning ("The problem of the twentieth century is the problem of the color-line . . ."), is primarily a historical account of the Freedman's Bureau. Other essays are personal recollections and reflections, powerfully evocative of a South and a Southern way of life that has not yet entirely passed. These contain some of Du Bois' best writing, and prove his extraordinary skill at adapting academic learning to the use of figurative prose. They remind us once again that neither bitter anger nor desperate rebelliousness—both charged against him—were the ruling passions of Du Bois' young life. One essay, "Of Alexander Crummell," is a eulogy of the character and services of one of Du Bois' early heroes. It is a laud, veritably a song of praise. Another, "Of the Coming of John," is a short story, almost a parable in tone and in intent. In a few, the literary charm—so highly praised by some of the friendly contemporary reviews—may now seem a bit obtrusive, but in most the manner is a perfect fit to the matter. And the matter is, always, a "gift of Spirit" from the Negro people: "Our song, our toil, our cheer, and warning have been given to this nation in blood-brotherhood."

It is impossible to say finally what makes a literary classic, for no two are alike. No two are alike for the simplest and best of reasons: each is the expression of an individual, of a *particular* genius. Classics have only this in common—they minister to universal emotional needs; they supply something vital to the universal intellect. *The Souls of Black Folk* does this by expressing the soul of one people in a time of great stress, and showing its kinship with the timeless soul of all mankind. *The Souls of Black Folk* will go on doing this. Not counting the European, this is the twenty-sixth edition. It will not be the last.

W. E. B. Du Bois and the black messianic vision

VINCENT HARDING

It is often considered polite in circles like our own to pay as little heed as possible to titles, especially when they prove to be as vexing as the one assigned to me: "Du Bois as a Negro Nationalist." On this occasion such a luxury is not possible, I fear. For it is only as we grapple with the kinds of issues which are implied in those words that we are able to do justice to the man we honor and assess today.

As far as I have been able to gather, Du Bois never referred to himself as a "Negro Nationalist," and indeed on one occasion he cautioned against his views being placed in that category. But his very need to raise the word of caution is a hint in itself: it reminds us that there were many points in his life and work when his thought could have been identified with a variety of nationalist ideologies.

Nor should this be surprising. Du Bois was born into a time of nationalism—a time when men believed in progress (with a capital P), and he later admitted that in his youth that chief of nationalists, Otto von Bismarck, was his hero. Of *that* fascinating relationship Du Bois wrote:

> Bismarck was my hero. He had made a nation out of a mass of bickering peoples. He had dominated the whole development with his strength. . . . This foreshadowed in my mind the kind of thing that American Negroes must do, marching forth with strength and determination under trained leadership.[1]

Paper, except for Epilogue, delivered at the opening session of the American Historical Association, December 28, 1968. This is part of a longer essay on the messianic elements of Du Bois' life and thought. Dr. Harding is Professor of History and Sociology at Spelman College and Director of the Institute of the Black World, founded in 1969, in Atlanta.

For the practitioners of many nationalisms it is obvious that all the painful, exhilarating acts of gathering a scattered people and stamping them with identity are seen as ends in themselves. For others the establishment of physical and spiritual homelands and states becomes the ultimate goal. Some of these views were shared by Du Bois, others obviously not, but even that is not the main burden of this paper.

Rather, I should like to suggest that while Dr. Du Bois was obviously concerned—often obsessed—with the ultimate destiny of black people in America, that dark, compelling destiny was almost always defined by him as fulfilling the national vocation. Indeed, he did not limit himself to that level; but for much of his life Du Bois saw the black people of the nation as critical transformers and redeemers of the destiny of the world. We understand Du Bois best, I would suggest, if we see him beyond the perimeters of nationalism, beyond even the dreams of Pan-Africanism. I think we are most faithful in our recording if we define his deepest hopes and convictions as those of a Black Messianism stretched over the boundaries of humanity. This, in his thought, was the calling of Africa's rejected children; and those of us in the American diaspora were to be in the vanguard of that awesome hope.[2]

To fulfill that messianic role, as Du Bois grew to sense it, there was an absolute necessity for black people here to develop economic, political, cultural, and moral force, strength—let us call it power. As both paradox and reinforcement of this need for black solidarity, it was clear to Du Bois that such power and fulfillment could not be achieved unless the bonds imposed by America on its black people were broken. So, for the task of breaking bonds and of convincing men that they needed to be broken, black people again had to organize, sometimes with whites (but often without them, according to Du Bois); *always* they had to organize *within* the race to prepare a broken people for its destiny. Often, he saw that inner organization as a form of black communalism, inspired by the African past, informed by the socialism rising all around him.

So neither power, solidarity, civil rights, nor aspects of nationhood were ends in themselves, even though Du Bois often tended to glory in their appearance. They were consistently put forward as means toward a new humanity. It was not until the end of his life that this messianic vision of the vocation of Africa's children in America was transferred to the homeland itself. But that moves ahead of the story.

Within the limits set by time and patience, we cannot possibly tell the full story of Du Bois' thought and action toward Black Messianism, but some particulars will be necessary. First, of course, it must be clear that this aspect of the thought of Dr. Du Bois did not develop in a vacuum. Its roots went back into Afro-American thought at least as far as the anguished *Appeal* of David Walker, and included the scholarly sermons, essays, and books of Alexander Crummell, a man known and loved by Du Bois.[3] Men like Walker and Crummell, in different ways, saw redemption coming forth from black America. W. E. B. Du Bois was born into a time when men, both black and white, still believed in redemption.

He was born, too, into the bosom of the North, and his experiences with the subtle color line of Great Barrington, Mass., must enter into the bill of particulars when we try to understand sources. As with all other aspects of the man's intellectual and ideological life, this one had deeply personal fountains. They were located not only in the quiet rebuffs of his schooldays, but in occasions like his first hearing the Hampton quartet, and being moved to tears as he "seemed to recognize something inherently and deeply my own." Thus, in spite of the fact that black Fisk was not his first choice of college, he was most likely right when he recalled that he was "beginning to feel lonesome in New England," and looked forward with anticipation to the black world of Fisk.[4]

The genius of Du Bois is that he was able to take his personal responses to the color line and turn them into matters of ultimate significance—matters of personal, racial, and human destiny. So Fisk was not only the place where he gloried in the opportunity to meet more beautiful black women than he had ever seen in all his seventeen years, but it was also the occasion for him to declare publicly:

> I am a Negro; and I glory in the name! I am proud of the

black blood that flows in my veins. . . . [I] have come here . . . to join hands with my people.[5]

His people included the poor blacks of the Tennessee countryside, as well as the middle-class sons and daughters of the University, so he went out during his two summers in the state to teach and learn. Later when he remembered those days the messianic commitment surely colored his memories, but he said that it was at Fisk and in the black rural areas of Tennessee that he "accepted color caste and embraced the companionship of those of my own color," then quickly added:

> This was, of course, no final solution. We Negroes were going to break down the boundaries of race; but at present we were banded together in a great crusade and happily so.[6]

From Fisk to Harvard

To break down the barriers of race in a lifetime was surely a divine vocation for any people—especially those who lived behind the barriers, within the veil.

After three years, he went on to Harvard and was away from the warmth of Fisk's inspirational environment. Nevertheless, Du Bois said, "I was firm in my criticism of white folk and in my dream of a Negro self-sufficient culture even in America."[7] Of course, there was never Du Bois without paradox, so even while convinced of the need of a self-sufficient Negro culture he was excitedly producing and directing a performance of Aristophanes, *The Birds,* in a black church in Boston.

Du Bois was never afraid to admit that dividedness in his own being, a dividedness which sometimes made it difficult for him to affirm with consistent intensity his sense of black vocation. Certainly that is why his years in Europe were filled with evocations of the greatness of German culture, with at least one love affair with a blue-eyed damsel, and with those "friendships and close contacts with white folk [which] made my own ideas waver."[8] (Beware of close contacts with white folk!)

It was especially in Germany that the outpourings of nationalism and patriotism which he often witnessed drove him relentlessly up against a series of agonizing questions concerning his own ultimate vocation and that of his black people in America. Du Bois later wrote:

> I began to feel that dichotomy which all my life has characterized my thought; how far can love for my oppressed race accord with love for the oppressing country? And when these loyalties diverge, where shall my soul find refuge?[9]

Whatever the ultimate answer to that question, it was also in Germany that Du Bois made his well-remembered dedication of his life to his "oppressed race." The ceremony on his twenty-fifth birthday must not be set aside simply because Du Bois later called it "rather sentimental," for one of his friends was right to call him a marvelous combination of the romantic and the rationalist. Indeed, one must add, too, that he also tended to combine all the strengths and weaknesses of the mystic and the materialist. So the dedication must be taken seriously, especially within the context of the present examination.

Significantly enough he began that ceremony by dedicating his library to his dead mother—calling on history, on the ancestors, at the moment of profound decisions for the future. Then he went on to make this vow, as he records it:

> I will seek [the Truth] on the pure assumption that it is worth seeking—and Heaven, nor Hell, God nor Devil shall turn me from my purpose till I die.

From the concern for Truth he turned to the world, and said:

> I am firmly convinced that my own best development is not one and the same with the best development of the world and here I am willing to sacrifice. That sacrifice to the world's good becomes too soon sticky sentimentality. I therefore take the world that the Unknown lays in my hands and work for the rise of the Negro people, taking for granted that their best development means the best development of the world. . . .[10]

Here, for our purposes is the central, tripartite dedication: to truth, to the world's good, and to the good of his people. Du Bois came to manhood when men believed such things possible, and for all of his life—with significant periods of doubt—he seemed to believe it too. In Germany, he began where he was, on the black and inner ground of his own life, hoping against hope that there was no basic incompatibility among these ultimate commitments he had made.

We shall not attempt here to delineate the development of Du Bois' life when he returned to America. Let it suffice to say that he gave every evidence of holding fast to the resolves made in north Germany. Indeed, the familiar, bloody, American ground seemed to carry him even more deeply into the messianic understanding of the nation's black aliens. This was surely the burden of the essay published by the American Negro Academy in 1897, *The Conservation of the Races.*[11]

It deserves careful examination, for in this essay we find much of the Black Messianism that Du Bois would carry with him in one form or another, at one level of intensity or another, until he was buried in the land of his forefathers.

In the essay, after having defined race in terms of common heritage, language, blood, tradition, and impulses, he adds that members of such a racial group are also "striving together for the accomplishment of certain more or less vividly conceived ideals of life." Out of that setting he continued: "Some of the great races of today—particularly the Negro race—have not as yet given to civilization the full spiritual message which they are capable of giving." In order to do this, Du Bois called for black solidarity and originality. He writes:

> For the development of Negro genius, of Negro literature and art, of Negro spirit, only Negroes bound and welded together, Negroes inspired by one vast ideal, can work out in its fullness the great message we have for humanity.

As Du Bois saw it, black people in America were "the advanced guard of Negro people," and had to remember that "if they are to take their just place in the van of Pan-Negroism, then their destiny is *not* absorption by the white Americans." Rather, he proclaimed that if blacks were faithful to their calling, America could become the place where it could be demonstrated that blacks "are a nation stored with wonderful possibilities of culture." If this was to begin, he said, then black destiny "is not a servile imitation of Anglo-Saxon culture but a stalwart originality which shall unswervingly follow Negro ideals."

Afro-Americans had "a distinct mission as a race" according to Du Bois. Put somewhat mystically, it was to be "the first fruits of this new nation," of an Africa reborn, "the harbinger of that black tomorrow which is yet destined to soften the whiteness of the Teutonic today." Obviously intoxicated with hope, Du Bois went on to say, "It is our duty to conserve our physical powers, our intellectual endowments, our spiritual ideals; as a race we must strive by race organization, by race solidarity, by race unity to the realization of that broader humanity which freely recognizes differences in men, but sternly deprecates inequality in their opportunities of development."

So Du Bois called upon black people to have faith in themselves, in their past, and in a glorious messianic vocation. His peroration—and in spite of himself he *was* a preacher—included these words: "We must be inspired [he wrote] with the divine faith of our black mothers that out of the blood and dust of battle will march a victorious host, a mighty nation, a peculiar people, to speak to the nations of the earth a Divine truth that shall make them free."

Of course, it takes no special wisdom or insight to see that Dr. Du Bois in this essay had grasped an Old Testament understanding of the messianic people and nation. That is, those who have a sense of common encounter—experience with the acts of God in their history and who are called by their prophets to a common vocation on behalf of all men. Not until sixty years later, after a lifetime of basic faithfulness to this vision, did W. E. B. Du Bois move in another related but significantly different direction. Even as he moved, though, he still believed that history defines both present and future.

Returning to the earlier period, it should be apparent that Du

Bois' program for the Talented Tenth grew naturally out of his messianic vision of the role of the black people in America, out of his nineteenth-century German–American–Old Testament understanding of leadership, and out of his mistrust of white leaders for black hosts. Whites, he said, could not be trusted "to guide this group into self-realization and to its highest cultural possibilities."[12] Therefore, the specially trained black minority was also part of his messianic commitment.

In an important sense, much of Du Bois' scholarship came out of the same messianic context, out of the same tripartite commitment to truth, the world, and his people. He saw his trust was not betrayed. Later he would constantly chastise and encourage black schools in the task of scholarship on the Afro-American experience as part of their role in building their people's sense of self as well as contributing to the broader truth.

Such an attitude was especially evident in his comments about his commitment to the clarification of African history. In his autobiography he wrote, "I am not sure just when I began to feel an interest in Africa." But he said [he knew that he became tired of] "finding in newspapers, textbooks, and history fulsome lauding of white folk, and either no mention of dark peoples, or mention in disparaging and apologetic phrase."

Reclaiming the past

It was at that point, Du Bois remembers, that "I made up my mind that it must be true that Africa had a history and a destiny, and that one of my jobs was to disinter this unknown past, and help make certain a splendid future."[13]

The insistent theme of black solidarity was somewhat toned down in *The Souls of Black Folk* (1903), but the profound love of black people came out in many of the essays, especially, for instance, the memoir of Alexander Crummell and the meditation on The Sorrow Songs. Of course, Du Bois could not write for public consumption without the messianic theme being stated on one level or another, and it was present—though muted—in that most famous of his writings. It was recognizable near the closing of the first essay, when Du Bois wrote:

> Work, culture, liberty—all these we need . . . each growing and aiding each, and all striving toward that vaster ideal that swims before the Negro people, the ideal of human brotherhood, gained through the unifying ideal of race . . . that some day on American soil two world-races may give to each other those characteristics both so sadly lack.[14]

It was in *The Souls of Black Folk,* too, that there appeared for the first time—as far as I can tell—the suggestion of a fear that remained with Dr. Du Bois all his life, a fear that Afro-Americans might betray their own messianic vocation. In the essay, "On the Wings of Atlanta," he asked these questions:

> What if the Negro people be wooed from a strike for righteousness, from a love of knowing, to regard dollars as the be-all and end-all of life? Whither, then, is the new-world quest for goodness and Beauty and Truth gone glimmering? Must this, and that fair flower of freedom which . . . [sprang] from our fathers' blood, must that too degenerate into a dusky quest of gold?[15]

By the time a half century had passed, Du Bois thought he had the answer, and it transformed his hope as well as his final days.

But in 1904 Du Bois still had much ground for hope. He shared it with his students and with young persons wherever he found them, challenging them to become leaders of the black messianic vanguard. In his *Credo,* published that year, he continued to affirm the creative tension of his convictions. Thus he proclaimed a belief in the brotherhood of all men, as well as a special belief "in the Negro Race; in the beauty of its genius, the sweetness of its soul, and its strength in that meekness which shall inherit the earth." So, too, he could believe "in pride of race" and also in "Liberty for all men."[16] Throughout his life the task was continually to keep these beliefs in tension. His record in accomplishing that task was mixed with success and failure, but I think the success clearly dominates the scene.

The Niagara Movement was, of course, an attempt to sustain the tension, to put action behind the creed, to gather together a black vanguard for the struggle. That story cannot be told here, but it must be seen in the context of the commitment to black solidarity and hope.

On the other hand, Du Bois often admitted that it was hard for him to trust whites, even those he knew were theoretically his allies in the building of a kingdom beyond caste. The raw nerves of his blackness and the long memories of racial pain made it difficult to know how to put together his hope for a new brotherhood beyond race with his sense of need for a committed black brotherhood. Later he wrote, for instance, about those first two decades of the twentieth century:

> I was bitter at lynching, but not moved by the treatment of white miners in Colorado or Montana. I never sang the songs of Joe Hill, and the terrible strike at Lawrence, Massachusetts, did not stir me, because I knew that factory strikers like these would not let a Negro work beside them or live in the same town. It was hard for me to outgrow this mental isolation.[17]

This suggests, of course, that it was often difficult for Du Bois to live up to the socialism that he and Niagara proclaimed—difficult because of his commitment to black people and his experience with whites. (It was in this context that he left the Socialist Party in 1912, believing that his devotion to blacks would not allow what he considered the luxury of wasted votes on a Socialist Presidential candidate.)

Du Bois' ever-deepening sense of commitment to black solidarity held profound implications for his relationships with the white-dominated NAACP. It is already apparent that one of his most important reasons for taking an executive position with the organization was the opportunity it afforded to have his own forum in *The Crisis*. Early in the game the founding editor began to use the pages of the periodical to put forward his own convictions, suggestions and intuitions for the building of black solidarity—often at the expense of the Association's stated goals and methods.

So by 1915 Du Bois was writing words which may have surprised others, but which grew out of the days of Fisk and Germany, and *The Conservation of the Races*. He said:

> The Negro must have power; the power of men, the right to do, to know, to feel and to express that knowledge, action and spiritual gift.

Besides, he repeated, "the first article in the program of any group that will survive must be the great aim, equality and power among men." His program for this empowerment included political, educational, and cultural organization among blacks. Finally he said:

> I thank God that most of the money that supports the National Association for the Advancement of Colored People comes from black hands; a still larger proportion must so come, and we must not only support but control this and similar organizations and hold them unwaveringly to our objects, our aims and our ideals.[18]

One of the natural products of his position was his call within a year for a black political party.

Du Bois' position was reaffirmed in his slim but significant book, *The Negro*. In addition to the immeasurable service it performed in introducing many black persons to their African roots, it continued the theme of black messianism, in a way that surely made the Spingarns and the Villards even more uncomfortable. Near the end of the work, Du Bois wrote:

> Instead of being led and defended by others, as in the past, American Negroes are gaining their own voices, their own ideals. Self-realization is thus coming . . . to another of the world's great races.[19]

Post–World War I attitudes

This was, of course, the time of the European holocaust, and the war had a significant effect on Du Bois' sense of the role of black people and all of what he called "the darker races." For instance, in 1916 he stated his conviction that the European struggle had vividly illustrated the bankruptcy of western civilization. Therefore, he said it was time for black people to reassess old ideals—from the African past.

Old standards of beauty beckon us again [he wrote] not the blue-eyed, white-skinned types . . . but rich, brown and black men and women with glowing dark eyes and crinkling hair. . . . Life, which in this cold Occident stretched in bleak conventional lives before us, takes on a warm golden hue that harks back to the heritage of Africa and the tropics.

Then, predictably, the messianic word was spoken again. Du Bois wrote, "Brothers, the war has shown us the cruelty of the civilization of the West. History has taught us the futility of the civilization of the East. Let ours be the civilization of no *man,* but of *all* men. This is the truth that sets us free."[20]

It is obvious, too, that Du Bois' angle of vision from the black side made it possible for him to see new aspects of the world through the carnage of the war, especially the significance of the Second Coming of the nonwhite peoples of the world. As a result of the war he was also able to develop new approaches to his long-standing interest in Pan-Africanism, a topic purposely slighted here, but surely important for our full understanding of Du Bois.

In America, "after the war" meant the riots of 1919 and a general resurgence of black suffering. It meant the rise of Marcus Garvey, and Du Bois had to come to terms with *that* variety of black solidarity—another issue that we must slight at this time. Almost predictably, the postwar period found Du Bois responding to the intensified problems of black people with more extended attempts to spell out his concerns for the inner organization of the black community. None of the institutions in that community escaped his scrutiny, and as we might expect, the colleges were especially exposed. For instance, when in 1926 Tuskegee and Hampton received multimillion-dollar endowments, Du Bois wrote of his hope that the funds would make them independent enough to "say to all whites: This is a Negro school." Tell them, he counseled:

In the long run we can imagine no difference of interest between White and Black; but temporarily there may be, or men may imagine there is; in such case we stand flatly and firmly for Negroes.

This school is not a sanatorium for white teachers or a restaurant and concert hall for white trustees and their friends.[21]

His constant demand of black schools was that they be faithful to their role—or, perhaps, that they first understand their role—in the struggle for survival and for fulfillment in which black persons were involved.

By 1929 Du Bois was proposing that the future road for black people lay in the direction of consumer and producer's cooperatives. As the depression began he urged the development of "an economic General Staff" for black America which would help chart the way ahead.[22]

As we approach 1934, the year that his black solidarity program and his criticism of the NAACP finally provided the occasion for his departure from *The Crisis,* several issues should be clearly stated. First, Du Bois' emphasis on the organization of the black community was not new to the depression period. Its roots went back in his own life to the nineteenth century. The pronounced emphasis on economics was more recent, and had been influenced by many factors, not the least of them being the brutal experience of blacks during the depression. Du Bois had also watched the success of Garvey for a period and could observe the economic achievements of Father Divine and his strange form of religious communalism. The socialist-communist movements had their effect. (Du Bois had visited Russia and was deeply impressed with what he saw.) At least as important as any other single factor was Du Bois' own conviction that blacks were still faced with a struggle of several generations before racial prejudice would be overcome.

So he called for what might be labeled "Black Socialism" or black communalism, from cooperative farms to urban communities, to socialized medicine—all in the hands of black people. He proposed that many of them be underwritten with Federal funds.[23] He refused to run from the term segregation, and used it almost as a goad, saying that since it existed and would continue to exist until deep levels of change came in the white psyche, that blacks should use it for their own good. He recognized the sense in which this might compromise his ultimate vision for blacks, and in March 1934 published this brief summary of the dilemma:

> 1. Compulsory separation of human beings by essentially artificial criteria such as birth, nationality, language, color and race, is the cause of human hate, jealousy and war, and the destruction of talent and art.

On the other hand, he put this proposition up for consideration:

> 2. Where separation of mankind into races, groups and classes is compulsory, either by law or by custom, and whether that compulsion be temporary or permanent, the only effective defense that the segregated and despised group has against complete spiritual and physical disaster, is internal self-organization for self-respect and self-defense.[24]

By then it was clear that his concern for the continuation of black spiritual life was equal to that of his concern for the physical, and he desired self-respect at least as much as self-defense. This was a natural response for one who sought to maintain a messianic hope for black people. They must endure, but they must endure with integrity, not as wards of the white society, Du Bois said, not as beggars at white doors.

He was even ready to face the possibility of black emigration if the nation made it impossible for this black solidarity and selfhood to develop. In several instances he compared the black situation in America to the Jewish predicament in Europe. But he never gave up his ultimate concern for the Truth of black people in America. In the last issue of *The Crisis* which he edited, he refused to back down against the NAACP's opposition and said:

> In this period of frustration and disappointment, we must turn from negation to affirmation, from the ever-lasting 'No' to the ever-lasting 'Yes.' Instead of drowning our originality in imitation of mediocre white folks . . . [we] have a right to affirm that the Negro race is one of the great human races, inferior to none in its accomplishment and in its ability.[25]

When he was attacked on the grounds that he now seemed to be changing his position, Du Bois said, "I am not worried about being inconsistent. What worries me is the Truth." He said he saw more segregation in the North in 1934 than in 1910 and wondered how black men would keep their souls while battling against the walls.

Interestingly enough, the following month, June 1934, Du Bois showed some concern for both consistency and truth when he inserted in *The Crisis* several paragraphs from *The Conservation of the Races,* dated 1897. They ended with the familiar issue of the distinct mission of black people versus "self-obliteration." Then he added a note, saying: "On the whole, I am rather pleased to find myself still so much in sympathy with myself."[26] In the light of the present mood of black America, it appears that Du Bois now has many more sympathizers than he could then imagine. But none of them was on the Board of the National Association for the Advancement of Colored People at that time, so the resignation of W. E. B. Du Bois was accepted—for reasons only partly related to black socialism.

Referring to the black communalistic emphasis of his messianic vision, Du Bois later wrote:

> I shall not live to see entirely the triumph of this, my newer emphasis; but it will triumph just as much and just as completely as did my advocacy of agitation and self-assertion. It is indeed a part of that same original program; it is its natural and inevitable fulfillment.[27]

Du Bois did not live to see our own black-conscious age arrive in America. Indeed, before he died he often appeared to despair of its borning. But we see it, and remembering his words, some of almost a century ago, we can do no less than stand in awe before this giant of a man.

What more we can do depends, I suppose, upon whether we still believe in fulfillment, redemption, new men, and new societies. Or—perhaps more importantly—what more we can do depends on whether we are convinced that a man can, in *this* age, still say without shame:

> I will seek [the truth] on the pure assumption that it is worth seeking—and Heaven nor Hell, God nor Devil shall turn me from my purpose till I die.

Epilogue

When it is complete, the last portion of this essay will attempt to establish several clarities. First, and perhaps most obvious, is the fact that in the wilderness of the western black diaspora W. E. B. Du Bois was in all likelihood the most significant voice to prepare the way for this current, newest age of blackness. He is the proper context for an adequate understanding of Malcolm, of Fanon, of Stokely Carmichael and Martin Luther King, Jr.

The last section will also examine the significance of legal desegregation in America for Du Bois' vision of the messianic role of black people here. I will suggest that by the 1950s he became convinced that his beloved people were "being bribed to trade equal status in the United States for the slavery of the majority of men." Many events—including the frightened response of black leadership to his own time of McCarthyite trial—reinforced that conviction. Black Americans were being led to a betrayal of their messianic calling.

Within that setting, finally, we understand more fully his decision to return to the land of his forefathers near the end of his life. Among the many other factors involved, W. E. B. Du Bois had evidently transferred his black messianic hope to the brothers in the homeland, especially those under Kwame Nkrumah's leadership. This was surely apparent in the words he spoke when he became a citizen of Ghana—just six months before his death, just six days before his ninety-fifth birthday. Du Bois said then:

> My great-grandfather was carried from the Gulf of Guinea. I have returned that my dust may mingle with the dust of my forefathers. There is not much time for me. But now, my life will flow on in the vigorous, young stream of Ghanaian life which lifts the African personality to its proper place among men. And I shall not have lived and worked in vain.[28]

Thus, at this next to the last moment of his life, the past, the present, and the future were joined as one in the thoughts of Du Bois and in his undying hopes for the glorious destiny of Africa, wherever they may be found.

References

1. W. E. B. Du Bois, *Dusk of Dawn: An Essay Toward an Autobiography of a Race Concept* (New York: Harcourt, Brace, 1940).
2. St. Clair Drake, unpublished manuscript prepared for delivery at Roosevelt University, Chicago (Summer, 1963).
3. W. E. B. Du Bois, "Of Alexander Crummell," *The Souls of Black Folk* (New York: Blue Heron Press, 1953).
4. W. E. B. Du Bois, *Autobiography of W. E. B. Du Bois: A Soliloquy on Viewing My Life from the Last Decade of Its First Century* (New York: International Publishers, 1968), pp. 105–106.
5. Francis L. Broderick, *W. E. B. Du Bois: Negro Leader in a Time of Crisis* (Stanford: Stanford University Press, 1959), p. 8.
6. Du Bois, *Autobiography,* p. 135.
7. *Ibid.,* p. 136.
8. Du Bois, *Dusk of Dawn,* pp. 101–102.
9. Du Bois, *Autobiography,* p. 169.
10. *Ibid.,* pp. 170–171.
11. Howard Brotz, ed., *Negro Social and Political Thought: 1850–1920* (New York: Basic Books, 1966), p. 485.
12. Du Bois, *Dusk of Dawn,* p. 70.
13. Du Bois, *Autobiography,* p. 343.
14. Du Bois, *Souls of Black Folk,* p. 22.
15. *Ibid.,* p. 69.
16. W. E. B. Du Bois, *Darkwater* (New York: Harcourt, Brace and Howe, 1920), pp. 3–4.
17. Du Bois, *Autobiography,* p. 305.
18. Francis L. Broderick and August Meier, eds., *Negro Protest Thought in the Twentieth Century* (Indianapolis: Bobbs-Merrill, 1965), p. 60.
19. W. E. B. Du Bois, *The Negro* (New York: Henry Holt, 1915), p. 231.
20. W. E. B. Du Bois, *An ABC of Color* (Berlin: Seven Seas Publishers, 1963), pp. 87–88.
21. *The Crisis,* 31 (March, 1926), p. 216.
22. *The Crisis,* 36 (November, 1929), p. 392; 40 (July, 1932), p. 242.
23. *The Crisis,* 41 (January, 1934), p. 1; 41 (February, 1934).
24. *The Crisis,* 41 (March, 1934), p. 85.
25. *The Crisis,* 41 (June, 1934), p. 182.
26. *Ibid.,* p. 183.
27. Du Bois, *Dusk of Dawn,* p. 311.
28. William Branch, New York *Amsterdam News* (Saturday, September 7, 1963). Accra, Ghana, dateline.

Cultural contributions of Dr. Du Bois

ERNEST KAISER

The Negro people, in their fight against chattel slavery and to obtain and keep their citizenship rights over the past century and a half, have needed political and cultural leaders and spokesmen who were giants. And they have produced them: Frederick Douglass, Carter G. Woodson, and W. E. B. Du Bois; men who could inspire and move a whole people.

W. E. B. Du Bois was born and grew up during the period which ran from the high point of Reconstruction democracy for Negroes and poor whites in the South after the Civil War to the nadir or lowest point around the turn of the century, from Negro voting and high office-holding, integrated schools, and gains in the struggle for land in the South through the overthrow of Reconstruction, the driving of Negroes and poor whites from power, the massacres, the many hundreds of lynchings, the burning of Negro schools and churches, the taking of Negro land, the forced free labor of the convict lease system, the plantation sharecropping and the enactment of stringent laws segregating southern Negroes and whites from the cradle to the grave. It was a period in which the Negro people were oppressed so hard in the South that compromisers like Booker T. Washington arose willing to be half men and to accept half a loaf.

And through all of this terrible period Du Bois was preparing himself at Fisk University, Harvard University, and the University of Berlin. At Fisk he wrote many articles, essays, and a novel, was editor-in-chief of the *Fisk Herald* and became quite an orator, debater, and public speaker. At Harvard he studied under many great men: William James in psychology, George Santayana and Josiah Royce in philosophy, Shaler in geology, Palmer in ethics, Barrett Wendell in English and Albert Bushnell Hart in history. Du Bois distinguished himself here, was graduated and received a Harvard fellowship to do graduate work in history and in what would be called social science today. This fellowship and its renewal carried him to his master's degree and through his dissertation for a Ph.D. degree, all on the suppression of the African slave trade. He was guided through this work by Professor Hart as a brilliant student and scholar. Du Bois worked on a number of general studies at Harvard and his dissertation, *The Suppression of the African Slave Trade to the United States of America, 1638–1870,* was published in 1896 as volume one in the Harvard Historical Studies series.

Then with a Slater Fund half gift and half loan, he went to Europe for two years of postdoctoral study at the University of Berlin. There Du Bois again distinguished himself in economics, history, and sociology, sitting under such outstanding German scholars as Gustav Schmoller and Wagner. It was at the University of Berlin in 1893 that Du Bois, at twenty-five years of age, dedicated himself, not grimly but with great determination, to the search for truth and to "work for the rise of the Negro people" since "their best development means the best development of the world; to make a name in science, to make a name in literature and thus to raise my race." All of the cumulatively Herculean and stupendous work of Du Bois' long and fruitful life fitted into his overall plan of making a name in literature and in the social science disciplines and (broadening his original view) doing other writing and organizing work in a more direct effort to raise and advance the Negro people. All of his great physical resources and all of his many and prodigal talents, even genius, he devoted unstintingly and perseveringly to the uplift of all peoples of African descent.

Dr. Du Bois' cultural contributions may be broken down roughly into three categories: literary-political works (essays, poetry, novels, autobiography); historical, sociological, biographical works (pertaining to the Negro in the U.S.); and his works as an Africanist. Tracing each of these groups chronologically, we get a concerted and cumulative view of this man's work and his impact as a towering Afro-American, a giant American intellectual and world thinker and scholar.

His literary-political work began with *The Souls of Black Folk* (1903), a now classic book of essays and sketches. Written in simple, beautiful, Biblical rhetoric, this book is a passionate polemic justifying Reconstruction, criticizing Booker T. Washington and giving a devastating picture of the Black Belt. It also demanded the right to vote, civic equality, the education of youth according to ability, and all rights implicit in the Declaration of Independence. Finally, the book set forth the cultural gifts of the Negro to America. This book, said James Weldon Johnson, had a greater effect upon and within the Negro race in America than any other single book published in this country since *Uncle Tom's Cabin*. *The Gift of Black Folk; Negroes in the Making of America* (1924) sets forth in great detail the cultural and historical gifts of Negroes to America. But before this book there were the novel *The Quest of the Silver Fleece* (1911), Du Bois' literary and militant editorship of the NAACP's *The Crisis* magazine beginning in 1910 and extending into 1934, and *Darkwater* (1920). *Darkwater* (at one time subtitled "the twentieth century completion of *Uncle Tom's Cabin*"; at another "voices from within the veil") is a continuation of the essays and sketches of *The Souls of Black Folk* and contains that famous and passionate poem "A Litany at Atlanta" about the terrible Atlanta, Ga., riot of 1906 and his beautiful "Credo" written in 1904.

Du Bois' works were part of the background for the Harlem Renaissance of the 1920s and early thirties. Du Bois participated in this movement as the encouraging editor of *The Crisis* during this period; also as the author of "The Black Man Brings His Gifts" for the book *The New Negro* (1925) edited by Alain Locke and of another novel *Dark Princess* (1928). In 1940 came his beautifully written autobiography, *Dusk of Dawn: The Autobiography of a Race Concept*. Here Du Bois uses his own life, as he had earlier in the booklet *A Pageant in Seven Decades* (1938), to probe the sociology and psychology of American racism. In 1940 Du Bois also founded at Atlanta University the quarterly literary magazine *Phylon,* a review of race and culture, which is still being published although more sociological now. In 1952 Du Bois returned to autobiography with *In Battle for Peace: The Story of My 83rd Birthday,* this time to tell inimitably and with masterful pen the story of that monstrous frame-up attempt, trial, and acquittal of himself and his colleagues of the former Peace Information Center on charges of failing to register as "foreign agents."

His *Black Flame* trilogy of novels, *The Ordeal of Mansart* (1957), *Mansart Builds a School* (1959), and *Worlds of Color* (1961), covering the story of the Negro people and Negro-white relations from the end of the Reconstruction era in the late 1870s to the middle 1950s is a tremendous achievement of American literature and written when Du Bois was in his late eighties and early nineties! Here he tries to sum up in historical fiction what has really happened in Negro and U.S. history since the Reconstruction period as he knows it from study and experience. Finally, at the time of his death in 1963, there appeared *An ABC of Color* edited by him and consisting of some of his important speeches through the years and excerpts (poetry and prose) from his books and magazine writings, mostly from *The Crisis* magazine. Also to be added here are the hundreds of articles over the many years from his prolific pen.

Du Bois' historical, sociological, and biographical works pertaining to the Negro in the U.S. began with his above-mentioned *The Suppression of the African Slave Trade to the United States, 1638–1870* (1896), an authoritative work of sound scholarship which was the first scientific history of the Negro. He turned quickly from history, when the opportunity opened at the University of Pennsylvania, to sociology, then in its infancy. He made a study of the Negro in Philadelphia, *The Philadelphia Negro: A Social Study* (1899), so thorough and complete that it has withstood the criticism of forty years and was the first scientific sociological study done in the U.S. This study showed the Negro group as a symptom and not a cause; as a striving, palpitating human group and not an inert, sick body of crime as the city fathers of Philadelphia had wanted him to prove.

From the University of Pennsylvania Du Bois moved to Atlanta University, where his careful monographs in the Atlanta University publications series (1899–1912) were the first genuine social science studies to appear in the South by whites or Negroes and much better done than any other attempted similar work anywhere in the world. These studies gained international attention. They dealt with the college-bred Negro American, the Negro common school, economic cooperation, efforts for social betterment, and morals and manners among Negro Americans;

also Negro crime, the Negro artisan, the Negro American family, the Negro church, and Negro health. Dr. W. M. Cobb of the Howard University School of Medicine calls the monograph *The Health and Physique of the Negro American* (1906), in this Atlanta University series, the first significant scientific approach to the health problems and biological study of the Negro. But, says Cobb, neither the Negro medical profession nor the Negro educational world was ready for it. Its potential usefulness was not realized by Negroes. Whites were hostile to such a study embracing the anthropology, psychology, and health of the Negro in all of their aspects. This study, Du Bois' single excursion into the health field, was, says Cobb, an extraordinary forward pass heaved the length of the field, but there were no receivers.

In 1909 came Du Bois' elegiac, brooding, prose poem biography of John Brown in which he treats the facts from a different point of view; that is, from the viewpoint of the little known important inner development of the Negro American. And viewed in this way, John Brown becomes the white American who perhaps came nearest to touching the real souls of black folk. Du Bois' *John Brown* and Oswald Garrison Villard's *John Brown* (1910), both commemorating the fiftieth anniversary of Brown's death in 1859, were two voices crying in the wilderness of the venomous anti-Brown American history and biography of that time.

His work on the Reconstruction period which began in 1910 when he read a paper on "Reconstruction and Its Benefits" before the American Historical Association (*American Historical Review,* July 1910), culminated with his great work *Black Reconstruction in America, 1860–1880* (1935). This book is a comprehensive defense of the role of Negroes and Radical Republicans during Reconstruction and a repudiation of the widespread opinion of the period as a tragic era productive only of evil and corruption. *Black Reconstruction* and James S. Allen's *Reconstruction: The Battle for Democracy, 1865–1876* (1937), published two years later, rescued this period from white historiography and forced American historians to revise and reconsider their biased work on Reconstruction.

As early as 1909 Du Bois started an Encyclopedia Africana project to commemorate the fiftieth year of the Emancipation

Proclamation (1913) and the 300th anniversary of the landing of the Negro in America (1919). Later in 1931 an Encyclopedia of the Negro project was initiated by the Phelps-Stokes Fund involving Negro and white scholars and with Du Bois heading the group. In 1945 Dr. Du Bois and Guy B. Johnson edited the *Encyclopedia of the Negro* (revised in 1946), a small preparatory volume with reference lists and reports but representing only a portion of the material which the editors had prepared from 1931 to 1943. This volume is all that the project has published. Du Bois, as Director of Special Research for the NAACP, also edited a lengthy, documented, published petition *Appeal to the World* which was presented to the United Nations in 1947 for redress of the grievances of and discrimination against U.S. Negroes.

Du Bois says that he became tired of finding in newspapers, textbooks, and history fulsome praise of white people and either no mention of dark people at all or disparaging or apologetic statements. He decided that Africa must have a history and destiny, and that one of his jobs was to dig up and reveal this unknown past and help make certain a splendid future. And so over a number of years, he did a lot of reading, writing, research, and planning as an Africanist and architect of African freedom. His very important work as an Africanist begins again with his doctoral dissertation, *The Suppression of the African Slave Trade to the United States of America, 1638–1870* (1896). His second book on African history was *The Negro* (1915), a volume in the Home University Library. There was his work at the great Races Congress of 1911 in Europe dealing with the scientific bases of racial and social relations of various ethnic and cultural groups. Then his Herculean work in helping to organize and participating in the six Pan-African Congresses of 1900, 1919, 1921, 1923, 1927, and 1945. These pioneering conferences brought together Africans, West Indians, American Negroes, and interested whites to discuss the problems of colonial peoples and African freedom. We must also include here Du Bois' many articles in books and magazines on Africa.

Black Folk, Then and Now (1939), an enlargement of Du Bois' *The Negro,* was an historical, anthropological, and sociological study of the Negro in Africa and in the Americas. After World

War II came *Color and Democracy: Colonies and Peace* (1945) which took up the post-war world peace plans from the point of view of the colored colonial peoples and presented a ringing challenge to the imperialist countries. Concentrating on the study of colonial peoples and peoples of Negro descent throughout the world as Director of Special Research for the NAACP, Du Bois produced *The World and Africa* (1947), a pioneering inquiry into and bold outline of the part which Africa has played in world history, the details of which may be filled in by William Leo Hansberry and other Africanists. Finally, after he went to Ghana in the fall of 1961, his six *Information Reports* (edited with W. Alphaeus Hunton) for cooperation toward a many-volumed, monumental *Encyclopedia Africana* and a provisional draft plan defining and setting the scope and contents of the *Encyclopedia* prepared for the December 18, 1962, conference on this great work at the University of Ghana.

Langston Hughes' poem "The Negro Speaks of Rivers," dedicated to W. E. B. Du Bois, echoes some of this African history and concludes with:

> I've known rivers:
> Ancient, dusky rivers.
> My soul has grown deep like the rivers.

Countee Cullen captures the life and career of this incredible Negro giant and genius of a man—Du Bois—with these lines:

> Men raised a mountain in your path,
> Steep, perilous with slime,
> Then smouldered in their own hot wrath
> To see you climb and climb.

W. E. B. Du Bois: philosopher

EUGENE C. HOLMES

Since before Fisk, which he entered in 1885, and through Harvard, where he secured his second A.B., then the University of Berlin for graduate work and Harvard again, where he won the Ph.D., Dr. Du Bois "followed knowledge like a sinking star." This scholar always followed that star, not for its own sake, but for knowledge purposeful and for knowledge working. In his "Portrait of Dr. Du Bois" in the *American Scholar,*[1] Saunders Redding observed that "the pursuit has given him one of the most catholic minds of the century." He added, "It is not a difficult mind to know."

In 1886, as an undergraduate at Fisk, his first important essay was entitled, *An Open Letter to the Southern People.* This struggling college, missionary and philanthropy dominated, could not provide the young Du Bois with the proper prerequisites of a sound education, so he went to Harvard College which he had always aspired to and two years later he won his second bachelor's degree in 1890. In the next year he won his M.A.

During his Harvard years, there were many luminaries in philosophy, Adams, Palmer, Royce, and James. The advances in science were made mainly in psychology which was being developed by William James. Geology under Shaler was one of Burghardt's favorite subjects. Most of the advances in Darwinian biology and the new anthropology were opposed if only in the academic halls. But there was Barrett Wendell in English, Albert Bushnell Hart in history, and Bingham in economic theory. His philosophy teachers wished that he would undertake the serious study of philosophy, but the young student probably decided that while philosophy would be his guide, it did not bake any bread. His decision was to stay in the social studies and to attempt to adapt the new sociological approach to the problems of Negro history and to Negro uplift.

In his graduate study at the University of Berlin, he studied long and hard under the great historians, economists, and philosophers—Schmoller, Wagner, Von Ranke, Trendelburg, Natorp, the post-Kantians, and the Hegelians. Marxism was very much in the academic air and Du Bois became friendly with the Fabians and other socialists who were in Berlin. Discussions with these students and professors were heady and enlivening. After a short stint as professor of Latin and Greek at Wilberforce, he returned to Harvard to complete his doctoral work, his dissertation being *The Suppression of the African Slave Trade to the United States, 1638–1870,* published the next year as the very first doctoral dissertation in the Harvard Historical Studies.

As a result of his term as an instructor of sociology at the University of Pennsylvania, he wrote a distinguished monograph, *The Philadelphia Negro.*[2]

> Finally, let me add that I trust that this study with all its shortcomings and errors will at least serve to emphasize the fact that the Negro problems are problems of human beings; not ungrounded assumptions or metaphysical subtleties. They present a field which the student must enter seriously and cultivate seriously and honestly. And until he has prepared the ground by intelligent and diligent research the labors of philanthropists and statesmen must continue to be, to a large extent, barren and unfruitful.
>
> W. E. B. Du Bois
> Atlanta, 1899.

At Atlanta, where at first he was professor of economics and history, he edited the famous Atlanta University *Studies of the Negro Problem.* He was well on his way to becoming the pioneer in a scientific approach to the social sciences and he would spare no efforts to give the swaddling discipline of sociology a scientific foundation.

With Dr. Du Bois, from the beginning of his professional career, it was always the problem of getting the truth about race by means of a scientific approach in the only ways and methods which would ensure proof and prediction, those of inference and the logic of induction. He vowed to search always for the truth as a scientist and "to work for the use of the Negro people since their best development means the best development of the world, to make a name in science, to make a name in literature and thus to raise my race." Never before in intellectual history had any man set himself such a titanic task.

Dr. Du Bois saw the truth as a tool for the better performance of the scientific task of probing and assaying "the scope of chance and unreason in human action." That he applied his scientific methods to the limited areas of race relations and Pan-Africanism was partly "because of the specialization of modern scholarship and partly because doing otherwise would have meant the rejection of race and a consequent upsetting of the balance between intellect and emotion."[3] In plain terms, Du Bois had come to see the problem of color in impersonal terms as a matter of social conditions and this condition itself was a matter of education, it was a matter of knowledge, one of scientific procedure within a world which had become scientific in concept.

Literally and historically, there had not been any philosophies of freedom up until Du Bois, who made it his basic theme in *belles lettres,* in his sociology, and in his history. He felt that when the slaves expressed their reaction to American reality, they seized upon the pessimistic symbols and images of Christianity—the only body of literature allowed them—and charged them with a concealed energy and optimism, whose meaning was revealed on the plane of action through the countless revolts and escapes that marked this period of American history. When the abolition of Northern slavery made Negro expression on a higher level a possibility, the free Negroes of the North made an alliance with the rising middle class and they named their first publication *Freedom's Journal.*

Du Bois saw what Emancipation, and later, Reconstruction, had done to break the militant alliance between the freedmen, the industrial capitalists, and the northern working men. With the liberation movement incomplete, Dr. Du Bois guided Negro writing into being concerned with the destiny of the Negroes in the new order and thus he began an examination and evaluation of Negro history and sociology with the discipline of advanced science. But not even the broad knowledge and imagination of Du

Bois grasped the real class nature of American Negro experience. This experience had passed too swiftly through historical space and its forms had not become developed into full consciousness within American institutional life. This Negro experience could be only vicarious and it was not until much later in his life that he came to understand it as a historical process.

Though he was not a mass man, the often aloof Dr. Du Bois derived his inspirations from the masses. More than anything, this was the materialist side of him. It was expressed in his faith in the democratic ethos, and, as a materialist, he was unlike "the laughing" Democritus and the mechanical materialist, Hobbes. For Du Bois, it was always "a passion for dignity on earth and for justice for all."

The philosophically untrained referred to "the old man" as an "idealist" or as "a realist." Dr. Du Bois' philosophical training and his turning toward the tools of scientific method in the social sciences led him inexorably to materialism and to construct models as a scientific historian and sociologist. The materialist draws his inspiration and chooses his models from the largest and most obvious fields of science, such as stellar evolution, the field of biological evolution, or, in Du Bois' case, the actions of human beings. This included the movement of social institutions, the study of the suppression of the African slave trade, the Philadelphia Negro, the laws of capitalist development into imperialism and all of the actual transformations of national life.

The philosopher-sociologist Du Bois always regarded his methodology as embracing the equal rights of human beings to strive to live and it was in that sense that his materialism was expressed in its sympathies for a democratic ethos. Within such a humanistic context, peace, and not war, was the only true good because it became a reflection of universal justice toward the poor of the earth and it included the aspirations of the enslaved of all nations for its goals.

Dr. Du Bois was among the first American scholars in the social sciences to teach Marxism, when he gave a graduate seminar at Atlanta University in 1904, "Marxism and the Negro." In this seminar and in the published Atlanta University *Studies,* he applied his knowledge to the economic structure of the heinous slave system, to the class struggle after Reconstruction, to the conflict between labor and capitalism, to the unequal development of free public education, and to the unholy alliance between the Booker T. Washingtons and philanthropy. Du Bois analyzed the impact of colonialism and the development of capitalism into imperialism. This analysis was applied with razorlike sharpness toward the efforts of the enslaved to be free of their chains. Thus, it was in the struggle against war and as a world leader for peace that the indomitable warrior spent most of his efforts.

World peace was always his aim, and even more so after World War II. "The real causes of war," he declared, "will persist and threaten so long as Europe and America are determined by means of cheap labor to control the wealth of the world." Thus his labors for world peace "were inseparably linked with his efforts to realize the vision of a world rid of colonial and racist domination and exploitation."[4] In 1949, to a great Congress on Peace, in New York, the great man declared, "And all this depends first on world peace. Peace is not an end. It is the gateway to real civilization. With peace, all things may be added. With war, we destroy even that which the toil and sacrifices of ages have builded."

As a materialist, it was only natural that ethically and economically Dr. Du Bois' sympathies were always along socialist lines of thinking. This thinking began nearly six decades before his death. In a commemorative speech in Accra, shortly before his death, the Reverend Howard Melish declared: "From Europe he returned with two indelible impressions that were increasingly to mould the balance of his life. The first was a consciousness of the utter destructiveness of war and its futility as an instrument of social progress. The second was his conviction that a radically different mode of human, social, and economic organization was no longer just a human dream, but now an imposing fact of history."

All of this deep philosophical analysis culminated in his dreams of Pan-African unity. From the first, in 1919, as the founder of the Pan-African movement and organizer of the Pan-African Congresses, until his death, this was the dream and the dedication —a federated Africa. As a social philosopher devoted to activity as well as to providing the theoretical basis for the solution of man's most pressing problems, Dr. Du Bois saw the triumph of Pan-African unity as a long step forward in the history of human freedom. His was never any metaphysical or pragmatist approach, but rather one of the fusion of theory with practice. Africa's plight was seen as a world predicament and Africa's needs were major issues of a world crisis and Africa's cures would be in the obvious interests of the common good.

Dr. Du Bois made a speech in 1950 before the national convention of the Phi Beta Sigma Fraternity in which he declared prophetically:

> What young Africa must learn and deeply understand is that if socialism is good for Britain and for most of the present world, as every wise man knows it is, it is also good for Africa, and that is true no matter what is taught by British Tories or in reactionary American schools. In Africa, as nowhere else in the world, lies the opportunity to build an African socialism which can teach the world; on land historically held in common ownership; on labor organized in the past for social ends and not for private profit, and on education long conducted by the family and clan for the progress of the state and not mainly for the development of profitable industry. What is needed—and all that is needed—is science and technique to the group economy by men of unselfish determination and clear foresight.

And on his ninetieth birthday:

> Socialism progresses and will progress. All we can do is to silence and jail its promoters. I believe in Socialism. I seek a world where the ideals of Communism will triumph—to each according to his need; from each according to his ability. For this I will work as long as I live. And I still live.

References

1. *American Scholar,* XVIII (1949), 93.
2. W. E. B. Du Bois, *The Philadelphia Negro: A Social Study* (Publications of the University of Pennsylvania, 1899 Series in Political Economy and Public Law, No. 14).
3. *Ibid.,* p. 94.
4. W. Alphaeus Hunton, "W. E. B. Du Bois: The Meaning of His Life," *Freedomways,* III, No. 4, 493.

. . . E. B. Du Bois: the historian

CHARLES H. WESLEY

The life and career of W. E. B. Du Bois provide fundamental emphasis for the declaration that history deals not only with the dead past, but also directly and indirectly with the life-giving spirit of the present and the promise of the future. His talents were devoted in his time span to all the avenues of literary expression as a prolific author, but his best historical efforts were at the beginning of his career. Basic to his writings was the profound influence of the historical and the philosophical-scientific methods of the social sciences, and it was rare for him to complete a book without involving historical backgrounds in it. It was along history's pathway that he made his literary route to the present and the future.

During the years 1883 to 1894, Du Bois was experiencing his formal education at high school in Great Barrington, Massachusetts, Fisk University in Nashville, Tennessee, Harvard University, Cambridge, Massachusetts, and the University of Berlin, Germany. As early as 1883, while in high school, he was writing "Great Barrington Notes" to the *New York Globe* and the *New York Freeman*.

This was the period also when American historians began their organization as professional groups. The American Historical Association was founded in 1884, and was preceded by the formation of local societies of scholars in history and the social sciences. The *Political Science Quarterly* was established in 1886.[1] Standards of scholarship in these fields were emphasized for the first time in the United States, and the works of scholars in history who were trained in American universities were published and were regarded not only as contributions to historical scholarship, but as stimuli to graduate students and younger colleagues.[2] A committee of the American Historical Association was appointed in 1896 to recommend a course of history study for secondary schools.

As a student at Fisk University, 1885–1888, Du Bois was not

affected by these happenings in history, and yet these years were regarded by him as "years of growth and development," during which he learned "new things about the world."[3] Primarily, coming from North to South, he saw discrimination as he had not seen it before. He came in contact with disdain, abuse, and violence based upon color, while he studied at Fisk in courses in Latin, Greek, history, natural science, politics, and religion. He served as editor-in-chief of the student newspaper, the *Fisk Herald,* 1887–1888. At his Fisk Commencement in 1888, his subject was "Bismarck," and his choice of this subject revealed to him, he wrote, "the abyss between my education and the truth in the world." His history courses had not led him to the understanding of European intrigue, the expansion of European power in Africa, the industrial revolution, the slave trade, colonialism, and the rivalries of European nations over the products of the lands of the darker people. As Du Bois said, "I was blithely European and imperialistic in outlook; democratic as democracy was conceived in the United States."[4]

At Harvard, he sat at the feet of writers of history, Albert Bushnell Hart and Justin Winsor, psychologist William James, philosophers Josiah Royce and George Santayana, litterateurs George Lyman Kittredge, Charles Eliot Norton, and economist F. W. Taussig. Specialists in the single area of history were rare in this day. Du Bois states in this connection that his education at Harvard turned from philosophy, centered in history, and then gradually in economics and social problems. Sociology had not been recognized at this time, but Du Bois believed that this would have designated his course then although he had interests in history; but he realized that Harvard's faculty leadership was not yet fully centered in this field of study. His course papers at Harvard in 1891–1892 included such historical themes as "Lee," "Unrepresentative Men," "Historical Conference," "Methods in History." His early interest in economics was manifested in a paper entitled, "A Constructive Critique of Wage Theory; An Essay on the Present State of Economic Theory in Regard to Wages."[5]

After two years at Harvard, his second baccalaureate, *cum laude,* the first being from Fisk, was received at Harvard where he was one of six commencement speakers, with his subject, "Jefferson Davis As a Representative of Civilization." However, the original title of the address was "Jefferson Davis and the African." From 1890 to 1891, he pursued graduate courses in history and political science as a fellow at Harvard and worked on a master's thesis, "The Suppression of the Slave Trade." The degree of Master of Arts was awarded to him in 1891. His master's degree study was first published under the title "The Enforcement of the Slave Trade Laws," in the Annual Report of the American Historical Association for 1891.[6] From 1892 to 1894, through a grant from the Slater Fund, he studied at the University of Berlin where he united his studies in history, economics, and politics, under historian Gustav Schmoller. At this time, Du Bois believed that through the pursuit of truth by investigation, race problems would have their solutions. There was a manuscript in historical research which came from one of his Berlin seminars in 1892 entitled, "The Plantation and Peasant Proprietorship Systems of Agriculture in the United States."

The first historical publication

The first of the major Du Bois historical works which earned for him the title of historian was through the publication of the volume, *The Suppression of the African Slave Trade to the United States of America, 1638–1870,* in partial fulfillment for the degree of Doctor of Philosophy awarded in 1895 at Harvard University. Du Bois was twenty-four years of age when he worked on this subject. There were twelve chapters and appendices embracing colonial and state legislation and typical slave trade cases in 335 pages, with voluminous footnotes and a bibliography. The title page showed that the author was a "Sometime Fellow of Harvard University and Professor in Wilberforce University." The irony of this situation at Wilberforce, as it relates to Du Bois as a historian, is that he was not teaching history classes and was not designated as a professor of history. He was instead a professor of Latin and Greek, 1894–1896,[7] or as he says, "the chair of classics," which he accepted with gratitude at the annual salary of $800.[8]

This volume was issued as the first of the Harvard Historical Studies, published under the direction of the Department of History and Government. The volume with two additional ones issued in 1896, and three announced for 1897, were to "comprise works of original research selected from the writings of teachers and graduate students in the Department of History and Government in Harvard University."[9]

This study was based upon historical sources, national and state, colonial statutes, Congressional documents, reports of anti-slavery societies and personal narratives. In his preface, Du Bois states that there was difficulty in separating the suppression of the slave trade from the system of American slavery and colonial policy, and yet he endeavored to "avoid superficiality" and "unscientific narrowness of view." And he adds, "While I could not hope entirely to overcome such a difficulty, I nevertheless trust that I have succeeded in rendering this monograph a small contribution to the scientific study of slavery and the American Negro."

The volume was received with good reviews and had little criticism in the *American Historical Review,* 1897; the *Annals of the American Academy,* 1897; the *English Historical Review,* 1897; and the *Atlantic Monthly,* 1897. The *Nation*'s reviewer stated that the volume would "long remain the authoritative work on the subject,"[10] and the reviewer in the *Atlantic Monthly* asserted that although Du Bois had been industrious in collecting his materials, his work disclosed "a lack of appreciation of the subject in its historical proportions."[11] Another reviewer regarded him as "the advocate rather than the historian," and it was true that he referred to the "cupidity and carelessness" of Americans and the lack of moral opposition "to the slave traffic."

In the *African Methodist Church Review,* H. T. Kealing, editor (1897), declared that "the book is epochal" and that "certainly for faithful and full verification of every statement, for impartiality, for grasp, correct summarizing of the essential meaning of widely divergent actions and seemingly antagonistic motives in the same section, Professor Du Bois' work is monumental among all the writings that the race has produced."[12]

This volume has stood through the years as a solid piece of historical research and writing. All subsequent historical studies of value concerning the slave trade to the United States have included in bibliographies or footnotes this Du Bois study of 1896.

Fifty-eight years after this first printing, in 1954, another edition of this volume was published by the Social Science Press, New York. He added an "Apologia" of two and one half pages to this new edition which the publishers placed in the back of the book. As an author looking back sixty years when he began the research, Du Bois has two major criticisms of it. The first is the separation of his subject from "the total flow of history" by an author, "when he knows nothing or little of the mass of facts of which his minute study is a part." Another self-criticism by him was his lack of knowledge "of the significance of the work of Freud and Marx." He had received some Freudian thought through William James but he did not "realize the psychological reasons behind the trends of human action which the African slave trade involved." In Germany, he heard more of Marxism, but he added that this was more in rebuttal, and there was "no complete realization of the application of the philosophy of Karl Marx to my subject." He concluded that he should have added to his research "the clear concept of Marx on the class struggle for income and power beneath which all considerations of right or morals were twisted or utterly crushed." Nevertheless he concluded that he was proud that at the beginning of his career in 1896 he had made no more mistakes than he did in this historical work.[13]

Continued historical production

During the same year in which his first historical publication was issued, 1896, Du Bois accepted an appointment as assistant instructor in the Department of Sociology at the University of Pennsylvania in order to undertake a special investigation into the conditions of the colored people of Philadelphia. This opportunity was of great influence on his career. He regarded himself as being "pushed aside by forces which, if not entirely beyond my control, were yet of great weight." He had offered to teach social sciences at Wilberforce, although this course would have been beyond his required schedule, but he was denied this opportunity by the authorities. The University of Pennsylvania now gave him the opportunity of a research project in the social sciences. Of this opportunity, he said, "My vision is becoming clearer. The Negro problem was in my mind a matter of systematic investigation and intelligent understanding."[14]

The fact that he was designated an "assistant instructor," although a Ph.D. from Harvard, made no difference to him. He had his opportunity and he would use it effectively and efficiently, for here was the "chance to study an historical group of black folk and to show exactly what their place was in the community." The result was *The Philadelphia Negro: A Social Study.*

Du Bois did not turn entirely from history to sociology, but there was more emphasis upon current social conditions and less upon the history of the Negro people in Philadelphia. His goals were directed to endeavors by white and black Philadelphians who were recipients of better opportunities and who should have reached and lifted the masses of Negroes. This was his concept of the challenge to the "Talented Tenth." His survey was revealing and became the basis for a history of this section of the city. Moreover, Gunnar Myrdal in his *American Dilemma* closed his description of what a study of a Negro community should be by calling attention to the Du Bois study of the Philadelphia Negro, "which best meets our requirements, a study which is now all but forgotten."[15]

Du Bois in this Philadelphia study seemed to be moving away from history, as he was pressed more and more by the revelation of conditions affecting adversely the darker people. He was still the scholar but devoted less emphasis to history. He began to differentiate pure research from reform and change, and saw clearly the need for the latter in the light of expressed ideals. He stated this view more clearly in a paper, "The Study of Negro Problems," in the *Annals of the American Academy of Political and Social Science* in 1899. He stated that "the sole aim of any society is to settle its problems in accordance with its highest ideals, and the only rational method of accomplishing this is to study those problems in the light of the best scientific research."[16]

The Philadelphia Negro, which Du Bois called "a huge volume of five hundred pages but not unreadable," was intended to be a first of a series of studies of the Negro population in several urban centers. He regarded it "as complete a scientific study and answer as could have been given with defective facts and statistics, one lone worker and little money." In 1901, he published a series in the *New York Times Magazine Supplement* of individual articles on New York City, Boston, and Philadelphia. While Du Bois did not follow up this study in other areas, such studies as were made could not ignore the trail blazed by this distinguished scholar, and by this date, sociologist.[17] Another brief study of this type was "The Negroes of Farmville, Virginia," under the auspices of the U.S. Department of Labor.[18]

From 1897 to 1910, he was associated with Atlanta University as professor of economics and history. He edited sixteen *Atlanta University Studies,* covering over two thousand printed pages dealing with Negro life and each of which had its basic background in history. However, this work was regarded as primarily sociological.[19] Also while at Atlanta, his collection of essays with historical and sociological overtones, *The Souls of Black Folk,* was published in 1903 and passed subsequently through twenty-seven editions, and was reprinted in 1953. This volume was again reprinted in 1961 in the Premier Americana Series, Fawcett World Library.

The one excursion of Du Bois in historical biography was in his publication in 1909 of *John Brown*. In thirteen chapters with chronology and bibliography, the author tells his story in 409 pages, admitting that materials were scarce but that "even in the absence of special material the great broad truths are clear, and this book is at once a record of and a tribute to the man who of all Americans has perhaps come nearest to touching the real souls of black folks." Du Bois said this book is "one of the best things that I had done," for he had considered John Brown from the point of view of the Negro-American rather than as a fanatic who had interrupted the normal course of events in American life and history.[20]

In 1915, Du Bois returned to history in a small volume in the Home University Library Series, entitled *The Negro*. In the opening lines he wrote:

> The time has come for a complete history of the Negro people. Archaeological research in Africa has just begun, and many sources of information in Arabian, Portuguese, and other tongues are not fully at our command; and, too, it must be confessed, racial prejudice against darker people is still too strong in so-called civilized

centers for judicial appraisement of the peoples of Africa. Much intensive monographic work in history and science is needed to clear mooted points and quiet the controversialist who mistakes present personal desire for scientific proof.[21]

The best historical sections of this book treat of African history, with emphasis on Ethiopia and Egypt, the West Coast of Africa, culture, the trade in men, the West Indies, and a chapter on "The Negro in the United States," and another on "Negro Problems." He included the theories of anthropologists Guiseppe Sergi and Franz Boas, criticized the Aryan myth, and stated the thesis of class conflict and the belief in the union of black and white workers for the creation of a better society. Writing vigorously and succinctly, Du Bois presented facts about African history and culture which were unknown in 1915, a time when the concept of racial inferiority and African savagery were rampant and dominant in the thought of the American people.

He returned to history in 1924, as a result of a subvention from the Knights of Columbus and issued *The Gift of Black Folk; The Negroes in the Making of America.* This was a book of 349 pages in the Knights of Columbus Racial Contribution Series.[22] The author admits that this book, "while basically sound, as I believe, [but] was too hurriedly done, with several unpardonable errors."[23]

The Reconstruction period had been a longtime topic for consideration by Du Bois. As early as 1909, Du Bois expressed his interest when a letter was sent to him by James R. L. Diggs, President of Virginia Theological Seminary at Lynchburg, suggesting the rewriting in a series of ten volumes or more of Reconstruction in the Southern states. Diggs stated that "southern writers present our white brothers' side of the question, but I do not find the proper credit given our people for what of good they really find in those trying days." Du Bois replied that the plan was excellent and would fit into his encyclopedia project, and that he would take it up in the fall.[24]

The next year, 1910, he prepared and presented a paper at the annual session of the American Historical Association on "Black Reconstruction and its Benefits."[25] Du Bois said that U. B. Phillips, defender of the South, was "greatly exercised," that William

Dunning of Columbia University and Albert Bushnell Hart of Harvard had praised it. As a result, Du Bois was convinced that Reconstruction had its "tragedy"—because here an attempt was initiated to make democracy and the tenets of the Declaration of Independence apply not only to white men but to black men."[26] While serving as editor of *The Crisis,* and with a grant from the Rosenwald Fund, Du Bois had undertaken a history of Reconstruction from the Negro-American's point of view. After two years as professor of sociology at Atlanta University, the project was completed and was published as *Black Reconstruction in America: An Essay Toward a History of the Part Which Black Folk Played in the Attempt to Reconstruct Democracy in America, 1860–1880.*

This volume directed attention to the achievements of Reconstruction by Negroes after the Civil War who, despite opposition, were creating a better American life but were prevented by reactionaries; that their strike during the war and their use as soldiers helped win the war and freedom; that Negro legislators made contributions to national and local government, and that they did not deserve the criticism of historians; that Negro suffrage had failures because it was not supported, north or south, except by individuals and was finally defeated by force.

Du Bois also criticized the works on Reconstruction by James Ford Rhodes, John W. Burgess and William H. Dunning in particular. According to Du Bois' view, Rhodes was an exploiter of labor, Burgess was a slaveholder, and Dunning was a Copperhead. He said that around these historians there had assembled a postwar group of graduate students from the South, who were propagating these biased views. He wrote:

> They had been born and reared in the bitterest period of Southern race hatred, fear and contempt. Their instinctive reactions were confirmed and encouraged in the best of American universities. Their scholarship, when it regarded black men, became deaf, dumb and blind. The clearest evidence of Negro ability, work, honesty, patience, learning and efficiency became distorted into cunning, brute toil, shrewd evasion, cowardice and imitation—a stupid effort to transcend nature's law.[27]

Du Bois believed in the final section of his volume entitled "The Propaganda of History," that "historians of Reconstruction, with a few exceptions, had ignored the Negro, or had distorted, misinterpreted the part which the Negro had played in Reconstruction mainly because of their loyalty to the lost cause and to the ideals of the South and fidelity to clan and class." He added, "In propaganda against the Negro since emancipation in this land, we have faced one of the most stupendous efforts the world ever saw to discredit human beings; an effort involving universities, history, science, social life and religion."

Black folk through the ages—a summary view

Du Bois undertakes a volume of history and social interpretation, which is brilliantly written, in *Black Folk, Then and Now; An Essay in the History and Sociology of the Negro Race* (1939).[28] This volume was an expression and outgrowth of his volume in 1915 under the title, *The Negro*. The author advised his point of view when he stated:

> I do not for a moment doubt that my Negro descent and narrow group culture have in my cases predisposed me to interpret my facts too favorably for my race; but there is little danger of misleading here for the champions of white folk are legion. The Negro has long been the clown of history; the football of anthropology; and the slave of industry. I am trying to show here why these attitudes can no longer be maintained. I realize that the truth of history lies not in the mouth of partisans but in the calm science that sits between. Her cause I seek to serve, and wherever I fail, I am at least paying Truth the respect of earnest effort.

The task before him then was not only an account of the history of the Negro people, but also a description of the bearing of these facts upon the inequalities of the modern world. In this volume, as in others, Du Bois shows that his primary interest is in the Negro, and that he is not only writing history, but he is making a case for the Negro people.

Du Bois devotes the largest part of the volume to Africa and its civilization, endeavoring to give re-evaluations in the light of new materials which appeared in recent publications. He refers to the word "Negro" and reveals the error of those who endeavor to restrict the word to a group of Africans and to regard the black and brown folk of Ethiopia, Egypt, and North Africa as "white." Such a division makes a sharp contrast with the American interpretation of including all persons of color as Negroes, even those who have only a remote kinship to any of the African peoples. Thus, the word "Negro" becomes a dual word to be used in accordance with the convenience of the writers.

Moving from Africa, the author continues the thesis of the quality of Negro contributions and intelligence into the modern period and endeavors to show that racial inferiority concepts are at the basis of anti-Negro manifestations. He also finds that the inferiority of the Negro is based primarily on economic causes which are manifested in his chapters on "The Trade in Men," and "The Western Slave Marts." Imperialism receives its share of criticism by him with a severe indictment of the European states which maintain their government and their exploitation for the benefit of themselves, but the author looks forward to the rise of the workers of Asia, Africa, and America. At the same time, the contributions of Negroes to literature, the arts, music, industry, and labor, receive recognition in the volume.

The book is reviewed by Carter G. Woodson in the *Journal of Negro History,* and the beginning lines are "This book is more black folk *now* than *then,"* by which the reviewer meant that more space was devoted to the former period than the latter, and that in fact, "the space devoted to Africa is quite inadequate." Woodson also asserts that the work was written mainly from secondary sources, and he says that the author did not use the more important ones. But Woodson would have credit given to him "for using such data as he has collected in the form of undigested quotations to show the culture of Africa. . . ."[29]

More than historian

While Du Bois wrote considerably outside of the field of history, much of that which he wrote was based upon it. His imaginary writings grew out of basic history, extending from *The Quest of the Silver Fleece* (1911) to *The Black Flame* trilogy (1957–62). As editor of *The Crisis,* his editorials were frequently based upon historical backgrounds. There was continuing emphasis on Negro art, drama, and literature. He advocated the study of Negro history in his first report on the Niagara Movement in *The Voice of the Negro* (1905), which contained as one of its purposes, "to study Negro history." He urged even the use of pageantry in the demonstration of Negro history, so that there would be impressions left in the minds of viewers and hearers by these theatrical pictures of the Negro in history. He did not hesitate to criticize some Negro members of the Board of Directors of the National Association for the Advancement of Colored People when he said that they were ashamed of their African heritage and wanted to regard themselves as Americans rather than Africans, resented and feared, as he declared, "any coupling with Africa."[30]

The Dusk of Dawn, planned as a biography, contains only parts of history and is not a historical autobiography. While the book gives a general review of the life of the author, there is much that is repeated and which has been known of Dr. Du Bois from other writings. While we may think of Du Bois as having been a writer of history, his reputation does not rest on history alone as a special area of his career. James Weldon Johnson declares that "the great influence Du Bois has exercised has been due to the concentrated force of his ideas. . . ."[31] And yet historians must concentrate their ideas as do other scholars. This is his major claim to greatness associated with the fact that he has enfused his ideas with historical backgrounds.

Following *The Suppression of the African Slave Trade to the United States of America,* there are few single valid and strictly historical works which have been produced. In fact, basically there has been history but it has been mingled with sociology, economics, and a pro-Negro corrective purpose. The latter is important, and each of his involvements make for the greatness of the man. If the historian is a writer of history, a chronicler, an analyst or one well-versed in history, or one who records and explains events and persons as steps in human progress, and pursues the truth as exact as he can get it, Du Bois would qualify, and more so than the specialized chronicler or analyst.

One of the last, and the earliest of the plans and programs of

Du Bois was centered in the *Encyclopedia Africana,* originally launched by him as the *Encyclopedia of the Negro,* the concept of which was started in 1909. With the assistance of the Phelps-Stokes Fund in 1931, this *Encyclopedia of the Negro* was initiated, and in 1945, Du Bois and Guy B. Johnson of the University of North Carolina edited the small preparatory volume with references. This program lay dormant in Du Bois' planning until the sponsorship of the Ghana Academy of Science, and the Government of Ghana had underwritten the cost of beginning the work with headquarters at Accra, Ghana, and with Du Bois as the Secretary for the *Encyclopedia Africana.* Correspondence with hundreds of persons brought promises of cooperation from scholars all over the world. It was decided that the *Encyclopedia Africana* should be written by African scholars from the considerable body of knowledge already produced, and that which was to be assembled and prepared. After Du Bois went to Ghana in 1961, information reports were prepared by him toward the *Encyclopedia Africana* and a draft plan was prepared for the conference on this work at the University of Ghana, December 18, 1962. This was a project of the sixties. In the meantime, *Color and Democracy, Colonies and Peace* appeared in 1945, and *The World and Africa* in 1947. The latter was intended as an inquiry into the part which Africa had played in world history.

Du Bois was more than a historian; he was an advocate, a crusader, a critic, a teacher, a booster of morale, and one who continuously urged that the darker peoples in the United States need not be ashamed of being Negroes. He promoted this idea despite controversies, and did not hesitate to enter the lists of verbal battle whenever it was necessary. As historian, he first made a scientific historical study. Then he was drawn from research by the very facts collected by him, as well as by the anti-Negro views of white historians who were his contemporaries. As editor, sociologist, essayist, publicist, and maker of history, he objected to the ways in which American historians had distorted the image of darker Americans in the writing of history. He found the Negro an average and ordinary American and a human being faced with pressures created by the masters of his environment, against which he was struggling almost in vain, but to him the struggle was worth it. He admitted his pro-Negro premises and proceeded to prove them. He was *for* Negroes in history, as so many others were *against* them. Du Bois knew that a people must believe in themselves, for, as he said, no people who did not had "written its name in history."[32] He knew that it was through the mind and pen of the historian that the achievements of persons and peoples were rescued from the dead past, and that the ordinary can become extraordinary through the mind and purpose of the craft of the historian. To say that the scientific historian has no business dealing with the dramatic or the picturesque or the literary, or with current life and the promise of a people is an irrelevant definition of the people's historian. However, literary cleverness is never satisfactory to the historian or his reading public, and it is inevitable through human frailty that there is a relativity in all historiography.

In his literary endeavors, Du Bois moved from the status of specialist in history, with the earmarks and trappings of the historian, to the concentration of facts and ideas on race and racism, the use of creative imagination, the exercise of dramatic expression, and the mastery of the style of the poet, the dramatist, and the phrasemaker, which moved him into the world of art and letters so that he could write:

> I sit with Shakespeare and he winces not. Across the color line I move arm in arm with Balzac and Dumas, where smiling men and welcoming women glide in gilded halls. From out the caves of evening that swing between the strong-limbed earth and the tracery of the stars, I summon Aristotle and Aurelius and what souls I will, and they come all graciously with no scorn or condescension. So, wed with Truth, I dwell above the Veil. Is this the life you grudge us, O knightly America? Is this the life you long to change into the dull red hideousness of Georgia? Are you so afraid lest peering from the high Pisgah between Philistine and Amalekite, we sight the Promised Land?[33]

And likewise, we who now march toward our Promised Land of Freedom and Opportunity should be basing our endeavors upon the worthy historical heritage created and developed in the writings of W. E. B. Du Bois!

References

1. Michael Kraus, *A History of American History* (New York: Farrar & Rinehart, 1937), p. 314.
2. F. N. Thorpe, "The Study of History in American Colleges and Universities," *Circular of Information* (Washington, D.C.: Bureau of Education, 1887), No. 2, p. 252.
3. W. E. B. Du Bois, *Dusk of Dawn: An Essay Toward an Autobiography of a Race Concept* (New York: Harcourt, Brace, 1940), p. 30.
4. *Ibid.*, p. 32.
5. Paul G. Partington, *W. E. B. Du Bois Bibliography* (Unpublished).
6. "The Enforcement of the Slave Trade Laws," *Annual Report of the American Historical Association for the Year 1891* (1892), pp. 161–174.
7. *Who's Who in America,* Vol. XXV (1948–1949), p. 686.
8. Du Bois, *Dusk of Dawn,* p. 49.
9. W. E. B. Du Bois, *The Suppression of the African Slave Trade to the United States of America, 1638–1870* (New York: Longmans, Green, 1896).
10. *The Nation,* December 31, 1896, p. 468.
11. *Atlantic Monthly,* April, 1897, p. 479.
12. *The African Methodist Church Review,* XIII, No. 3 (January, 1897), 359.
13. W. E. B. Du Bois, "The Apologia," *The Suppression of the African Slave Trade, 1638–1870* (New York: Social Science Press, 1954), p. 329.
14. Du Bois, *Dusk of Dawn,* pp. 57–58.
15. Gunnar Myrdal, *An American Dilemma: The Negro Problem and Modern Democracy* (New York: Harper & Row, 1962), p. 1132.
16. W. E. B. Du Bois, "The Study of Negro Problems," *Annals of the American Academy of Political and Social Science,* XI (January, 1898), 16; Francis L. Broderick, *W. E. B. Du Bois: Negro Leader in a Time of Crisis* (Stanford: Stanford University Press, 1959), pp. 39, 40.
17. W. E. B. Du Bois, *The Philadelphia Negro: A Social Study,* together with a special report on domestic service by Irabel Eaton (Publications of the University of Pennsylvania, 1899 Series in Political Economy and Public Law, No. 14).
18. W. E. B. Du Bois, *The Negroes of Farmville, Virginia: A Social Study,* Bulletin of the U.S. Department of Labor, III (January, 1898), 1–38.
19. W. E. B. Du Bois, "The Laboratory in Sociology at Atlanta," *Annals of the American Academy of Political and Social Science,* XXI (May, 1903), 160–163.
20. W. E. B. Du Bois, *John Brown* (Philadelphia: George Jacobs, 1909).
21. W. E. B. Du Bois, *The Negro* (New York: Henry Holt, 1915), Preface.

22. W. E. B. Du Bois, *The Gift of Black Folk: The Negroes in the Making of America* (Boston: Stratford, 1924), Introduction by Edward F. McSweeney.
23. Du Bois, *Dusk of Dawn,* p. 269.
24. Herbert Aptheker, *A Documentary History of the Negro People in the United States* (New York: Citadel Press, 1951), II, 874.
25. *American Historical Review* (July, 1910).
26. Du Bois, *Dusk of Dawn,* pp. 318–319.
27. W. E. B. Du Bois, *Black Reconstruction* (New York: Harcourt, Brace, 1935), p. 276.
28. W. E. B. Du Bois, *Black Folk, Then and Now: An Essay in the History and Sociology of the Negro Race* (New York: Henry Holt, 1939).
29. Carter G. Woodson, *Journal of Negro History,* XXXIV, No. 1 (January, 1939), 462.
30. Du Bois, *Dusk of Dawn,* p. 275.
31. James Weldon Johnson, *Along This Way: The Autobiography of James Weldon Johnson* (New York: Viking Press, 1934), p. 204.
32. W. E. B. Du Bois, "The Conservation of Races," *American Negro Academy Occasional Papers,* No. 2 (Washington, D.C., 1897).
33. W. E. B. Du Bois, *The Souls of Black Folk* (New York: Blue Heron Press, 1953).

. E. B. Du Bois' influence on African history

WILLIAM LEO HANSBERRY

W. E. B. Du Bois was blessed with a wide variety of human talents at their best. That he made maximum use of these exceptional natural endowments finds eloquent testimony in the extraordinary achievements of his long and fruitful life. He attained, as the series of essays in this memorial issue of *Freedomways* makes abundantly clear, true eminence as a scholar, teacher, philosopher, historian, humanitarian, social scientist, man of letters, and leader of men—in short his was many distinguished careers rolled into one. The fact that so many authors have been asked to review different aspects of his many-sided career is but another indication of his manifold interests and accomplishments. My own particular assignment in this timely undertaking is to review Dr. Du Bois' achievements and influence as a pioneer in the study of Africa's storied and unstoried past.

The editors of this memorial volume have indicated that I have been given this particular assignment, first, because of my own and Dr. Du Bois' rather parallel efforts to ferret out the facts about Africa's ancient past; and, second, because of the very important part, as I had previously disclosed to them, which Dr. Du Bois had played in shaping and giving direction to my own somewhat unusual career as a devotee of Clio's Art. I have long cherished a suitable opportunity to make public acknowledgment of the positive manner in which Dr. Du Bois influenced my own career as a student of the history of the misnamed "dark continent;" and since the editors have specifically asked that I take note of that fact in this review, I have consented to comply with this request.

Thanks to a reasonably well-stocked library left to me at the age of three by my deceased father—a teacher of history at Alcorn College in Mississippi—I acquired, while still quite a youth, a deep interest in the stirring epic of human strivings in the distant and romantic ages when Clio's craft was new; and by the end of my freshman year in college at Old Atlanta University I had become, largely through independent reading—and in my own estimation—something of an authority on the "glory that was Greece" and the "grandeur that was Rome." While carrying out these self-imposed reading assignments, I had made a diligent effort to learn something about what had been the course of human affairs in Black Africa during what was then widely believed to have been the "Golden Age" of the Ancient World; but my quests in these respects proved of but little avail. Apart from an occasional, and usually tantalizingly enigmatic or obscure reference to the ubiquitous Kushites and the "blameless Aethiopians," picked up while perusing the excitement-packed historical chapters of the Old Testament, and "blood and thunder" narratives in many of the nineteenth-century "Outline Histories of the Ancient World," I acquired little else that added to my exceedingly limited knowledge of Black Africa's story in olden days.

I was then quite ignorant of the fact that under the combined influence of ethnocentrism and colonialism there were widespread tendencies in certain circles in the Western world to ignore or suppress most types of Africana which presented black peoples in a favorable light. I was tempted at times, I confess, to wonder if it were indeed true, as was then commonly believed, that Black Africa was altogether devoid of any history worthy of serious academic concern prior to the landing of Prince Henry the Navigator's hunters of men on "Africa's coral strand" in 1442. But the scattered bits of information which I had picked up about Ancient Kush and Old Aethiopia, together with a kind of intuitive faith in the basic equality of all the major divisions of the human race, made it impossible for me to believe that Africa—the second largest of the continents—had remained throughout untold ages a cultural wasteland until Christian slave traders from "enlightened" European lands "sowed the seeds of civilization" for the first time on her "culturally barren shores."

But how and where would I be able to find in adequate amounts, tangible and incontrovertible historical evidence which would confirm and amplify my intuitive learnings in these respects? Being myself of African descent, how could I prove to myself and others that I was not being tricked by my own ethnocentric impulses into reading more into the scattered and inconclusive references to the Ancient Kushites and the Old Aethiopians than the master craftsmen in the quiet halls of the Muse of History would or could approve? Although he was not aware of the fact until several years later, it was Dr. Du Bois who rescued me from the horns of these academic and psychological dilemmas; let us review briefly how this rescue was brought about.

Following the completion of my freshman year at Old Atlanta University in June 1916, I went, as I had done the two preceding summers, to Brown's Wells—a small health resort, near McComb, Mississippi—where I spent three months operating—or trying to operate—a pressing shop, and reading any book or magazine I could buy or borrow which treated in anywise of Africa and the African at home or abroad. A particularly favored and fruitful item in this assortment of readings was, of course, *The Crisis,* which under Dr. Du Bois' editorship was then the most influential and widely read of all publications devoted primarily to the interests of the "darker races" of Africa and the Americas. In a certain issue it was indicated that the Home University Library, a division of Henry Holt and Company, had recently published a new volume, *The Negro,* by Dr. Du Bois, which was, in part at least, a review of the then available evidence bearing upon the history of Black Africa in earlier times. I ordered a copy immediately and when it arrived I soon discovered that the little book contained just the type of information for which I had been searching for many months.

Its two hundred and forty-two pages were packed with innumerable facts not only about Ancient Kush and Old Aethiopia but about a whole series of kingdoms and empires which had flourished elsewhere in Black Africa—notably in the Balad es Sudan—in historical antiquity and in the Middle Ages, but of which, up to that time, I had never read or heard a single word. There were well-documented passages taken from Herodotus and Diodorus Siculus and other classical and oriental authors which indicated that there were mighty kingdoms and highly developed cultures in Ancient Kush and Old Aethiopia which were already hoary with age when Hellas was still an infant and Rome was yet unborn; and there

and queens were apparently individuals who had been well endowed with goodly amounts of Ethiopian or Kushite blood. Specifically mentioned in this connection was Queen Nefertari, the venerated ancestress of the great Eighteenth dynasty, who is described as "a Negress of great beauty, strong personality and unusual administrative force." In the same category is placed Queen Hatshepsut "who sent the celebrated expedition . . . to Punt." To these were added the great Pharaoh whose reign is described as "one of the grandest in Egyptian history"—the reference here being to Thutmose III whose statues and recovered mummy reveal him to have been a man of "strong Negroid countenance."

On the strength of ideas and concepts acquired in the course of my earlier readings, I was more or less prepared for what Dr. Du Bois had to say about the heroic character of the kings and queens of Ancient Kush and Old Aethiopia; but certain of the details which he revealed about the cultures, kingdoms, and empires of the Balad es Sudan in the African west, were so contrary to previously acquired concepts about that much maligned part of the continent that certain of these details, on first thought, seemed almost beyond belief.

Could it be true, as the learned Doctor had avowed, that "the known history" of the West African empire of Songhay "covered a thousand years" during which period three dynasties with a total of sixty kings had followed one another on the imperial throne? Did the first of these dynasties, said to have numbered thirty kings, begin indeed as early as the year A.D. 700 and last until 1235? Was Sonni Ali (1464–1492), the seventeenth and last ruler of the second dynasty, the great warrior prince he was pictured as having been; and did his renown, as was said of him, "extend from the rising to the setting sun"? Under his successor Askia the Great (1492–1528), did the Songhay empire reach, as was reported, "from Lake Chad to the Atlantic;" and during his administration did there "reign everywhere great plenty and absolute peace"?

Was it true that the kings of Ghana in the Middle Ages lived in palaces adorned with sculpture and furnished with glass windows; and if circumstances required could these kings put into the field, as was claimed, armies totalling as many as two hundred thousand men? On his pilgrimage to Mecca in 1324, was it possible, as Dr. Du Bois' sources reported, that Mansa Musa, the emperor of Mali, carried along with him eighty camel-loads of gold—valued at five million dollars (sterling?)—to pay his own expenses and the expenses of his entourage which is said to have amounted to sixty thousand persons? And finally, could it be true that when Christian Europe's slave trading missionaries first established themselves in Guinealand at the end of the Middle Ages, they found there, as Dr. Du Bois avowed, an abundance of evidence indicating that the building, metallurgical, and plastic arts had been carried on at exceptionally high technical and artistic levels throughout this region "without interruption for centuries"? Particularly impressed was I by Dr. Du Bois' citations concerning the remarkable technical and artistic skill which was said to be reflected in the Ashanti gold weights, the Yoruba glass and terracotta *objets d'art,* and the Yoruba and Benin castings in bronze and brass.

Inasmuch as most of the agents and agencies of Western inculturation—geographers, missionaries, colleges, public schools, and the press at large—had always pictured these and other parts of Africa "south of the Sahara" as gigantic jungles which were then and always had been hardly more than the haunts of "savage beasts and still more savage men"—it is easy enough to understand how it was not altogether easy for me to accept at the very first all of Dr. Du Bois' iconoclastic observations at full face value. After a little reflection, however, on Du Bois' long demonstrated ability to utilize social and historical evidence and testimony with the caution of a true scholar, I concluded that he must be basically right, despite the Western world's prevailing notions to the contrary.

All of the cultures, kingdoms, and empires mentioned up to this point lay north of the equator, but the southern half of the continent was by no means overlooked. As Dr. Du Bois pointed out, when Diogo Cam, the Portuguese navigator, discovered the mighty Congo in 1482, he was astonished to learn that there was a large, powerful, and well-governed kingdom of the same name which extended from the mouth of the great river deep into the African interior. Further on toward the east was another even larger and more powerful African state known as the empire of the Monomotapa. This mighty African empire, along with the neighboring coastal kingdom of Sofola, had been renowned for ages as regions rich in mines of gold, silver, copper, tin, and precious stones—there were, indeed, those who had contended that it was in this part of Africa that was situated the famous "Land of Ophir" from which King Solomon's "gold, silver, ivory, apes, and peacocks" were derived.

Stretching northward from Sofola along the balmy and beautiful East African seacoast, so Dr. Du Bois next pointed out, lay a series of adjoining city-states which were known collectively to Moslem writers of the Middle Ages as the "empire of the Zenj" or the "kingdoms of the Blacks." According to Masoudi, an Arab author writing in the tenth century of the Christian era, one of the great black overlords of a part of the dominions of the Zenj could put into the field an army of three hundred thousand men; and in his broad domain "ivory and gold were abundant, and there was a plentiful supply of millet, meat, milk, and honey." Dr. Du Bois quoted Ibn Batuta, who visited the Land of Zenj in 1330, as saying of Kilwa, one of its principal cities, that it was composed of "handsome houses built of stone and mortar" and furnished with "windows like those of the Christians;" and from a Portuguese author, Duarte Barbosa, who wrote a revealing eyewitness account of the city in 1515, there was a quotation to the effect that the houses were terraced and stood in well-watered gardens where many fruit trees flourished; the wealthy people of the city, according to the same author, were reported to have been clothed "in gorgeous robes of silk and velvet." To the rear of Kilwa and its sister principalities along the coast, there had formerly flourished, according to Dr. Du Bois' sources, a number of other powerful and well-organized central African states, the most notable of these being the Katwara empire of which parts of the present-day kingdoms of Uganda were but attenuated reminders of its pristine past.

Following his rather inclusive regional survey of the principal areas of the continent in which political and cultural practices and institutions had reached significant levels of development in earlier times, Dr. Du Bois turned his attention to a brief but remarkably succinct and revealing review of the devastating and demoralizing effects upon the indigenous cultures and kingdoms of Black Africa, first, by Mohammedanized Arab and Berber slave traders who invaded the continent by way of the north and east; and second, by slave-trading Christians from Europe and the Americas, who carried on their wholesale trade in men from numerous military and missionary centers scattered along African coasts on the west and south. It was Dr. Du Bois' estimate that the combined Moslem and Christian slave trade, which lasted for more than a thousand years, must have cost "Negro Africa well over 100,000,000 souls."

Though exceedingly shocking in their effect, Dr. Du Bois' remarks in this connection provided me with my first clue to what must have been one of the primary causes for the decline, decay, and final collapse of the cultures, kingdoms, and empires which had flourished in Black Africa in earlier times. For our author went on to say that as a consequence of "organized slave trading in every corner of Africa . . . whole regions were depopulated, and whole tribes disappeared. . . . Family ties and government were weakened . . . native industries were disorganized . . . and future advances in civilization became impossible. . . . It was the rape of a continent to an extent never paralleled in ancient or modern times."

Here then is something of an outline of Dr. Du Bois' initial contribution to my quest for knowledge concerning the age-old epic of the triumphs and failures of humankind in what my mentor so aptly described as "at once the most romantic and most tragic of continents." After the day and night which was spent in devouring the contents and ingesting the purport of his actually small, but to me truly Gargantuan volume, my historical horizons were widened a hundred fold. But that was only the initial impact of Dr. Du Bois' influence so far as my historical outlook and academic goals were concerned; for in addition to the information contained in its main text, Dr. Du Bois had appended at the end of his little volume, a long list of books which he recommended as "further reading" for those who wished to acquire additional information about the history of the cultures, kingdoms, and empires which he had so briefly, yet revealingly sketched. These books, it was indicated, were of unequal merit in their contents and in the objectiveness of their points of view. Those which Dr. Du Bois regarded with most favor or upon which he himself had leaned most heavily, were marked by an asterisk to set them off from the rest.

I promptly decided that I would read the books on this starred list as soon as I could lay hands on them; but it is hardly necessary to say that no one of these volumes could be found at Brown's Wells, nor were they perhaps available, for that matter, elsewhere in Mississippi. On returning to Atlanta University in the fall of 1916 I discovered, to my great disappointment, that only three of the thirty-odd starred volumes on Dr. Du Bois' list, which treated specifically of Africa's early civilizations, were in our school's library; and only one additional volume could be located in the other libraries in Atlanta which were open to me. But these four available volumes included not one of the books I was most eager to see. In discussing this situation with Professor John Bigham, a graduate of Harvard and the head of the combined departments of History and Sociology—a position previously held by Dr. Du Bois—I was informed that most of the publications on the starred list could be found only in the Library of Congress or in great metropolitan or university libraries such as those at Harvard and Columbia or Boston and New York; and he advised, in passing, that after I had completed my work at Atlanta, I should enroll in the Graduate School at Columbia or Harvard where I could carry out a research program in African history in partial fulfillment for the Master of Arts degree.

But what Professor Bigham did not know was the fact that I was a young man in a terrible hurry to read the starred books—and others—on Dr. Du Bois' recommended list. As a consequence, after spending two weeks at the beginning of my sophomore year at Atlanta, I packed my trunk and headed for Harvard. Knowing as they did, how limited were my finances, the members of my family and my faculty friends at Atlanta viewed this move with the gravest misgivings but they—particularly Dean Adams and my widowed mother—pledged all the help they could possibly give. My immediate and major objective—though I kept strictly silent about the matter—was to read the books on Dr. Du

Bois' list; and—pick up one or two Harvard degrees along the way if possible! The details of what followed during the next four years—though a human interest story of grit, gall, and guts of the first order—are largely irrelevant to the needs and purpose of this review; here it is sufficient to say that by June 1921, I had read practically all of the books concerned with ancient Africa which were on Dr. Du Bois' list, and many others as well, and had managed, meanwhile, to meet the rigorous requirements for Harvard's widely coveted and justly prized Bachelor of Arts degree.

Although some of them have already been mentioned in passing, it will be both fitting and revealing to comment briefly on certain of the other more notable publications to which Dr. Du Bois' list had directed my attention and from which he had drawn the historical information and made it available to the interested public. In terms of their literary authenticity in content and wide influence in uprooting the popular misconception that the early history of Africa south of the Sahara was a matter unworthy of serious academic concern, the two most outstanding books in this respect were written, paradoxically enough, by two gifted authors whose names were for decades household words in circles where the conquest of Africa for imperial purposes was one of the primary objectives of the age.

The earlier of these two volumes, listed under its translated English title as *Timbuctoo the Mysterious* and published in 1896, was written by an exceptionally talented Frenchman, Felix Dubois, and was based in the main upon information extracted from a remarkable aggregation of old historical manuscripts which he acquired in the early 1890s during an unusually fruitful visit to the Valley of the Niger—the heartland of the once mighty Songhay empire. The second of these volumes, mistitled—so far as main theme was concerned—*A Tropical Dependency* and published in 1906, was written by the gifted English author Flora Shaw—better known as Lady Lugard. Though undertaken initially with the purpose of describing contemporary Nigeria, one of Britain's largest and richest crown colonies, the book turned out to be, in the end, the most inclusive and best-written digest of the great kingdoms and empires which had flourished in central and western Africa in the Middle Ages, which had ever been published up to that time—it is indeed, despite certain limitations, the great classic among books of its kind.

In addition to much valuable background information about the history of the Balad es Sudan in late antiquity and in the Middle Ages, there are in Lady Lugard's deceptively named volume some admirable summaries of the writings of a number of Arab, Moorish, and Sudanese authors whose works are of primary value in the study of Black Africa's past; but of these authors and their works, the scholars of the Western world—except for a handful of orientalists—were almost wholly ignorant prior to the appearance of Lady Lugard's book. Among the earliest of such summaries is an excellent introduction to the history and civilization of Ghana in the Middle Ages as these are revealed first in the illuminating pages of El Bekri's *Roads and Realms* which was published in 1067; and second, in El Idrisi's *Book of Roger* which appeared in 1154. Then comes Lady Lugard's excellent digest of the history and internal conditions in the empire of Mali as these are reported in the eyewitness account of Ibn Batuta who travelled widely in the Lands of the Blacks between 1349 and 1352; and in Ibn Khaldun's great *History of the Berbers* which was first published in 1406.

Then followed Lady Lugard's rather detailed outline of cultural and political developments of the great Songhay empire as these are so effectively revealed in Leo Africanus' *History and Description of Africa,* completed in 1526; and in the great *Tarikh es Sudan,* written between 1590 and 1656, by Abderrahman es Sa'di, who was perhaps the greatest of the historians which Black Africa ever produced in bygone times. There was also in Lady Lugard's book an excellent digest of the then available historical information on the Hausa states and the great medieval empire of Kanem-Bornu.

In contrasting what her inquiries had revealed concerning the cultural, social, political conditions in the Balad es Sudan with what was known of comparable conditions during the same period in western and northern Europe, Lady Lugard startled many of her countrymen by declaring in effect that the levels of civilization reached by the peoples of Black Africa in medieval and early modern times were quite superior in many respects to those attained by their Celtic, Teutonic, and Nordic contemporaries. In other words Flora Shaw, the talented wife of Sir Frederick Lugard—one of England's ablest empire-builders and practicing advocates of the "white man's burden"—did not permit her loyalties in these respects to blind her to what seemed to be the incontrovertible facts—despite popular notion to the contrary. By this prevailingly objective attitude toward the vast mass of historical facts which she brought together in *A Tropical Dependency,* Lady Lugard and her Gallic counterpart, imperial France's Felix Dubois, did more, quite unwittingly it is true, to stimulate African opposition to European colonialism than did any other non-African authors of the period. For ironically enough, it was the stirring stories of the departed glories of the great empires of Ghana, Mali, Songhay, and Kanem-Bornu, as these were recounted in *A Tropical Dependency* and in *Timbuctoo the Mysterious,* which did so much to alert many Africans to the fact that they had built, under their own direction, great states for themselves in the past and were thoroughly capable of doing likewise in the present and future.

To these two significant publications must be added another which had a tremendous influence in the same direction. The reference here is to *Christianity, Islam and the Negro Race* by that great preacher of African patriotism, Dr. Edward Wilmot Blyden, who preceded, indeed, Felix Dubois and Lady Lugard, as an effective pioneer to the African past; and who did more than either to inspire the African to become again master in his own house. It is certain that Dr. Du Bois, by his favorable references to and citations from the works of these three authors, was primarily responsible for calling their inspiring contents to the attention of so many of the men who have taken the lead in fashioning Africa's modern Renaissance as a consequence of the inspiration derived from a knowledge of the continent's heroic past.

From a purely academic point of view, however, Dr. Du Bois' greatest influence as a historian was through the part he played in directing the attention of professional students of Africa's early history to the modern editions of original works of the great Arab, Moorish, and Sudanese geographers and historians upon which the volumes by Lady Lugard, Felix Dubois, and Dr. Blyden were so largely based. Worthy of special mention in this connection was

Dr. Samuel Lee's English translation of Ibn Batuta's *Travels in the Balad es Sudan,* which was published in 1829; and the Hakluyt edition of Leo Africanus' *History and Description of Africa* which was translated and published in three volumes by Dr. Robert Brown in 1896. And here too, particular notice must be taken of Es Sa'di's great *Tarikh es Sudan* which was translated into French by Octave Houdas for the School of Living Oriental Languages which had it published in Paris in the year 1900.

Though belonging in a different category but of primary value to African historians were two other publications to which Dr. Du Bois directed attention by not only including them on his starred list but by including many citations from each in his own text. The earlier of these was the remarkably detailed and revealing account of the African explorations and investigations of the great German traveler Heinrich Barth which was published in five volumes in English in 1857–1858 under the title, *Travels and Discoveries in North and Central Africa.* In this great work Barth, through innumerable excerpts and digests from then unavailable manuscripts, provided Western scholars with their initial acquaintance with the rich contents of the writings of various Arab, Moorish, and Sudanese authors whose works are of the greatest value in the study of Black Africa's past. Barth also revealed the astonishing fact that the old royal family of Songhay, which was overthrown by an invasion from Morocco in 1591, had survived as the ruling house in one of the isolated or unconquered provinces of that once great empire—thus making it one of the world's oldest royal families that had come down to the present from the past. Next in importance to Barth's volumes in this particular category was an incomparable mélange of travel-notes and reports on archaeological explorations carried out by the German explorer Leo Frobenius in southern Nigeria between 1910 and 1912, and which was translated and published in 1913 under the English title *The Voice of Africa.* More, perhaps, than any other African explorer before or after his time, Frobenius was able to sense the true character and greatness of the African *Weltanschauung* in the palmy days of old when the continent's ancient way of life had not yet been disrupted by unwelcome intruders from the Moslem East, and by merciless marauders from the Christian West.

As has already been repeatedly implied, Dr. Du Bois was profoundly impressed with the abundance and richness of the historical materials which he canvassed in the course of his initial effort to acquaint a largely disinterested and skeptical public with the fact that Black Africa was far from being the unsung waif of History which the Western world was so wont to believe. We are informed, indeed, that in the course of this effort, Dr. Du Bois was himself astonished at the wealth of the available historical facts relating to Africa's storied past, but about which he had previously known so little "despite a varied university career." But notwithstanding the magnitude of the information acquired in the course of his initial review of Africa's role in world history and the demands which were made upon his time and energy by other numerous commitments, Dr. Du Bois continued throughout his long life to assemble and disseminate more and ever more of the little known facts about the early history of his beloved continent.

In *Black Folk, Then and Now,* published in 1939, he made available to the general public and in his characteristically engaging style, many new and little known facts about Africa's past which he had brought together since the appearance of *The Negro* in 1915; and in 1947 he published *The World and Africa* which was yet another volume in which the early history of the homeland of his immemorial grandsires was his principal theme. To his list of works relating primarily to Africa in bygone times must be added *The Suppression of the African Slave Trade to the United States of America,* published as early as 1896, and which was the first volume in what subsequently became the world-renowned Harvard Historical Studies.

It is true that Dr. Du Bois' achievements as a historian fall rather short of the level of excellence attained by Herodotus and Thucydides and many of the other giant-craftsmen in the past who labored in the same broad and exacting field of literary endeavor. In this connection it needs, however, to be remarked, that unlike most truly great historians for whom historiography was both a vocation and a profession—Dr. Du Bois' efforts were, on the contrary, sideline and secondary activities. Instead of being able to give his full attention to *Africana antiqua* he usually found it possible to devote only an hour or two at a time to such efforts on those rare occasions when there were momentary lulls in the demands of his professions as a teacher, journalist, and defender of human rights. Then only would he be permitted now and then to scribble a note or pen a paragraph for some projected chapter devoted to the early history of Ancient Kush, Old Aethiopia, or the Balad es Sudan.

The volumes which were produced under such limiting circumstances may not have been comparable in scope of content to Flavius Josephus' *History of the Jews,* nor as majestic in style and inclusive in detail as Gibbon's *Decline and Fall of the Roman Empire;* but in many passages in Du Bois' historical writings there are clear evidences of the same type of genius which sparked each of these and other immortal masterpieces of united scholarly and literary effort. It is revealed in such passages that Du Bois, like most of the great predecessors similarly engaged, had a passion for truth and justice and was skilled in ferreting out and making critical but effective use of facts. For it is indicated that though he was, as most truly great historians have been, a consummate storyteller, he, as they, had the capacity for keeping the imagination within proper bounds as was demanded by the available evidence. And finally, for example—he was both a man of action as well as a man of thought—in short, he could and did do battle in defense of the Goddess of Justice in the heat of day, and wield a quiet pen in the cause of the Muse of History in the cool of night. Although Du Bois' achievements in the latter respect may have their limitations, they were, nevertheless, in terms of the African story as a whole, the most inclusive and influential publications of the kind that had found their way into print up to the time they appeared—they are indeed still—along with the tireless, if yet widely unappreciated, labors of Joel A. Rogers—exceptionally useful guideposts to, and compendiums of, much little known knowledge about Black Africa's past.

Had William Edward Burghardt Du Bois been free, or inclined, to limit his efforts to prying out and piecing together the surviving remnants of the torn and tattered annals detailing the story of ageless Africa's pristine past, he might well have turned out to be an African Homer and Herodotus rolled into one; for he was by temperament and talent not only a potentially great epic poet but a pre-eminent historian as well. Du Bois elected, however, to restrict himself to no single branch of human endeavor but chose rather to work untiringly for numerous human causes which his many extraordinary natural endowments enabled him to serve so well. As the editor of the *Encyclopedia Africana*—with its manifold demands upon a great variety of human talents at their best—he was still engaged, at the age of ninety-five, in these diverse labors of love to which he had given his long life, when the Fates called him to his new abode in Memory's bright mansions above.

The formative years of 'Phylon' magazine

MOZELL C. HILL

Looking over the world today we see as incentive to economic gain, as cause of war, and as infinite source of cultural inspiration nothing so important as race and group contact. Here if anywhere the leadership of science is demanded not to obliterate all race and group distinctions, but to know and study them, to see and appreciate them at their true value, to emphasize the use and place of human difference as tool and method to progress; to make straight the path to a common world humanity through the development of cultural gifts to their highest possibilities.

Phylon, Vol. 1, No. 1., p. 3

The above statement represents the conceptual strategy of W. E. B. Du Bois as he placed it into the context of an "apologia" for the launching of a new quarterly magazine, *Phylon,* The Atlanta University Review of Race and Culture. The statement appears in the first issue of the magazine, first published in 1940; it is a unique, erudite, yet readable magazine now in its twenty-fifth year of continuous publication.

Phylon and W. E. B. Du Bois are inseparable. Truly *Phylon* is one of Du Bois' many creative contributions. Thus, in order to fully comprehend this magazine, especially in its formative stages, it must be viewed against the backdrop of the intellectual and cultural framework within which its creator lived and worked. When this is done, it becomes readily apparent that the format, style, and editorial slant reflect the philosophy, temperament, and broad perspectives of W. E. B. Du Bois.

In 1897, Du Bois, a very energetic and enthusiastic young man, went south to Georgia to become one of the first professors of sociology in an American university. It was at Atlanta University that he went about his work with a zeal seldom found in college teaching and research. It was here that he developed the foundation studies of the position and the special problems affecting the life and culture of Negroes in the United States. His approach was a mode of inquiry that was scientific; his studies were longitudinal in nature, designed to stretch in time over a period of one hundred years.

Du Bois' disciplinary training at Harvard University in the social sciences, especially history, social philosophy, and sociology, had provided him with a breadth of outlook and a penetrating depth for understanding into the nature of human nature—the hows and whys of men's actions when they come in contact with each other. Moreover, his academic experience in European universities had helped him to examine the philosophical bases for meaningful research into the problems that engulfed black peoples the world over. Thus the breadth and depth of his academic training plus his unmatched philosophical orientation restrained Du Bois to avoid the trappings of being captured by merely slanting his studies toward programs of social reform. He insisted that his studies were not merely focused upon solving the so-called race problem as an end in itself. He stressed this point of view when he wrote:

> We seem to see today a new orientation and duty which will not call simply for the internal study of race groups as such, but for a general view of that progress of human beings which takes place through instrumentality and activity of group culture; . . . not even to confine our investigations to those darker races whose advance is least known or appreciated; but rather to look at all groups of men. Naturally we shall usually proceed from the point of view of black folk where we live and work to the wider world.

It was to be expected that Du Bois' very first studies would investigate the social and cultural conditions bearing upon the new world Negroes. As far as we know, these were the first scientifically designed studies which concentrated on the problems faced by American Negroes. However, after twelve years of painstaking research, Du Bois noted in 1910 the urgency of the plight of the black man in the United States. He observed the full force of the backwash and collapse of Reconstruction at the turn of the century. He also noted the emergence of the "Plessy-Ferguson separate-but-equal" philosophy, along with the actions of state legislatures throughout the nation. These among many other actions against the presumably emancipated black man placed him in what Du Bois termed "an impossible situation." The reign of terror expressed in burnings, lynchings, disfranchisement, night riders, whippings, etc. created a condition which, in Du Bois' words, "demanded immediate action to prevent social death."

It was for this reason that Du Bois left Atlanta University—meaning that his studies were interrupted. He assumed a new role—"A minister of propaganda," he explained. He became the Director of Publications and Research for the newly formed National Association for the Advancement of Colored People, an organization he helped to incorporate in 1911.

Du Bois' activities with the NAACP and his editorial craftsmanship with its official organ, *The Crisis,* need not detain us here. However, as he threw himself into his new role as "minister of propaganda" for NAACP, he found time to make his second trip to Europe, when his actions took on broader dimensions. He began to see that his urgent struggle to help black men to full citizenship was not to make them simply American, but to begin to build the ideal America—a truly interracial culture—from which black men could assume human dignity.

Between 1918 and 1928, Du Bois made four additional trips to Europe. It was during this period that he became absorbed in Hegelian dialectics and the doctrine of Karl Marx. Du Bois had now become convinced of the Marxian notion of economic determinism. He took on the view that "the economic foundation of a people largely determines the direction of their thought, culture, and actions."

Now a mature, mellow scholar with strong Marxian orientations, Du Bois returned to Atlanta University in 1934 as a teacher, researcher, and writer. Here he sat down to the primary task of filling in the background of certain historical studies concerning black peoples. He published scores of articles, monographs, and books between 1935 and 1940. Two of these publications, *Black Reconstruction* (1935) and *Black Folk, Then and Now* (1939), introduced an entirely new conceptual view from which to assess the economics and culture of black peoples. At the same time, Du Bois was intensely interested in restoring the program of systematic study of the Negro problem on a worldwide scale. He felt that such an all-encompassing study was not only indicated, but was of an almost immediate necessity. One of his projects was the establishment of the Negro Land-Grant College Social Research Program. Another was a proposed project for the publication of an encyclopedia of the Negro. Although he labored enthusiastically to bring these proposals to fruition while he was at Atlanta University, he did not receive sufficient financial support to get either one of them under way.

It was within this context that Du Bois focused his energies upon the establishment of a scholarly journal of comment and research on race and culture. He decided to give this new magazine the title *Phylon*—race—which was a transliterate from the Greek. This unique name was not selected to represent a pedantry of learning, but rather the title was intended as a thought-provoking designation which would catch on and be easily remembered. He was careful in setting the editorial policy of the new magazine; he did not want to duplicate the work of already established magazines, such as that being done by the *Journal of Negro History,* under the leadership of the late Carter G. Woodson, and the *Journal of Negro Education,* edited by Charles Thompson. What the editor of *Phylon* had in mind was to develop a new view of the social sciences in respect to the treatment of the life and culture of black folk. He firmly believed that an accurate account of the problem could only be presented by comprehending the actions of men and then isolating these actions for study within a system of thought. Du Bois wanted to bring into being a scholarly magazine which would serve as a vehicle for students interested in a reinterpretation of history, education, and sociology. He set the tone for *Phylon* when he wrote:

> We shall strive to abolish the present economic illiteracy and paralysis; and openly hold to frank criticism that widespread assumption that the industrial organization of the nineteenth century was something permanent and sacred and furnished a final word which

stops the twentieth century from facing the problem of abolishing poverty as the first step to real freedom, democracy, and art among men, through the use of industrial technique and planned economy.

In establishing *Phylon* and serving as its first editor-in-chief, it was clear to Du Bois that anything short of the abolition of poverty would not free the minds of black peoples not only in the western industrial world, but in every other section of the entire universe when peoples meet and come to grips with each other.

The editor-in-chief approached his new role by burying himself in the maze of details that had to be organized into an author-printer-publisher complex. His emphases were upon original research both direct and indirect, essays on widely separate subjects, the painstaking task of chronicling of events, and intelligent review of opinion and literature.

Du Bois, who retired from Atlanta University in 1944, worked and nurtured his "new venture in social science" through its first four years of publication. He was assisted by a distinguished editorial board which included Ira De A. Reid, Managing Editor, William Stanley Braithwaite, and W. Mercer Cook, among others.

'John Brown' by W. E. Burghardt Du Bois

A REVIEW BY ERNEST KAISER

Virtually all American historians castigate and deride old John Brown. Their writings are replete with expletives and invective denouncing the "sage of Osawatomie." These historians are echoing what they have read in biased, distorted American histories or have been taught by generations of anti-Abolitionist, anti-John Brown professors. The anti-John Brown posture and attitude are *de rigueur* for American historians now. In addition to the Civil War and general histories by Bruce Catton, David Donald, J. G. Randall, C. Vann Woodward, Allan Nevins, Michael Krause, and others that attack Brown, there are full-length biographies and anti-Abolitionist studies berating and denigrating him such as J. C. Furnas's *The Road to Harper's Ferry* (1959), Robert Penn Warren's *John Brown; The Making of a Martyr* (1929) and Hill P. Wilson's *John Brown, Soldier of Fortune; A Critique* (1913).

After the good biographies of Brown by R. J. Hinton, F. B. Sanborn, and J. Redpath in the mid and late nineteenth century, Oswald Garrison Villard's *John Brown, 1800–1859; A Biography Fifty Years After* (1910, reprinted in 1929) and W. E. Burghardt Du Bois' *John Brown* (1909) in the American Crisis Biographies series, both commemorating the fiftieth anniversary of Brown's death in 1859, were two voices crying in the wilderness of the venomous anti-Brown American history and biography of that time. Michael Gold's little pamphlet *Life of John Brown* in the Haldeman-Julius series appeared in 1925 followed by Stephen Vincent Benét's long narrative poem *John Brown's Body* in 1928. While this poem sneered at that great Abolitionist Wendell Phillips and had other weaknesses, it was pretty good for its time. In 1932, the literary critic and English teacher at C.C.N.Y., Leonard Ehrlich, published his fine historical novel about John Brown, *God's Angry Man,* which was reprinted in 1938 as a paperback and distributed by the Readers Book Club in 1941.

David Karsner's *John Brown, Terrible "Saint"* came out in 1934. Muriel Rukeyser's long poem *The Soul and Body of John Brown* appeared as a very large book and limited edition in 1940. Theodore Ward, the American Negro author of the plays *Big White Fog* and *Our Lan',* had his play *John Brown* produced in New York City in 1950. Another Negro playwright William Branch, author of the plays *A Medal for Willie* and *A Wreath for Udomo,* got a pretty good run for his drama of Frederick Douglass and John Brown, *In Splendid Error,* in 1954.

The period around the centenary, 1959, of Brown's death saw the publication of Delight Ansley's very good *The Sword and the Spirit; A Life of John Brown* (1955) for young people, Allan Keller's inspiring *Thunder at Harper's Ferry* (1959), the excellent *A John Brown Reader* (1960), edited by Louis Ruchames, a good chapter on John Brown in Oscar Sherwin's *Prophet of Liberty* (1959) (a biography of Wendell Phillips), Herbert Aptheker's hard-hitting pamphlet *John Brown, American Martyr* (1960), Truman Nelson's big historical novel *The Surveyor* (1960), about John Brown, and the new 1962 centennial edition of W. E. B. Du Bois' biography *John Brown.*

This centennial edition has a new preface, some new comment in the text and new socialist conclusions and analyses by Dr. Du Bois (in italics except for the preface to differentiate the new material from the original text). Du Bois admits in the original preface that he has no special material and that his book is eclectic and draws on the biographies already in print in the 1900s. But his excuse for writing another biography of Brown is to treat the facts from a different point of view, that is, from the viewpoint of the little known but important inner development of the Negro American. And viewed in this way, John Brown becomes the white American who has perhaps come nearest to touching the real souls of black folk. The new preface raises the question as to how far force and violence can bring peace and good will. Du Bois says that John Brown's violence made Kansas a free state; that although Brown's plan to seize the armory at Harper's Ferry and arm the slaves failed in 1859, it was actually arms and tools in the hands of a half million Negroes that won the Civil War.

Du Bois has written here an elegiac, brooding, prose-poem biography of John Brown. There is an evocation in this book in the same poignant, simple, Biblical rhetoric that Du Bois employed in that classic book of essays, *The Souls of Black Folk* (1903), published six years before. Although he recites the bare facts of Brown's life, it is not the facts so much as the way Brown felt about and reacted to life that interests Du Bois. John Brown was in essence deeply religious or mystical; a shy, nature-loving boy who was born into a religious family, he was a young frontiersman similar in many ways to Abe Lincoln. Stern but tender with his children, Brown who felt deeply and was tender and honest must have been hurt to the quick by the tragedies and the eleven deaths in his family (a wife, nine children, and a grandson) over the years of his hard life. He thought that God had visited this sorrow upon him because he had done so little to increase the amount of human happiness. And so Brown called for action! action! against human slavery. The Du Bois who wrote this book was also deeply religious and linked up with Brown in this way; the book is written in the language of Biblical parables: "a great unrest was on the land;" "he lay down his life;" "the land was big with the tragic fate of his people."

Du Bois masterfully paints a rounded, poetic, yet horrible and devastating picture of southern slavery from 1800 to the Civil War with many slave revolts occurring in different places. Only the escape of the more militant fugitive slaves and the Underground Railroad prevented blood baths aplenty. Running through the book is a brilliant, telescoped history of the United States as well as a history of Negro Americans, especially the struggle of the free Negroes and Abolitionists, Negro and white, of the North.

Born in Torrington, Connecticut, in 1800, the year of the Gabriel-led slave insurrection in Virginia, John Brown was taken by his family to Ohio in 1805. Brown's life from 1805 to 1854 was almost wholly spent on the western slope of the Alleghanies in a small area of Ohio and Pennsylvania in a half dozen small towns but chiefly Hudson, Ohio. Here he grew to manhood roaming the wild Ohio forests and fraternizing with the Indians; he had very little schooling but much of religion, the church, and the Bible. Brown worked as a tanner, a postmaster, married two wives, had many children, speculated in land, was a bank director, a surveyor, a sheep-farmer, a racehorse breeder, went into bankruptcy, had a wool-merchant firm which involved going to Europe, and moved his family to North Elba, N.Y., in 1849 after the wealthy New York Abolitionist Gerrit Smith gave Adirondack farms to Negroes in 1846. This was a period of rising, prosperous cotton, woolen, and iron manufacturing and trade and of frightful economic panics. Brown attributed his financial disasters to his failure to worship and serve God.

When John was twelve years old, he saw a half-naked, wretched Negro slave boy beaten with a shovel, harshly abused verbally, and made to sleep at night in the bitter cold. Young John asked: "Is God their [the slaves'] Father?" Owen Brown, John's father, was an Abolitionist. John from earliest boyhood saw and felt the fearful cost the country was paying for slavery; he grew to understand that the cost of liberty was less than the cost of slavery or repression. Brown started early, about 1825, to aid fugitive slaves who were sent to him for help. As his dislike for slavery grew, he and his family had a plan to get a school started for Negroes or to help the free Negroes of the North. This was from 1828 until sometime after 1834. In 1839 Brown and his family swore blood feud with slavery. They were bound in a solemn compact to make active war on slavery and to labor for emancipation. Brown wanted to settle in a border state and educate slaves openly or secretly and send them out as emissaries. By 1839 Brown and William Lloyd Garrison saw that slavery was the great central problem of America and were ready to act against it.

Brown tried to divide the profits of the wool business more equitably between the producers of raw material and the manufacturers, but a combination of manufacturers forced him out of business in a few months. A man of principle and prophetic vision, he did not know how far the manufacturers would go in crushing people in order to make money. Brown did not want to spend all of his time getting or losing money. He had plans of larger usefulness, of nobler toil and nobler satisfaction. As he learned more and more of slave revolts and Negro resistance to slave catchers, Brown's fight against slavery became his primary work, God's work. Slaveholders were to him men of great wickedness and should be killed. As Brown found out about the great work and sprawling network of the Underground Railroad, he conceived the idea of central depots for running off slaves in the inaccessible portions of the South, and he began studying southern geography, especially the Alleghanies, with this in view. Frederick Douglass visited Brown in 1847 and heard of Brown's plan for a slave raid. Brown founded the all-Negro League of Gileadites in 1851 to prevent by force the taking of fugitive slaves after the passage of the new Fugitive Slave Law in 1850. The League did effective rescue work. The reenslavement of Anthony Burns in Boston in 1854 disturbed Brown deeply, for he knew the sorrow and fear of the Negroes who could be taken back into slavery.

After the passage of the Kansas-Nebraska Bill in 1854 repealing the Missouri Compromise that had prohibited slavery in the Kansas-Nebraska Territory, five of Brown's sons started for Kansas. Brown attended the Syracuse convention of Abolitionists in 1855 and later in the year started for Kansas with munitions, a sixth son, and his son-in-law. Brown and his sons fought several battles against Missouri slavers in bleeding Kansas in 1855 and 1856. He and his sons struck a telling blow for a free Kansas at Pottawatomie in the Swamp of the Swan. Then Brown and his sons went east. He toured New England to raise money in 1857. But slaves were already in Kansas and the Dred Scott Decision of March 1857 legalized them there. Brown went west again and returned east in 1858. He saw Frederick Douglass and others. He tried to get a black contingent among the Negroes in Canada in 1858. There was Hamilton's massacre in Kansas. Brown postponed his plans; he went back to Kansas. Kansas remained free because John Brown and the Free Soilers (who hated not slavery but slaves and wanted Kansas to be a free white labor state only) fought bravely. There was the raid into Missouri to free the slaves in December, 1858. Brown took the fugitive slaves thus freed to Canada in 1859. A sick man, he went to Harper's Ferry; he gathered twenty-two men (six or seven were Negroes) and munitions from June to October. (There were about fifty men, including the seventeen Negroes reported killed and those slaves who helped and escaped.) They attacked October 17, 1859. Col. Robert E. Lee and one hundred marines captured Brown on

October 18. Brown was tried and hanged at Charleston, Virginia (now West Virginia). He was buried at North Elba, N.Y., December 8, 1859.

All of this and much more is eloquently told in great detail by Du Bois. He quotes sections from many sources in describing the fighting and guerrilla warfare in Kansas and the proslavery Missourians invading Kansas. Brown knew that the federal government was proslavery and was aiding the Missourians against the Kansas free state settlers. Brown started the war that ended American slavery. His final message uttered in chains, in the very shadow of death, was a mighty Abolition document which shook the foundations of slavery more than any other single thing. For it was the South and slavery that were on trial—not John Brown. He felt in his soul the wrong of slavery and was glad to die in freedom's cause. His legacy to us is to teach us that the cost of freedom is much less than the cost of repression; that this Negro question is still to be settled; and that the end of it is not yet.

'The World and Africa' by W. E. Burghardt Du Bois

A REVIEW BY RICHARD B. MOORE

Still timely, though long overdue, is the current republication of *The World and Africa* by W. E. Burghardt Du Bois. Despite continuing demand, for some unknown and seemingly inexplicable reason, the publishers of the original edition of 1947 failed to bring out another edition of this truly significant work. Was this the result of adverse pressure brought to bear by the great Euroamerican power structure which had turned upon Dr. Du Bois, the dean of Afroamerican letters, with ruthless, degrading, and destructive venom, because of his unyielding insistence upon human rights, liberation of the African and other colonial peoples, and his courageous and powerful advocacy of man's supreme need, the vital requirement above all of *peace?*

Whatever the hindrance, this has happily now been overcome and so this revealing book about Africa and her relations with the rest of the world is once more available to the people. What is more: there have been added some seventy-three pages in this more durable book form of ten articles originally published in the *National Guardian* during February 14 to April 10, 1955. International Publishers is indeed fortunate to have secured the rights to this republication. These publishers are to be congratulated upon the restraint exercised, without which these unique and historic writings of Dr. Du Bois might have been overlain and obscured with current and unnecessary interpretation.

Here is the mature thought of a deeply delving and widely ranging scholar, who at the very beginning of this century realized the growing significance of Africa and the African peoples. Thus began his investigation and research which finally flowered in *The World and Africa: An Inquiry into the Part Which Africa Has Played in World History.*

In his foreword Dr. Du Bois has himself pointed to this development. There he refers to "the little volume called *The Negro,* which gave evidence of a certain naive astonishment on my own part at the wealth of fact and material concerning the Negro peoples, the very existence of which I had myself known little despite a varied university career."

Desiring to enlarge upon this earlier work after World War I, Dr. Du Bois wrote *Black Folk, Then and Now.* "But it happened," the Doctor tells us, "that I was writing at the end of an age which marked the final catastrophe of the old era of European world dominance rather than at the threshold of a change of which I had not dreamed in 1935. I deemed it, therefore, not only fitting but necessary in 1946 to essay again not so much a history of the Negroid peoples as a statement of their integral role in human history from prehistoric to modern times."

Going over *The World and Africa* again, this reviewer concludes that the author was eminently successful in the task which he set himself. Not only are many important but hitherto hidden facts about African life and culture brought to light; the arrogant assumption of white supremacists has been refuted by the masterful marshaling of facts—that thesis has been demolished which was expressed by Guernier: "Alone of all the continents Africa has no history!" Yet the style is lucid and at times reaches heights of beauty.

In the chapter treating upon Egypt, Du Bois wrote penetratingly:

> It is one of the astonishing results of the written history of Africa, that almost unanimously in the nineteenth century Egypt was not regarded as part of Africa; it was even asserted that Egypt was in reality Asiatic, and indeed Arnold Toynbee's *Study of History* definitely regarded Egyptian civilization as "white" or European! The Egyptians, however, regarded themselves as Africans. . . . There can be but one adequate explanation of this vagary of nineteenth century science: it was due to the slave trade and Negro slavery.

While generally critical of "race" theories, considerable vestiges of "race" yet remain in this book, as when the good Doctor refers to Seligmann's *Races of Africa,* which makes a European hodgepodge of most of Africa, as "priceless and marred only by his obsession with the Hamites." Contrary to the foregoing, the following statement is directly to the point:

> There was, however, persistent exception to this general agreement; under Caucasoid were included men of widely different physique inhabiting Europe; the term Mongoloid was even more vague and indefinite and nearly fell into disuse. But the term "Negro," as a definite and scientific race designation, persisted, and its use was defended with bitter determination by men who otherwise ranked as leading scientists. Despite the fact that the number of human beings corresponding to the current definition of the word "Negro" was narrowed again and again in space and number to a small remnant even in Africa, nevertheless in the usage of many distinguished writers there really emerged from their thinking two groups of men: Human Beings and Negroes.

Today it would appear that the conclusion must now be reached that the name "Negroe" or "Negroes," having been put beyond the pale of "Human Beings," it is proper and beneficial to abolish the use of this degrading term "Negro" and insist upon the use of the accurate and honorable terms *African* and *Afroamerican.*

While the growth of knowledge will date some statements in this epoch-making book, it would seem that most of it will remain true, and in some respects timeless, particularly as an unusually penetrating and far-visioned statement of its day and time.

Needless to say, *The World and Africa* should be read by every Afroamerican. No less should it be read by the Euroamerican majority who seriously need this historical antidote to destructive race prejudice and callous inhumanity. The cloth edition should be recommended, since this is a book to keep and to refer to, read to the youth, and hand down to posterity. But the paper edition brings this illuminating study within the price range of all.

PART THREE

W. E. B. DU BOIS AS AN ACTIVIST

W. E. B. Du Bois: the meaning of his life

W. ALPHAEUS HUNTON

Dr. W. E. B. Du Bois will be acclaimed as one of America's greatest sons. I recall one of the hundreds of tributes paid him during his lifetime, which expresses best, I think, the meaning of his life for the country of his birth. It was written over twelve years ago on the occasion of his eighty-third birthday. It read:

> The nineteenth century, in American Negro history, was the era of Frederick Douglass; the twentieth century is the era of William Edward Burghardt Du Bois.
>
> Each suffered the justice of hell and each, for a crucial moment, felt overwhelmed. Douglass: "The dark night of slavery closed in upon me;" Du Bois: "Whither? To Death? *Amen! Welcome* dark sleep!"
>
> But the moment passed, and the fire tempered, it did not devour. "Without struggle there is no progress," wrote Douglass. "No sound effort is in vain, least of all a struggle with high ideal and personal integrity," writes Du Bois.
>
> Whence come the strength and the wisdom? From the people; from the dispossessed and thus the uncorrupt; from the innumerable and thus the unconquerable.
>
> Into the choicest go these virtues. They went into Du Bois. Here was the people's own wisdom, their own selflessness, their own courage, their own integrity. And from this issued magnificent poetry and prose, lasting history, anthropology and sociology, creative editing, constructive statesmanship, brave organizing—and always passionate devotion to freedom, peace and human dignity.*

It is a strange and fateful circumstance that the news of the passing of Dr. Du Bois in Accra should have reached the United States at the very moment when hundreds of thousands of Negro

* From an article by the noted historian, Dr. Herbert Aptheker.

Americans and their white comrades-in-arms were assembling in Washington, D.C., for the mammoth protest demonstration of the insistence of twenty million black Americans that the Government of the United States act *now* to end once and for all the denial of equal rights which has left them second-class citizens ever since the Emancipation Proclamation a hundred years ago.

The vast assemblage in Washington was stunned by the news of Du Bois' death, and one of the leaders of the demonstration delivered a moving eulogy in tribute to the man whose life and work laid the foundation for the struggle which now has reached a level and a point of crisis from which no retreat, no sidestepping is possible.

What is happening in the United States today on the battlefront of democracy vs. racism stems back more than a half century to the Niagara Movement which was inaugurated at a meeting in Buffalo, New York, in July 1905, and which led to the establishment of the National Association for the Advancement of Colored People five years later. Dr. Du Bois was among those present at the inaugural meeting of the Niagara Movement, and when they met again the next year at Harpers Ferry, Virginia, on ground hallowed by the martyrdom of John Brown, Du Bois delivered an historic address in which he declared:

> We will not be satisfied to take one jot or tittle less than our full manhood rights. We claim for ourselves every single right that belongs to a free-born American, political, civil and social; and until we get these rights we will never cease to protest and assail the ears of America. The battle we wage is not for ourselves alone, but for all true Americans.

In his books such as *The Souls of Black Folk* and in the pages of *The Crisis,* monthly organ of the NAACP, which he founded in 1910 and edited for almost a quarter of a century, he continued to express this clear, unqualified demand for the complete liberation of his people from the heritage of slavery. His influence was felt by untold thousands of young Negro Americans in all walks of life—farm workers in the South, industrial laborers in Birmingham and Detroit, writers, artists, lawyers, teachers—who came to revere him as leader, mentor, father.

A signal contribution of Du Bois to the struggle for democratic rights in the United States was his refusal to accept the white American bourgeoisie's conception of Negro advancement as a purely domestic affair to be resolved only by and in the United States; and his insistence upon portraying this struggle in the world context of the liberation of *all* subject and oppressed peoples in Africa, Asia, and the Americas from the domination of colonialism, imperialism, and monopoly capitalism.

Thus in Dr. Du Bois' mind there was a perfectly logical consistency in joining the battle against the Color Bar—or Jim Crow, as it is called in the United States—with efforts toward cementing Pan-African unity. His labors to win respect and equal justice for Negro Americans by setting right the record of the Reconstruction period and of the role of Afro-Americans in the history of the United States went hand in hand with his pioneering work in sweeping aside the prevalent falsifications regarding the African peoples and their history and bringing to light what African culture was before the night of slavery and colonialism descended upon it. His lifelong aim as a scientist was to assemble in encyclopedic form the full truth about African history and culture.

During the first two or three decades of the twentieth century, Pan-Africanism was interpreted to mean the unity of all peoples of African origin and descent, and at that time, when Africa lay completely prostrate in colonial chains, it was natural to assume that the main drive for Pan-African unity and liberation must come from Afro-Americans in the West Indies and the United States.

But the picture changed radically with the emergence of the Soviet Union as a new world power and symbol of a new way of life, with the crisis of the capitalist economy which became evident in the widespread "depression" of the thirties, and with the events attending World War II and the growth of militant African nationalist movements.

When the Fifth Pan-African Congress met in Manchester in 1945, with Dr. Du Bois presiding, and George Padmore and Dr.

Kwame Nkrumah serving as joint Secretaries, there was no longer any question but that the center of gravity for Pan-African unity and struggle must henceforth be *among Africans in Africa.*

The year following the Manchester Conference, Dr. Du Bois, as Director of Special Research for the NAACP, submitted a memorandum to the Secretary and National Office Staff of that organization. He advanced in one section of the memorandum, this idea:

> We must look beyond the facade of luxurious cities, behind which modern civilization masquerades, and see and realize the poverty, squalor, slavery, ignorance, disease and despair under which the mass of men labor even today in our own slums, on our farms, and especially among the 200,000,000 colonial and semi-colonial peoples. Above all, we American Negroes should know that the center of the colonial problem is today in Africa; that until Africa is free, the descendants of Africa the world over cannot escape chains. . . . The NAACP should therefore put in the forefront of its program, the freedom of Africa in work and wage, education and health, and the complete abolition of the colonial system.

It is unfortunately necessary to say that the NAACP as a national body has not even yet fully embraced this proposal made by Dr. Du Bois, notwithstanding anti-colonial and anti-apartheid resolutions passed at annual conferences and occasional petitions to the United Nations in support of African causes. On the other hand, it can hardly be doubted that the great majority of articulate Negro Americans are becoming increasingly aware that their own freedom is ultimately dependent upon the complete liberation of Africa.

By becoming a citizen of Ghana on February 17, 1963, just six days before his ninety-fifth birthday, Dr. W. E. B. Du Bois simply formalized the fact that he was also a son of Africa. Through all his long life Africa was in his heart, in his mind, and in his blood. He traced his ancestry on his mother's side back to a great-great-grandfather kidnapped on the coast of West Africa.

Another cause to which Dr. Du Bois devoted much of his time

and energies during the years after World War II was that of world peace. As a student of history, Du Bois recognized fully that imperialism bred war. "The real causes of world war," he declared, "will persist and threaten so long as Europe and America are determined by means of cheap labor to control the wealth of the world." Thus his labors for world peace were inseparably linked with his efforts to realize the vision of a world rid of colonial and racist domination and exploitation.

To a great assembly of partisans of peace in New York in 1949 Dr. Du Bois declared:

> I tell you, people of America, the dark world is on the move: It wants and will have freedom, autonomy and equality. It will not be diverted in these fundamental rights by dialectical splitting of political hairs. . . .
>
> The white race may, if it will, tax itself into poverty, and arm itself for suicide, but the vast majority of mankind will march on and over them to freedom and selfrule.
>
> But this catastrophe is the last which we of the darker world wish or will. We have no time for revenge or for sneering at white men's tragic mistakes. What we want is a decent world, where a man does not have to have a white skin in order to be a man. Where poverty is not a means to wealth, where ignorance is not used to prove race superiority, where sickness and death are not part of our factory system.
>
> And all this depends first on world peace. Peace is not an end. It is the gateway to real civilization. With peace, all things may be added! With war, we destroy even that which the toil and sacrifice of ages have builded.

Du Bois voiced forthright criticism of the United States delegation for backing the colonial powers at the San Francisco Conference which established the Charter of the United Nations; he presented reasoned arguments against the Marshall Plan and Atlantic Pact, demonstrating that they served the interests of European imperialists; and he openly attacked various other aspects of the Cold War foreign policy of the United States government.

He claimed the right and duty of doing so as an American citizen.

Without bothering to argue that point, the administration proceeded to put the screws on him and to try to silence him. His separation from the NAACP was effected in 1948. His passport was withdrawn and he was denied the right to travel abroad. And in 1951, as a consequence of heading an organization of American citizens seeking to maintain world peace at a time when Senator McCarthy and his ilk were clamoring for war against the Soviet Union, Dr. Du Bois found himself one day standing in a criminal court in Washington, D.C., fingerprinted, handcuffed, searched for concealed weapons, and charged with being an agent of a foreign power.

The evidence against him was the flimsiest. But in that period of political madness, the requirements of law were often ignored. It was rather the loud protest raised in the United States and around the world that won Dr. Du Bois a verdict of acquittal. He never retracted one word he had uttered or written, and he continued to speak out as before against imperialism and war—more strongly.

The alternative to imperialism and war? Socialism. This was another great cause to which Du Bois gave his life. His advocacy of socialism developed from wide reading and study, from an extraordinary abundance of travel and observation in both capitalist and socialist countries, and from the functioning of a disciplined and penetrating intellect. Someone will some day trace the unfolding of the idea of socialism in the long succession of his published works which began in 1896 and continued down to the year of his death. It will suffice to say here that in his later years his convictions regarding socialism became the core of his life and of his thinking.

In *The World and Africa,* published just after the end of World War II, he had written:

> Accomplish the end which every honest human being must desire by means other than Communism, and Communism need not be feared. On the other hand, if a world of ultimate democracy, reaching across the color line and abolishing race discrimination, can only be accomplished by the method laid down by Karl Marx, then that method deserves to be triumphant no matter what we think or do.

Du Bois repeatedly warned Africa of the danger of copying a corrupt and outmoded system of capitalist exploitation:

> Refuse to be cajoled or to change your way of life so as to make a few of your fellows rich at the expense of a mass of workers growing poor and sick, and remaining without schools so that a few black men can have automobiles.
>
> Africa, here is a real danger which you must avoid or return to the slavery from which you are emerging. All I ask from you is the courage to know; to look about you and see what is happening in this old and tired world; to realize the extent and depth of its rebirth and the promise which glows on yonder hills.

Nearing his ninetieth birthday in 1958, Dr. Du Bois remarked bitterly that in the United States *youth* was applauded and *age* scorned, reversing what mankind had believed for thousands of years. (Shortly he was to come home to Africa where "Old Man" is an expression of respect and veneration instead of contempt.) He wrote:

> I would have been hailed with approval if I had died at 50. At 75 my death was practically requested. If living does not give value, wisdom and meaning to life, then there is no sense in living at all. . . .
>
> I do not apologize for living long. High on the ramparts of this blistering hell of life, I sit and see the Truth. I look it full in the face, and I will not lie about it, neither to myself nor to the world. . . .
>
> Socialism progresses and will progress. All we can do is to silence and jail its promoters. I believe in socialism. I seek a world where the ideals of communism will triumph—to each according to his need; from each according to his ability. For this I will work as long as I live. And I still live.

The rich legacy of Truth that Dr. W. E. B. Du Bois has left all mankind will long continue to live.

W. E. B. Du Bois as a prophet

TRUMAN NELSON

In the beginning the prophet sees preconditions, the explosive present and the transcendental future like a man sitting by the window of a darkened room, reading by strokes of lightning. A flash of insight, of foreboding, flares across his consciousness, and then he is plunged back into the confusions and the doubts of the ordinary mortal, groping his way through what may always be a total darkness and incomprehension of his private world and his fate in it. In time the flashes come closer and closer until the world he is destined to illume lights up under his hand with an incandescent glare and he is able to hold its crimes and secrets, its dungeons and despairs, to a steady cleansing glow which crackles and consumes like a forest fire.

The world of W. E. B. Du Bois was the world of color, and its people the majority of all the earth's people. I think of him as WORLD MAN ONE. No man ever moved within a wider bracket of humanity. Early in his life he "made it" with the whites; there were no intellectual prizes nor artistic achievements that he could not have taken from them at will, if he had chosen . . . chosen to be the "exception" whites are reluctantly willing to thrust upward to prove that they are "democratic." He did not want this, ever. Not only because it was morally wrong, and Du Bois was one of the most consistent moralists of all time, but because it was a false notion. The whites permit "exceptions" because they think of themselves with complacent blindness as the majority, and thus quite safe from being overturned by a handful of alien, inexplicable men of genius from outside, or *below,* where they usually place them.

What a searing lightning bolt W. E. B. Du Bois launched against this false, jerry-built elevation back in 1911. "The coming world man is colored. For the handful of whites in this world to dream that they, with their presently declining birthrate, can ever inherit the earth and hold the darker millions in perpetual subjection is the wildest of wild dreams." But it was a successful dream the whites had, because, as in a dream, they could choose their own landscape and the people in it, and as they moved on in the cataleptic trance of their own skin, they kept always just outside the penumbra of their consciousness, so as to be invisible, the "dark race" and the "dark Continent" from which they came.

I know this is true because I am white-skinned and I was taught not to see Negroes, to avert my eyes and not stare curiously with a child's innocence, at their strange black faces, so as not to embarrass them as they moved quite happily and uncomplainingly in their own subterranean world, so simple and primitive that if they had "work" and some free time to make music and dance, they would never cause trouble to anyone. The very sad thing about this attitude was that it was not intended to be cruel, but highly compassionate, like not staring at a cripple making his contorted way down the street or at some bedraggled tramp or drunkard passed beyond reclamation into a decent, orderly society.

This ethic of "not looking" was fortified in school where the black man never appeared humanly in the histories, and where such white men who had devoted their lives, as William Lloyd Garrison, or literally given them, as John Brown, to Negro liberation, were themselves ignored or explained away into "madness" or "fanaticism" as the black man was into subhuman inferiority and invisibility.

Du Bois changed all this. After reading him the black presence invades the whole consciousness. Grandeurs of intellect, perception, revolutionary thrust and power become apparent. And so does that ideology of lies which props up those centuries of white "liberalism" in which everything is judged by the words, by its "sentiments" and never by its fruits. In which "liberty and justice for all" means liberty and justice for *some* . . . of the white people, by the white people, and for the white people. In which all our talk about the perfectibility of a man end with the perfectibility of *me* . . . the white, superior me, first, and the black man can wait for the half loaf, or the crumbs, or whatever is left over as "time" settles this vexing problem.

W. E. B.'s first exposure of this widening gap between words and deed, and his first flash of prophecy, came in 1891, at the Eighth Annual Meeting of the American Historical Association. There, surrounded by droves of college presidents, pundits of the most exalted rank, and Henry Adams, he "read a scholarly and spirited paper on the 'Enforcement of the SLAVE TRADE LAWS!' . . . Mr. Du Bois showed that the prohibitory act of 1807 was not enforced . . . the infamous business was continued, for the United States would not permit the right of search . . . Vessels were fitted out for this traffic in every port from Boston to New Orleans. Mr. Du Bois estimates that from 1807 to 1862 not less than a quarter of a million of Africans were brought to the United States in defiance of law and humanity."

This burst on the meeting with the impacted force of several years of the most intensive scholarship by a young man of genius, accorded, by his very appearance at this gathering, one of the highest accolades of American pedagogy. It was flung into the faces of teachers, and teachers of teachers, who had, to a man, taught that the founding fathers had been opposed to slavery, and that the proof of this came with the provision in the Constitution abolishing the slave trade, whereupon, according to the popular and still operating American myth, slavery itself would disappear . . . and but for the unexpected invention of the cotton gin, you know how the story goes, slavery would never have persisted in the Land of the Free. Du Bois said, this is utter rot, you abolished nothing with your *ersatz* law, but an honest tradesman's approach to the selling of men, women, and children like meat in the market.

And he had to sit there, amongst his peers, on probation toward being human, whilst the President of this upper, upper elite of American scholars, William Hirt Henry said, in his inaugural address, "As regards the African race there is little to lament (about slavery) in comparison with the great benefits slavery conferred on the slaves. From a state of barbarism it raised the race into a state of civilization, to which no other barbarous people have ever attained in so short a time. The late African slave is now rated by our government as superior to the American Indian and to the native of the celestial Empire of China, and is entrusted with the highest privileges of an American citizen."

Just hear this: "our government" writing its Nuremberg laws some forty years before Adolf Hitler, setting up its racial ladder and looking down, then and now, from the topmost rung. It was not precisely there that Du Bois launched another one of his prophetical lightning bolts but I can well imagine the thunderheads collecting over this obscene complacency and condescension by the best brains the country had been able to gather together. The bolt came later. "This is the modern paradox of Sin before which the Puritan stands open-mouthed and mute. A group, a nation, or a race, commits murder and rape, steals and destroys, yet no individual is guilty, no one is to blame, no one can be punished. The black world squirms beneath the feet of the white in impotent fury or sullen hate."

It was this impotent, this virtually silent fury that reoccupied his early years of prophecy. Frederick Douglass, Charles Lenox Remond, Henry Garnett, were gone as spokesmen of the race. He stood alone against American racism, the worst in the world, buttressed and concealed as it is by the best, the kindest, the most advanced consciousness the country can produce. What he had to do now was organize intellect, black intellect, black articulateness, to countervail forever this degradation, this sullenness that is taken for apathy or ignorance and which destroys the psyche far more than guilt over a sudden act of violence ever will. In itself it was a stupendous task, a one-man-directed Renaissance, but his greatest opposition came from within the race itself.

No one knew better than he the great potential of the black race. His profound historical sense (for the prophet is a historian above all else) drove him to find the evidence to reverse the whole historical canon, deliberately falsified, which pictured the Reconstruction period as proving that the Negro was not competent to rule himself. After the Civil War, "Industry gave the black freedmen the vote, expecting them to fail, but meantime to break the power of the planters. The Negroes did not fail; they enfranchised their white fellow workers, established public schools for all and began a modern socialistic legislation for hospitals, prisons and land distribution. Immediately the former slave owners made a deal with the Northern industrial leaders for the disenfranchisement of the freedmen . . . the freedmen lost the right to vote, but retained their schools, poorly supported as they were by their own meager wages and Northern philanthropy."

"Northern philanthropy," by controlling the moneybags, forced upon the Negro a failure of nerve, convincing their leader, Booker T. Washington, that all was lost and that the Negro school and college had to be used as a saving remnant . . . and these schools to be mainly work-training schools. Washington and his lieutenants began to retreat and to even cringe before the white avalanche of ridicule and abuse which swept away or buried their will to resist. Du Bois could not contain his anger at this. He did what every prophet must do at some time or other, turn on his own people when they are wrong, when they are suicidal. With the cruelty of the light beam of a doctor's exploration of some putrid sore in the secret membranes, he showed them what they were becoming by not resisting at all levels the pressures of reaction.

He was a master at rediscovering and correctly analyzing the hidden continuities between events and trends which seem to have no surface connection. Booker T. Washington's retreat into proving the Negro's case by his ability to "work hard and save," his tactic of trying to shrink a great race into a mere petty bourgeoisie while they were still standing and struggling as *men,* did just what Du Bois predicted it would—brought on increasing spirals of suppression and degradation, coming full circle after the election of Woodrow Wilson, in the resegregation of the Capital itself, and culminating, in the country, with a foul wave of lynching, terror, and newly enacted racist law, nearly as bad as in slavery times.

Du Bois wanted them to fight, every day, for everything the white man had, right across the board. He called for an education that was a real education, not mere job training, and those jobs of the menial sort. Work was not education—education was the development of power and ideal—the source of art, of understanding. Work was too often to the Negro only a way of being used. He wanted black boys and girls to storm the heights held by Beethoven and Rembrandt, by Shakespeare and Pasteur. Why not? Du Bois was no diplomat, he drove a hard truth. Nor was he a pacifist; nor did he ever want to shed "our" blood before "theirs."

"Let no one," said Du Bois in 1913, "for a moment mistake that the present increased attack on the Negro along all lines is but the legitimate fruit of that long campaign for subserviency and surrender which a large party of Negroes have fathered now some twenty years . . . only the blind and foolish can fail to see that a continued campaign in every nook and corner of this land, preaching to white and colored, that the Negro is chiefly to blame for his condition, that he must not insist on his rights, that he should not take part in politics, that Jim Crowism is defensible, and even advantageous, that he should humbly bow to the storm until the lordly white man grants him clemency—the fruit of this disgraceful doctrine is disenfranchisement, segregation, lynching. Fellow Negroes, is it not time to be men? Is it not time to strike back when we are struck? Is it not high time to hold up our heads and clench our teeth and swear by the Eternal God we will *not* be slaves and that no aider, abettor, and teacher of slavery in any shape or guise can longer lead us?"

In 1913 and 1914 Du Bois' flashes of revelation began to fuse and stay lit and the pages of *The Crisis* for these years are one great coruscating glare. No wonder, said Du Bois, the sly Mister Dooley said the black man was "aisily lynched," they had made themselves the mudsills for the western world; when their wives were called prostitutes and their children bastards, they smiled; when they were called inferior half-beasts, "We nodded our simple heads and whispered, 'we is.'" When they were accused of laziness, they shrieked "ain't it so." They laughed at jokes about their color, about their tragic past and their compulsions to steal chickens. And what was the result? asked the prophet. "'We got *friends!'* I do not believe any people ever had so many 'friends' as the American Negro today. He has nothing but 'friends' and may the good God deliver him from most of them, for they are like to lynch his soul."

Then came World War I and his great soul was torn from the plight of his own people to the suffering of the world. He had to think now of all men. He went to Europe . . . "Fellow blacks," he said, "we must join the democracy of Europe," for there he found the dirty race hatred of America did not exist. He became aware of the Russian Revolution: that it was the one saving remnant of the bloody war. He went to the Soviet and said, "If what I have seen with my own eyes and heard with my own ears in Russia is Bolshevism, I am a Bolshevik!" Coming back to the United States he was in an agony of soul over what it did to his people, seen clearly from distant shores. *"It lynches . . . it disfranchises its own citizens . . . it encourages ignorance . . . it steals from us . . . it insults us . . . and* it looks upon any attempt to question or even discuss this dogma as arrogance, unwarranted assumption and treason."

It was the great American tragedy of this period that the rising tide of radicalism, of socialism, had little in it for the Negro. The revolutionary impulse which permeated the America of the thirties, for instance, was based on the trade union movement; the sit-down strike, the hunger marches, the action in Detroit on picket lines and in occupying factories. But the Negro was invisible there, too; he tagged along, but no one for a moment let him put his hand on the lever of mass power. Du Bois knew sadly that when he saw the Union Label on anything, it was almost always a sign that no Negro had worked on it. He knew all the arguments for unity of black and white . . . but why did so many unions, such as the International Typographical Union, exclude every Negro, with very few exceptions, from membership, no matter what his qualifications? This was unbearably tragic to him, for he understood more than most men that the people, the workers, give the world the homes, the bread, fulfill every human need out of their toil and devotion, and in turn, do all the fighting, suffering, and starving. He has a mythical old Negro put the matter this way: "If what *you,* [capital] gives us gives *you* the right to say what we ought to get, then what we gives *you* gives us a right to say what *you* ought to get; and we're going to take that right someday!"

He realized with the ultimate political sophistication that all workers were disenfranchised in respect to the wealth and power they create and felt that the workers should determine the policies of all public services through owning them themselves. There was no question about him being a socialist (he had joined the Socialist Party in 1904), but when he looked around him and saw, over and over again, the black man being excluded from trades or held down to the lowest grade of job, and heard on the other hand the radical parties extolling the organized Union as the vanguard of the revolutionary class, he cried out in anger and frustration, "Black brother, how would you welcome a dictatorship of this proletariat?"

It is a sign of the true prophet that although he cries out in the wilderness and into the unheeding voice of the whirlwind, he wants to gain the hearts and minds of all men . . . he wants to join the millions: he is not in the least exclusive. Over and over again, by pleading, by flogging, by toil and example of the very highest order, Du Bois tried to lead his people into the promised land of equality and fulfillment. He created a Negro intelligentsia, poets and exhorters who sometimes equaled and occasionally surpassed him in their denunciation and awareness of their white oppressors.

Obviously there was no majority for them here on American soil, but in the world, and particularly in Africa, there was a spiritual majority which could buoy them up and sustain them as they moved their frail, despised twenty million souls against the towering mass of white indifference and actual oppression. Du Bois tried to make them feel the confidence of being in a majority. "Most men in this world are colored. A faith in humanity, therefore, a belief in the gradual growth and perfectibility of men must, if honest, be primarily a belief in colored men." But where could he demonstrate this perfectibility? Where but in the home place, the motherland! His prophet's instinct told him that Africa could be the great base for the transformation of black people everywhere.

He brought this presence to black Africa's table, scraped bare and gouged and splintered by white imperialist greed and looting. First, in 1900, there was a Pan-African Conference in London, called by a West Indian. There were only thirty people there, among them Du Bois, and it had no roots in Africa itself, but it was a beginning. Then, after the Allied victory in World War I, hearing the pious disclaimers of the victors that they wanted, not blood and loot, but only "self-determination for all nations," Du Bois went to Paris to ask Wilson why he could not begin with the self-determination of the African colonies held by the defeated Germany. This is the way of the prophet; he demands the transformation of flowery words into solid fruit.

This idea was greeted with official indifference and in the press with scornful laughter. "An Ethiopian Utopia, to be fashioned of the German colonies, is the latest dream of the Negro race . . . Dr. Du Bois's dream is that the Peace Conference could form an internationalized Africa, to have as its basis, the former German colonies, with their 1,000,000 square miles and 12,500,000 population . . . to this, his plan reads, could be added by negotiation, Portuguese and Belgian Africa . . . within ten years, 20,000,000 black children ought to be at school . . ." (*Chicago Tribune,* January, 1919).

Du Bois organized a congress around this idea, to sit simultaneously with the Versailles Conference, enlightening and rebuking it, showing it the way to real peace, with an example of the nonexploitation of people.

The official American reaction to this was made clear in a typical State Department release to the press. "It was announced recently that no passports would be issued for American delegates desiring to attend the meeting." But it was already taking place, with Du Bois at the head of the table. The resolutions passed, the plans offered, came fresh baked from the warm ovens of his capacious brain; they may have sounded Utopian, but they could have been the bread of life to a hungry, stirring, re-borning continent.

Resolved that: the African land would be held in absolute trust for the native and they would have effective control over all acreage they could develop.

That: capital and investments be regulated beyond its power to exploit the native, revokable at any time, and its profits taxed for the complete social and material benefit of the native.

That: Labor would not mean slavery, and its conditions proscribed and regulated, humanely, by the state.

That: every native child should be taught to read his own language, and that of the trustee state, that all who wished would have higher technical instruction, that all who wished would have the highest cultural training, and all who wished would be trained as teachers.

That: the natives would be allowed, at once, to resume their participation in their ancient forms of local and tribal government, that this participation, when education and experience permitted, would be extended to the higher offices of the state until Africa was ruled totally by the consent of Africans.

This was "Utopia" for the white world. Well, you can hardly blame them for this . . . they haven't made it; obviously the natives of this land of the free have not effective ownership of their own land, they have no "higher" technical or cultural education that is *free,* the state does not protect them in the least, from the exploitation of capital and investments . . . nor is it ever possible, under present conditions, for anyone but a millionaire, or the hired creature of a billion-dollar corporation, to "extend" his political participation to the "higher offices of state."

This ideological base was fortified and armed, again and again, by African Congresses coming in 1921, in 1923, in 1927, coming to a climax in 1945. Much of the expenses of these congresses were paid for out of Du Bois' pockets, although he had to subsist on the meager earnings of a scholar and editor.

Someone else is telling the story of the African revolution and his part in it, but it is part of the making of a prophet to record all his triumphs and failures, and by the stupendous irony of time, just at the moment when Kwame Nkrumah heard first the locks open on his prison door, and walked then into the office of the alien Governor of his occupied country, to hear, then, himself asked to form the first free government his country had known since their enslavement by imperialist England, Du Bois heard the clank of an American prison door, opening to close him in.

The time had come when he had to face his mob. It was the whole country, it was the government, the courts, the press, the Congress, the F.B.I., the State Department, the Justice Department, all bearing down on him with a malignancy that would seem insane, except that motives had at the core the central truth that he, with his wisdom and prophecy, was threatening their overthrow. That lynch mob of the rotten center which goes by the name of "law and order" and "security," had decided that because he had been on a committee to achieve nuclear disarmament in a world on the brink of self-extinction, that he was an agent of a foreign power and subject to a fine of ten thousand dollars and five years in jail.

When he heard of his indictment in February of 1951, he was aghast at the presumption, at the disgrace. "Never in any single year has the frustration and paradox of life stood out so clearly as in this year, when, having finished some 83 years of my life in decency and honor, with something done, and something planning, I stepped into the 84th year with handcuffs on my wrists." He felt that this was the utter rending of the fabric of his work; that all his achievements were blotted out as he stood, as the government's lynch mob made him stand, in open court with handcuffs on his wrist, when they put him into a medieval cage with human derelicts, when they fingerprinted him, searched him for concealed weapons and performed all the other barbarous acts of insult that people, presumed to be innocent before trial, have to endure when they fall into the hands of the police.

His arraignment took place in February 1951, his trial in November. So the lynch mob ran at him for six months, screaming at the top of its lungs that he was an agent of Russia and that some well-proven treasonable activity on his part had brought him to trial. It was at the time of the Korean War, which was traitorous to resist. He was retired on a small pension and had very little money. He had to raise cash for his own defense in an agonizing series of talks and pleas to groups all over the country . . . this great man, this giant who had crushed the grapes of liberation for a whole continent, had to go around raising handouts for his own defense. For a long while he could not wholly understand why this was happening to him: he knew he was innocent, he had never taken, never seen any money or support for his committee from a foreign power. But then between the hammer and the anvil of the process experience, he began to renew, in its final essence, the revolutionary impulse that was deep in the marrow of his life.

He realized that he was on trial as a criminal because he had been the most prominent American in the circulation of the Stockholm Appeal, which said, "We consider that the first government henceforth to use the atomic weapon against any country whatsoever will be committing a crime against humanity and should be treated as a war criminal." He did not know, but he might have sensed, that the U.S. Government was meditating the use of atomic weapons against the people of Korea, people of color like himself. As the war went on and the immorality of American policy in Asia became clearer he realized why he, although other people were on trial with him, was singled out as the real culprit and why it was always said of him, in the newspapers, that he was a Negro. He felt that his persecutor's "real object was to prevent American citizens (particularly those of the Negro race) of any sort, from daring to think or talk against the determination of big business to reduce Asia to colonial subserviency to American industry, to reweld the chains on Africa, to consolidate U.S. control of the Caribbean and South America; and above all to crush Socialism in the Soviet Union and China. That was the object of this case."

More and more he became conscious that this was a war against people of another color, akin to his own, and that his towering presence as a Negro nuclear pacifist was extremely embarrassing to a government using Negro troops against other colored people . . . "worst of all is the use of American Negro troops in Korea. Not only is this bound to leave a legacy of hate between the yellow nations and the black, but the effect on Negroes of America, in a sense compelled to murder colored folks who suffer from the same race prejudice that they do at home, to be dumb tools of business corporations, this is bound to result in the exacerbation of prejudice and inner conflict here in America."

His defense cost him $35,150, and it was all for nothing; the case was dismissed after some days of trial, without ever going to the jury. The government had no case, said the judge. And the protests from countries all over the world who saw the condemned man as a giant among dwarfs, bore down on a nervous and uneasy State Department. So his only punishment for his innocence and truth was six months and more of agony as an indicted criminal, begging literally for his life . . . for who stays long in jail, or in life, at the age of eighty-three? The state was wrong, but who punishes them? "A nation steals and destroys, yet no individual is guilty, no one is to blame, no one can be punished."*

After his trial, after the establishment of his innocence, he was still tainted in the eyes of the rotten center, the lynch mob. The soaring crescendos of the African liberation movement exploded like fireworks. White pundits from Minnesota, from Walla Walla, from everywhere and anywhere but Africa, came in droves to TV and radio to "explain" the African revolutions. Across the river from the tower on the Empire State Building lived the man who had prophesied it and helped make it. Nobody asked him; nobody put in a ten-cent phone call to have him explain it. Now he was in exile. America acted as if he did not exist. Great countries outside wanted him for their honored guest; a few colleges dared listen to him briefly, but all that dammed-up wisdom and experience had no outlet into the mainstream of American life.

This was the final tragedy. The prophet silenced: isolated by petty defamation, by suspicion, by officially contrived alienation. Oh the waste of this! His country wasted him as some great natural resource is wasted; like a mountain wasted for a carload of ore, a forest splintered to make newsprint for the publication of trivia and lies. Wasted as Frederick Douglass and Garrison were wasted; Nat Turner and John Brown. Du Bois could have been greater than any of these, if only by the sheer longevity of his presence amongst us. If only because he embodied in his person the whole process experience of the American Negro from the time he was freed until now . . . and in his intellectuality and integrity, in his selflessness and lack of race chauvinism, gave to his own people a sense of their own attainable human grandeur, and to the whites an inescapable reminder of their racial shamelessness. When will the people learn to cherish their prophets, to defend them with their lives, to let them be heard, to *make* them be heard? When will they realize that wasting them like this means in due time, the tragic waste of themselves, or their sons sometimes, perhaps always, on bloody battlefields where their young blood and promise runs out into the unremembering earth!

The small, nobly erect and intact figure began to bend a little

* The trial is covered in pages 119–139, *In Battle for Peace.*

from weariness and pain. This enforced silence was for him a damned defeat. But then he had his final triumph . . . greater than Moses, greater than all the prophets. There are few moments in history more moving than when Kwame Nkrumah, in all the erectness and power of a young manhood that had wrested a new nation from a continent thought to be eternally dark and despised, and filled it with effusions of light, came to the old man and said, "Father, we want you to come home."

And so the great prophet returned to the land of his ancestors, to walk its bustling streets, full of the buoyancy of people living a life of revolutionary promise and advance, seeing in the faces of passers-by the reflected glory of his presence. He died there, and the cold sea rolls between us now. He was my great man and I miss him, but the indestructible terrain of his life and work, his writing and prophecy unite me with him, and transmit his warmth, as the stony bed of the ocean valley carries warmth and unites Africa to these troubled shores.

Du Bois and 'The Social Evolution of the Black South'

J. H. O'DELL

No section of America or of the world has a greater claim to share in the noble legacy of W. E. B. Du Bois than does the embattled Freedom Movement in the South. Of the broad spectrum of humanist concerns to which Dr. Du Bois devoted his energies throughout an exceptionally long life, none received more of his creative attention than did the problem of the social emancipation of the Negro people in the Deep South.

As is well known, he graduated from Fisk University in Nashville, Tennessee (Class of 1888), before going to Harvard and abroad for graduate study. In 1911, Du Bois wrote a pamphlet entitled *The Social Evolution of the Black South.* This was published as one of the American Negro Monograph series, in which Dr. Du Bois was identified as having been "for the past ten years Professor of History and Political Economy at Atlanta University." In a topical sense, at least, the title of the pamphlet suggests the foundation subject of Du Bois' intellectual commitment.

Predating this work of 1911, was a number of socio-economic studies by Du Bois, which in effect were related to the subject of the social evolution of the black South. Among the earliest and least known about was one entitled *The Negroes of Farmville, Virginia,* published in 1898. Many readers will immediately recognize that Farmville is Prince Edward County, which in our present decade became the only county in America to close down its public school system rather than grant equal educational opportunity for black and white children alike.

Du Bois, thorough scholar that he was, provides us with a review of the historical setting in which Prince Edward County developed and tells us that "before the Civil War, 75 per cent of the farms in this area were 100 acres or more, worked by gangs of from 10 to 50 slaves;" "the county is a geographical center of a historic slave state and is near the economic center of this state's greatest industry, tobacco culture. . . . Farmville is the metropolis and county seat and a center of social, political and industrial life for the county." Du Bois describes the types of Negro businesses and it is interesting that the population that he cites from the U.S. Census of 1890 shows that the population at that time was only 1,600 fewer than the 1960 census. Especially pertinent for our time is the following observation made by Du Bois:

> The town of Farmville has no school for colored children but sends them to the district school just outside the corporation limits. The schoolhouse is a large, pleasantly situated frame building with five rooms.
>
> It is not at present, if the general testimony of the town people is to be taken, a very successful school. It is practically ungraded, the teachers are not particularly well-equipped, except in one, possibly two cases, and the school term is six months—September 15 to April 11th.

More than a half century later, Negro parents in Prince Edward County were among the original plaintiffs involved in the historic Supreme Court's decision of 1954 (Brown vs. Board of Education). Their involvement in this case actually began three years earlier when students at Moton High School went on a strike in protest against inadequate facilities, a "direct action" which predated the southwide student sit-ins by almost a decade.

After the Supreme Court's desegregation decision of 1954, Prince Edward County became the center of Virginia's "massive resistance" program. Aided by the Federal Court in Richmond, the county Supervisors were granted delays for a five-year period and then in 1959 abandoned the whole public school system, leaving some 1,700 Negro children without any formal schooling for a period of over four years. The public schools were finally reopened in September 1964. The Negro students who had received any formal education at all during this period attended schools outside the county and state; some went as far as Springfield, Massachusetts.

Du Bois describes domestic work in Farmville:

> Just as the field hand of slavery days developed into the métayer [sharecropper], so the house servant easily developed into the

day worker. Thirty-three single women and 114 housewives go out regularly at day work in families or take family washing into their homes . . . being a subsidiary employment for most families. . . . Those who work in families are either paid like house servants, by the week, or if they work by the day, from 30 to 50 cents a day. Much neglect of their own household duties and of children, especially of growing girls, is a result of the absence of the mother from home. Those who take in washing receive from 50¢ to $1.25 a month for their washing. In this way, many a Farmville mother helps her husband support the family, or during dull times keeps them all above want.

Concerning the unemployment in Farmville, Dr. Du Bois writes:

One of the principal causes of idleness is the irregular employment. A really industrious man who desires work is apt to be thrown out of employment from one-third to one-half of the year by the shutting up of the tobacco factories, the brickyard, or the cannery. If he wants to get on in the world or accumulate property he often finds that he must seek better wages and steadier employment elsewhere; or if he can not himself go, he sends a son or a daughter. Fully one-half, if not two-thirds, of the property owned by Negroes in the town has been paid for in large part with money earned outside the town. On the other hand, if the man be of only ordinary caliber, he easily lapses into the habit of working part of the year and loafing the rest. This habit is especially pernicious for half-grown boys, and leads to much evil. Undoubtedly the present situation prolongs some of the evils of the slave system. It is also true that larger, better, and steadier industrial opportunities in a town like Farmville would in time be able to counteract the tendency of youth to emigrate, would build up a faithful and efficient laboring community, and would pay good dividends to the projectors of new enterprises. The great demand is for steady employment which is not menial, at fair wages.

The women, too, demand enlarged industrial opportunities outside of domestic service, and of a kind compatible with decency and self-respect. They are on the whole more faithful and are becoming better educated than the men, and they are capable of doing far better work than they have a chance to do. As it is, they can only become servants, and if they must serve they prefer $12.00 a month in New York to $4.00 in Farmville. This explains the growing excess of colored women over colored men in many northern cities.

With some adjustment, this is a description of dozens of semi-rural towns in the South today, more than sixty years later. One calls to mind personal observations in such places as Montgomery, Alabama, Vidalia, Louisiana, Woodville, Mississippi, Albany or Waycross, Georgia. An updated version would read something like this. . . . "They prefer $35.00 a week on a sleep-in job on Long Island, New York, to $12.00 a week and carfare in Montgomery."[1]

Apparently one of the major considerations in Du Bois' analysis of the social evolution of the black South was his concern for education, sharply reflected in his important article *Of the Training of Black Men,* written in 1902.[2] Reviewing the period following the overthrow of Reconstruction, Dr. Du Bois states the following:

> The Negro colleges, hurriedly founded, were inadequately equipped and illogically distributed and of varying efficiency and grade; the normal and high schools were doing little more than common (elementary) school work, and the common schools were training but a third of the children who ought to be under them, and training these often poorly. . . . In the midst, then, of the larger problem of Negro education sprang up the more practical question of work, the inevitable economic quandary that faces a people in transition from slavery to freedom and especially those who make that change amid hate and prejudice, lawlessness and ruthless competition.

That the period of "transition from slavery to freedom" has been agonizingly prolonged into our own lifetime and the present decade, by the institutions of American society, is obvious to all who are aware of the activities of the Civil Rights Movement. However, nothing underscores the relevance of Du Bois' observation, cited above, than does a recent study (1962) on the academic standing of Southern Negro schools. This study, published by Randolph Macon College in Virginia, reports that on an average 75 per cent of the Negro high schools in Alabama, Georgia, Louisiana, Mississippi, and South Carolina are of such poor quality that they are not accredited by the Southern Association of Colleges and Secondary Schools.[3] In effect, this means that a Negro student receiving a diploma from one of these high schools would have to take remedial courses before being eligible to enter a first-rate college even in the South. For most Negro students it simply means that they are graduating from high school with what academically amounts to about a tenth-grade education. This may appropriately be called educational colonialism, which, of course, is rapidly becoming the educational pattern in the deprived black ghettos of the North as well.

With great intellectual power and self-confidence, Du Bois poses a challenge for American education which is as valid today as it was in 1902 when he wrote:[4]

> We have a right to inquire, as this enthusiasm for material advancement mounts to its height . . . that ever-recurring query of the ages, Is not life more than meat, and the body more than raiment? . . . And above all, we daily hear that an education that encourages aspiration, that sets the loftiest of ideals and seeks, as an end, culture and character rather than bread-winning, is the privilege of white men and the danger and delusion of black.

And in reply to Southern white defenders of the status quo of 1902 who (then as now) kept making references to their figures concerning the "Negro crime rate," Du Bois answers:

> Even today, the masses of the Negroes see all too clearly the inequalities of their position and the moral crookedness of yours. The arch crime was slavery and lynching and lawlessness its twin abortion.

And then, as if looking three generations ahead to the present decade of social protest, Du Bois states in the same article the following:

> The dangerously clear logic of the Negro's position will more and more loudly assert itself in that day when increasing wealth and

more intricate social organization preclude the south from being, as it so largely is, simply an armed camp for intimidating black folk. Such waste of energy cannot be spared if the south is to catch up with civilization.[5]

It is perhaps some encouragement to the battle-weary to see that the Southern "moderates" are today beginning to show signs of catching up with this analysis of the South made sixty-odd years ago.

In examining the social evolution of the black South, Du Bois was not unmindful of the need to take into detailed account the *economic* position of the black community. At the turn of the century, 90 per cent of the Negro people lived in the South, a percentage figure which had been more or less constant since the first United States Census in 1790.[6] And in the South, we were confined, in the main, to the rural areas of plantation economy, a holdover from the slavery period. This fact basically determined our economic, political, and social status in American life and, indeed, our "social evolution" under American conditions.

In this context, Du Bois wrote one of his pioneering economic studies, *The Negro Landholder of Georgia,* published in 1901. He selected Georgia as an area of study because it had the largest Negro population in the country (today, it is the third largest) and he selected for special attention "the 56 counties containing the mass of the black population." As background, Du Bois graphically traces the evolution of the slave economy in Georgia during the nineteenth century and the distribution of the black population in Georgia from its early beginnings in Liberty County and Savannah, along the seacoast north to Augusta and across central Georgia to Columbus, then southwest into Albany (Dougherty County). In the 56 counties of black majority population, Du Bois, in analyzing the census reports found the average Negro farm owner held 79 acres. Today, more than 40 of these counties are still black majority population and the last agriculture census showed 72 acres average farm ownership among Negroes. Du Bois' pioneer study was written before the scientific revolution in American agriculture had had its impact on land tenure in Georgia, and elsewhere in the South. A case in point is the following:

TRENDS IN NEGRO FARM OWNERSHIP IN GEORGIA[7]

Year	*Number of Farms*
1920	13,684
1954	9,320
1960	6,068

As seen by this table, Negro farm ownership in Georgia declined by almost 60 per cent (while ownership among white farmers dropped about 33 per cent). During the period (1920–1954), the size of the average Negro-owned farm increased 5 acres while among the whites in Georgia, the increase was 25 acres. Many specialists in the study of Southern economic development make a point of calling attention to the decline of sharecropping as a sign of "progress." However, the decline in farm ownership among the small-farm owners is also a substantial feature of the Southern scene. In the South as a whole, in 1960, only one fourth of the black farmers owned their own farm. It will surprise some to learn that this is the same figure as 1910.

As for the decline in sharecropping, many former sharecropper families have become farm laborers, which is a step further down on the ladder of rural poverty and insecurity. Others have been forced to migrate to the cities, in search of employment at unskilled jobs which are gradually disappearing from the economy due to changes in technology. For tens of thousands of Negro families this whole developmental process in Southern agriculture leads to a condition of relative and absolute impoverishment.

Du Bois in an address to the American Academy of Political and Social Science (April 12, 1901) gave this description:

> I have seen in the black-belt of Georgia . . . a black farmer fall in debt to a white storekeeper and that storekeeper go to his farm and strip it of every single marketable article—mules, plows, stored crops, tools, furniture, bedding, clocks, looking-glass, and all this without a warrant, without process of law, without a sheriff or officer, in the face of the law for homestead exemptions, and without rendering to a single responsible person any account or reckoning.[8]

Let us compare this description by Du Bois in 1901 with the description of selected black-belt counties across the South contained in the report of the United States Civil Rights Commission in 1961. (We quote:)

> Political candidates totally disregard the Negro either as a registered or a potential voter. They neither address Negro groups nor seek Negro votes. Campaign issues do not acknowledge the interests of the non-white majority. When the Negro is the subject of campaign oratory, he is usually its butt. Since those running for office ignore them, the few Negroes who do vote have only a limited basis on which to do so. Excluded from every significant stage in the political process, the Negro citizen has little or no political existence except in the role of the "governed." His isolation is profound. . . .
>
> That governing is the reserved bailiwick of whites is demonstrated everywhere in the 17 selected counties. The elected officials are white, the registrars are white, the judges are white, the juries are predominantly, if not exclusively white, the policemen are generally white, the firemen are white—almost all official positions, excepting only menial ones, are held by whites. In instances where Negroes hold responsible positions—as policemen, teachers, agricultural extension agents, and the like—their duties are carefully limited and they deal only with other Negroes. Within the stable order of things, there appears little need to remind the Negro of his place. He is already in it.[9]

These descriptions and the census figures cited above demonstrate that the rural black South is today faced with the same problems of unrepresentative political institutions and lack of capital, due to poverty of land ownership, characteristic of undeveloped nations and communities, newly emerging from or still under colonial subjugation in such areas as southeast Asia, Africa, and parts of Latin America.

The real significance of Du Bois' writings in the period of the first decade of the twentieth century is appreciated when we take note of the political and social atmosphere of the country at that time, especially as it relates to the Negro in the South. Segregation, as a functional variety of colonialism, operating *within* the United States, had been firmly established and with it a society of racial despotism. The South was presenting the nation with several dozen lynchings each year; and the Hollywood movie industry had but recently been born and was taking its place in the institutional arrangement of American society as the chief dispenser of mass media "culture." Among Hollywood's early contributions to American film culture were such movies as[10] *The Wooing and Wedding of a Coon* (1905), which was described by the producers as "a genuine Ethiopian comedy;" then there was *Rastus in Zululand* (1910) and another *For Massa's Sake* (1911), which depicted a Negro character who was so loyal to his slave-master that, once free, he sold himself back into slavery in order to pay off the slave-master's gambling debts. Another example of film "entertainment" was the movie *Coon Town Suffragettes,* an obviously ludicrous reference to the historic Women's Suffrage Movement of that period, struggling to gain the right to vote for women. But such is the Hollywood mentality regarding issues of social significance. The ambitious businessmen of the young movie industry knew the "accepted way" of getting ahead in the world.

In this general setting, as if to further complicate matters, while "Teddy" Roosevelt was in the White House, the dominant sections of the white power structure had decided upon the selection of a Negro leader for the black South to follow; a policy, which for decades, had been tested in controlling the American Indian populations. Dr. Booker T. Washington was endowed with this role as *the* "Negro spokesman" and for more than a decade, he had been dutifully engaged in articulating the philosophy of the Atlanta Compromise.

With the gathering clouds of World War I causing a rapid decline in the immigration of cheap labor from Europe, the captains of American Industry reached into their colonialist reserve in the rural South for a black labor supply. Thus, the process of urbanization of the black population was accelerated to serve the needs of Northern industry; this process continued down to World War II and into the postwar decade which marked the beginnings of automation.

In a fundamental sense, therefore, the "social evolution of the black South" proceeds in response to the particular set of historical circumstances created and imposed by the existing institutional arrangement in our country. Conversely, the institutional arrangement, itself, is under pressure from the black South struggling for full emancipation. This interaction between the institutions of American society and the aspirations of the historically deprived and exploited black American community for freedom and equality represents a deepening and antagonistic contradiction profoundly effecting the course of social development in the United States.

Today, in the sixth decade of the twentieth century, the year 1965 finds the Freedom Movement in the South on the threshold of a new period in its development, in which the struggle for elementary civil rights is largely (but not completely) behind us, and the struggle for equality will increasingly command the main energies of the Movement. The struggle for black equality involves the question of gaining a *just share of the economic and political decision-making power of the country*. Consequently, the central problem facing the Movement and its leadership in this new period, is *the development of an adequate theory of social change to guide the practical activities of the Movement;* an adequate system of ideas deeply rooted in the scientific disciplines of economics, government, political behavior, as well as the science of organization.

A good starting point for developing an adequate frame of reference upon which to retool the program and policies of our Movement is to study in detail the Reconstruction period, because that was the only period in the entire history of the country in which the black population in the South had any real decision-making power in Government. Today, with a population of twenty-two million, we have six Negro Congressmen, but none from the South. Ninety years ago, we had sixteen Congressmen and two United States Senators—all of them from the South. In addition, the black South had scores of representatives in the state legislatures, compared to only three in the Southern states today. The Du Bois classic *Black Reconstruction,* is an indispensable weapon for deepening our understanding of the roots of today's problems in the South, and a motivational tool for more effective practical work.

In the course of staff training work in voter registration in the South, I have met scores of active, intelligent campus leaders of the Student Movement (and many adult community leaders as well) most of whom had never heard of W. E. B. Du Bois, were eager to know more, and were being introduced to his book *Black Reconstruction* for the first time during our training sessions. For most black Americans knowledge of this vitally important period in our American experience consists of a few scattered bits of information, handed down from one generation to another, almost like a folk legend out of some nebulous past. And, even this scanty knowledge has been diluted by racist slanders of the Reconstruction period, learned from public school history textbooks —many of which are authored and published in the North for Southern school systems. If there is any frame of reference for the black community in the South to measure its progress by (as well as its goals), it is the levels of political power achieved during Reconstruction. Qualitatively speaking, anything short of those levels amounts to "tokenism."

The two million black voters in the South today are faced with a historic challenge and opportunity to break the trap of landlessness, educational deprivation and the ever-widening, twenty-two-billion-dollar yearly income gap which prevents black America from exercising equality with white America. The Freedom Movement in the South is compelled to become a pacesetter of fundamental political change in America, if for no other reason than that the experience of the Movement is one of having been forced to function under conditions in which the political machinery of the state has been used more often in an effort to suppress the Movement than to uphold Constitutional rights.

More than sixty years ago in his article *The Social Evolution of the Black South,* Du Bois enunciated an elementary guiding principle for American leadership when he wrote:

> I do not believe that the systematic deception concerning the situation in the south, on the part of white men or black men, will in the long-run help that situation a single particle.

The life of Du Bois brings to mind a kind of tribute written on the life of the greatest of the Arabic historians, Ibn Khaldun, by the translator of his works at Yale:

> With great single-mindedness . . . he endeavored to master the intellectual development of humanity at its contemporary level. His background and upbringing had taught him to consider these the most desirable achievements in this world . . . realizing that the more enduring achievement of intellectual leadership is largely incompatible with the search for worldly success . . . aided by great ability and endurance, as well as by circumstances that, though harsh, were favorable to his aspirations, he became the great thinker and doer he set out to be.

These words, concerning the great fourteenth-century African historian of Arabic culture, provide us with an appropriate description of the greatest of the Afro-American scholars of the twentieth century—William Edward Burghardt Du Bois.

References

1. "The Negro People in the Southern Economy," *Freedomways* (Fall, 1963).
2. W. E. B. Du Bois, "Of the Training of Black Men," *Atlantic Monthly* (September, 1902).
3. J. Kenneth Morland, *Southern Schools—Token Desegregation and Beyond* (New York: Anti-Defamation League, 1963).
4. *Atlantic Monthly* (September, 1902).
5. *Ibid.*
6. "The Negro Population in the United States, 1790–1915," U.S. Census Table 3, p. 33.
7. U.S. Agriculture Census: 1954 and 1959.
8. W. E. B. Du Bois, "America's Race Problems" (Philadelphia: American Academy of Political and Social Science, 1901).
9. Report of United States Civil Rights Commission (1961), vol. on voting, p. 161.
10. Peter Noble, *The Negro in Films* (London: S. Robinson, 1948), pp. 27–29.

'The Brownies' Book': A pioneer publication for children

ELINOR DESVERNEY SINNETTE

> *This is* The Brownies' Book, *a monthly magazine for the children of the sun—designed for all children, but especially for OURS. It aims to be a thing of joy and beauty, dealing in happiness, laughter and emulation, and designed especially for kiddies from six to sixteen.*

Thus begins an exciting and memorable adventure in writing for children. The editor of *The Brownies' Book* was W. E. B. Du Bois. The idea of this scholarly historian editing a magazine for children at first may seem incongruous. With the discovery of a complete set of these magazines which were produced monthly from January 1920 until December 1921, there begins further insight into this man's greatness. He was indeed many years ahead of his times.

The purpose of *The Brownies' Book* as outlined by Dr. Du Bois was, "To seek to teach universal love and brotherhood for all little folk, black and brown and yellow and white." The meaning of this publication for all children is further stated by Dr. Du Bois.

> To make colored children realize that being colored is a normal, beautiful thing, to make them familiar with the history and achievements of the Negro race, to make them know that other colored children have grown into beautiful, useful, famous persons, to teach them delicately, a code of honor and action in their relations with white children, to turn their little hurts and resentments into emulation, ambition and love of their own homes and companions, to point out the best amusements and joys and worthwhile things of life, to inspire them to prepare for definite occupations and duties with a broad spirit of sacrifice. This is a great program—a tremendous task.

We want the advice of all mothers and fathers of all men and women and children in helping us accomplish it. We can conceive of no more splendid duty at this critical hour.

The time—October 1919.

Many of the older generation may remember *St. Nicholas:* Scribner's Illustrated Magazine For Girls and Boys, edited by Mary Mapes Dodge. This was published periodically from November 1873 to May 1943. This publication passed through the hands of hundreds and thousands of boys and girls in the United States. In the seventy years of its existence, *St. Nicholas's* theme was light-hearted, stressing gaiety and happiness. It is considered the landmark in magazine writing for children and is regarded fondly by parents, librarians, and teachers. As one leafs through its pages, volume after volume, one looks in vain for a brown face, a black face, evidence of that important part of United States history conveniently swept under the rug. One looks in vain for the story of a brown Dan or Alice who live with their family in New York, or on a farm in South Carolina or in Philadelphia, Chicago, or Florida.

The purpose of the *St. Nicholas* magazine was to "Make the spirit of St. Nicholas (Santa Claus) bright in each boy and girl in good, pleasant, helpful ways. And to clear away clouds that sometimes shut it out." Nowhere did this vital publication in the field of children's literature attempt to recognize the existence of an important segment of the population—the Afro-American child and his family. This child, developing from a heritage of slavery, seeking his horizons in a hostile environment, searching for images of himself and his people, heroes and hope, strength and fortitude. What did this child find in the pages of *St. Nicholas?*

He found the admonition directed to all American children to "keep cool, hold hard, and we'll get around the bend all right." He found a poem which the editor of *St. Nicholas* discovered in a book "a dear little girl had in a meadow." The pictures are, we are told, "enough to split the sides of the soberest." The poem is called "Ten Little Niggers."

> Ten little nigger boys went out to dine
> One choked his little self and then there were nine . . .

In another story we find "Sam, a po' nigga, the only nigga the stingy man had." We find the black child in cartoons, an object of ridicule and a buffoon. The impression of the Afro-American child as presented to the white reader is clearly that this black creature is not a part of his society but "something" apart. While New York schoolboys, 30,000 strong, were pictured parading in the May Day Americanization Parade (July 1920 issue of *St. Nicholas*) and a group of white children are seen sitting on guns aboard the *Pennsylvania,* flagship of the Atlantic Fleet, feeling "proud to be nieces and nephews of Uncle Sam," the January 1920 issue of *The Brownies' Book* showed Afro-American Sunday school children marching in protest to the lynchings and brutalities in the South.

To further compare—In the Watchtower, the current events department of *St. Nicholas,* we are told in April 1920: "Those restless people beyond the Rio Grande spent the month of April in their favorite pastime—Civil War."

The Brownies' Book took a different tone, a more mature attitude.

> There has been a revolution in Mexico. President Carranza has been expelled and General Obregon is at the head of most of the opposing forces. The trouble seems to have been that Carranza was not willing to have what his rivals considered a fair election.

In the *St. Nicholas* are stories written by the finest writers for children of the day. African life, when mentioned, was a gross caricature and helped to foster and perpetuate the stereotype of the "dark continent." The editor encouraged the young readers to submit their work and it was an honor to receive recognition from this publication. However, this magazine did not begin to serve the needs of the colored child or parent. There was need for something special and the editor of *The Crisis, A Record of the Darker Races,* saw it well.

Dr. Du Bois became *The Crisis's* editor in 1910. With the help of business manager Augustus Granville Dill and literary editor Jessie Redmon Fauset, he propelled it to a magazine of high literary standard through which he encouraged Negro writers and artists to give expression to their talents. By 1920 many young American Negro writers had been published first in the pages of *The Crisis.* The magazine also encouraged the finest in graphic arts and provided a forum for the work of Hilda Rue Wilkinson, Marcellus Hawkins, Laura Wheeler Waring, and others. Primarily for adults, there was however a special issue each year. The October issues of *The Crisis* seemed to have been prepared with the education of young people in mind. In July 1918 and October of the same year there appeared an Education Number and a Children's Number. The children's issue was full of pictures of beautiful brown babies, on the cover, above the editorial page masthead, and throughout. There were poems and stories for children in this October issue and the editorial pleaded with parents to send children to school. In October 1919 the Children's Number of *The Crisis* had pictures of children, a poem called "Father Love" by Leslie Pinckney Hill and a fairy story by Carrie S. Bond. It is in this issue that we read an article called "The True Brownies."

> The children's issues of *The Crisis* have been published annually for nine years and are easily the most popular number of the year. It makes the widest appeal to our readers. This is as it should be. Of course, we are and must be interested in our children above all else, if we love our race and humanity.

Dr. Du Bois stated further that he was distressed by the impact of the record of horror and strife in our children's world. What impression was it all making on them? He had received a letter from a twelve-year-old who wrote, "I hate white people as much as I know they hate me. I want to know more about my own people." This disturbed him and proved beyond a doubt that something had to be done.

> We must not lose our children to hatred. To educate them in human hatred is more disastrous to them than to the hated, to seek to

raise them in ignorance of their racial identity and peculiar situation is inadvisable, impossible. There seems to be one alternative. We shall publish hereafter not one children's number a year but twelve.

A whole generation of children was growing and developing without reading materials and concrete evidence dealing with their existence. Nothing to truly capture their interest and reflect their life. Nothing to tell them they were alive, important, worthwhile. Writing in *Dusk of Dawn* in 1940, Dr. Du Bois commented on the lack of identifying materials for our young people.

> One cannot realize today (in 1910) how rare it was. The colored papers carried few or no illustrations. The white papers none. In many great periodicals, it was the standing rule that no Negro portrait was to appear and that rule still holds in some American periodicals.

We may comment that the rule has held firm in most media until quite recently. At the same time, an entire generation of white children was growing and developing without a notion that there were children of other colors and cultures in their midst, totally unaware of differences, or sameness. Herein lay the source of potential strife and misunderstanding, of revolt and tumult. The mounting records of lynchings and violence committed against his people in the South, riots, labor strikes in the North, gave full evidence that his children were finding it impossible to heed *St. Nicholas* magazine's advice and get around the bend by keeping cool and holding hard.

Dr. Du Bois had formed a publishing company with Augustus Dill. It was this company which published *The Brownies' Book*. *The Crisis* team of Du Bois, Dill, and Fauset, became The Brownies' team.

Augustus Granville Dill, Harvard graduate and successful business manager of *The Crisis,* showed an interest in young people of talent in all the art areas. His "Five Twenty's," a series of musicales held at his bookshop, permitted young performers to show their skills. The literary editor was Jessie Redmon Fauset, a lady of distinction, from similar background and education as Dr. Du Bois, who most certainly knew well the so-called "better class" of Negroes and who brought them to life through her books. She is described by one reviewer as "a gentlewoman whose pen dips choicely into the lives of black folk who go to school and come home to the simple niceties of living just like white folks do."

This teacher, holder of a Phi Beta Kappa key, author of *There Is Confusion, Plum Bun, The Chinaberry Tree,* and *Comedy American Style,* found the same attractiveness in her people, black people, as Dr. Du Bois. She was moved by their beauty, warmth, understanding, tolerance, and fellowship. She believed her people would find themselves through searching in the past. As a teacher in the New York City schools, she saw daily the need for children and young people to have insight into their past and hope and pride in their future. She believed in giving Afro-American children a sense of identity early in their childhood. The unhappy characters in her novels never had this and were forever searching for values. It was she who gathered stories, poems, biographical material, words of wisdom for the children. She and Dr. Du Bois sought out and encouraged young writers to contribute their talents for the children, the Brownies.

And what of Dr. Du Bois, this man of vision whom we associate with the world of scholarship and philosophy? What of his qualifications to be editor of a children's magazine? We may find a clue to this aspect of the Doctor's personality in *13 Against The Odds* by Edwin R. Embree. Dr. Du Bois is described as being: "In constant warfare against the wrongs of color-caste in the United States and throughout the world."

Here too is a glimpse of the young Du Bois, the teacher in the rural South. "Reading and spelling with his class, picking flowers, singing and listening to stories of the world beyond the hill." And: "Although restrained, and dignified, with hundreds of devoted admirers—few friends, he showed a tenderness and ease with his grandchildren and with other young people that he seldom had with adults."

Here is Du Bois, the teacher, encouraging, understanding, relaxed, and as informal as he would ever be. He had the determination and vision to provide good literature to the Brownies. Literature which reflected scholarship, sincerity, awareness of current events, because he saw each child as "the future of humanity."

The Brownies' Book closely followed the format and arrangement of its companion publication, *The Crisis*. The quality of paper was excellent, the print was clear and attractive even to the younger reader. The many illustrations were appealing and beautiful. The photographs were numerous and well done. One which bears mention is the frontispiece of the February 1920 issue. It is a full-page photograph of a small Afro-American boy standing with hands on hips, cocky, sizing up the situation at the huge steelworks in Birmingham, Alabama. The caption reads, "The World That Awaits Him." One cannot help wondering what indeed was awaiting him in Birmingham over the next forty-five years. Birmingham, Alabama, city of police dogs and fire hoses. Had Birmingham lived up to his dreams and expectations?

Each issue had about thirty-two pages, with advertising kept to a minimum. The advertising which appeared was mainly to promote books, schools, courses, and self-improvement through education. As an example, the following ad appeared on the back cover of the June 1920 issue.

> Have you told your children of the part which Negro American soldiers played in the Great War? Then let them have before their eyes *The Crisis* Calendar for 1920 which contains twelve pages each carrying the picture of a Negro American Hero of the Great War with military citations. The cover reproduces Roscoe C. Jamison's inspiring poem, Negro Soldiers.

Cover art work was done by leading Afro-American artists. Each cover of the twenty-four issues was outstanding. Between these covers was a wealth of literature, poetry, music, biographical information on men and women of history, games, plays, riddles, puzzles, and current events.

Dr. Du Bois spoke in *The Brownies' Book* as "The Crow."

> The crow is black and O so beautiful, shining with dark blues and purples, with little hints of gold in his mighty wings. He

flies far above the Earth, looking downward with his sharp eyes. What a lot of things he must see and hear and if he could only talk—and lo, *The Brownies' Book* has made him talk for you.

Through this current events page, Dr. Du Bois presented to his boys and girls, the world, its inhabitants, and his interpretation of events happening over the globe. Dr. Du Bois respected young people and expected them to be interested in other people and to respect them.

In this department he reported news of the uneasy peace, and the suffering that followed World War I. He pointed out the many problems of the League of Nations and in each issue he included items pertaining to the struggle for freedom within the United States. The title of this feature was called, "As The Crow Flies." In his role of The Crow, Dr. Du Bois never failed to remind his young readers of the beauty of their color.

> I like my black feathers—
>   don't you?
> Whirl, whirl, up, whirl and fly
> home to my sweet, little, black
> crowlets . . . Ah, but they're black
> and sweet and bonnie.

It is significant to note that when the end came for *The Brownies' Book,* The Crow sometime later returned to fly through the pages of *The Crisis.*

There was a wide selection of story material in each issue of *The Brownies' Book*. We discover folk tales, fables, and legends from Spain, the African continent, Denmark, the Caribbean, and Mexico. There were adventure stories, girls' stories, and boys' stories written by A. O. Stafford, Augusta E. Bird, Yetta Kay Stoddard, Arthur Huff Fauset, and many others. Mary Effie Lee also contributed regularly. Later known as Effie Lee Newsome, her *Gladiola Garden,* a collection of verse, was a significant addition to the field of children's literature. The widely acclaimed writer, Langston Hughes, appeared in many of the 1921 issues. Even at that time his poems, plays, and articles were reaching young audiences. Other contributors of poetry were James Weldon Johnson, Jessie Fauset, and Georgia Douglas Johnson. Nina Yolande Du Bois, the daughter of Dr. Du Bois, was among the contributors of prose and illustrations.

Many of the issues carried a biography of an important black hero or heroine. Samuel Coleridge-Taylor, Alexander Dumas, Denmark Vesey, Harriet Tubman, Alexander Pushkin, Katy Ferguson, Blanche K. Bruce, Sojourner Truth, Charles Gilpin, Phyllis Wheatley, Bert Williams, Frederick Douglass, Toussaint L'Ouverture, Benjamin Banneker, and Crispus Attucks were the subjects of these biographical sketches. All were well written and served to inspire young minds as well as to engender a sense of self-respect.

Other departments of the magazine were "The Judge," a page of lively advice to children. One realizes that Jessie Fauset captured the interests of three separate age groups when she addressed her remarks to her friends, Billikens, William, and Wilhelmina.

"The Jury," another department, was devoted to letters from readers. This letter written by a young girl in Philadelphia points out the bitterness that smoldered in the hearts of Negro children as a result of many painful school experiences.

> Sometimes in school, I feel so badly. In the geography lesson, when we read about the different people who live in the world, all the pictures are pretty, nice-looking men and women, except the Africans. They always look so ugly. I don't mean to make fun of them, for I am not pretty myself; but I know not all colored people look like me. I see lots of ugly white people, too; but not all white people look like them, and they are not the ones they put in the geography. Last week the girl across the aisle from me in school looked at the picture and laughed and whispered something about it to her friend. And they both looked at me. It made me so angry. Mother said for me to write you about it.

What better reply could there have been to this pathetic letter than the short article by Kathleen Easmon written for the June 1921 issue entitled, "A Little Talk About West Africa." The article included a full page photograph of West African students posing proudly outside their school much in the same way as high school students in Philadelphia.

This article written by an African portrayed life as it was being lived in West Africa. Miss Easmon wrote, "Our people in the bush have heard that you call them savages, a word which they translate as meaning the people who have no sense. It is unfair to call a person who does things well but in a different way from yours, a savage." Forty-four years later many nations and many people have yet to fully understand the meaning of this statement.

Another feature was "The Grownups Corner," directed to parents. In the January 1921 issue, the editors summed up the first year of publication in this Grownups Corner. A gentlemen from Boston wrote that the magazine was teaching one group of American children to respect themselves and another group to show them respect. The editors also pointed out that 98 per cent of the work appearing in the magazine was done by colored men. The editors further stated that all of the original drawings, save one, had come from the pen of such notable colored artists as Laura Wheeler, Albert Smith, Hilda Wilkinson, Marcellus Hawkins, Louise Latimer, and others. These competent craftsmen contributed in full measure to the beautiful profusion of graphic material included in the issues. The young readers were continually encouraged and invited to submit their original work for publication. The excellent art work helped to stimulate this kind of reader participation.

"Little People of the Month" was a feature usually accompanied by lovely photographs of a Brownie with a comment on his special accomplishments. Many issues contained photographs of recent graduates. The July 1920 issue contained four full pages of photographs of graduates with a notation of their schools and their special interests. These were Brownies on their way up the ladder of academic achievement who would serve as inspiring examples to smaller Brownies.

Dr. Du Bois' literary contribution to *The Brownies' Book* appeared as a story in the August 1920 issue. It was called, "Honey (Rewritten After Maeterlinck)." It was in the form of a charming conversation between Boy and his mother. While the story is a description of the life of a bee, many other concepts are discussed. The ideals of Life, Love, Death, Work, and Sharing are beautifully interwoven in this story for children.

> Yes darling. But love is a great and holy thing and always near to death; that is why death is beautiful. *And:* Yes, Boy; of all crimes idleness is worst. Work is Love. Love is Life. Life is flowers and honey and work.

One calls to mind these same concepts expressed for the adult world in *Dusk of Dawn.*

> I have met life face to face. I have loved a fight and I have realized that Love is God and Work is his Prophet; that His Ministers are Age and Death. . . .

The Brownies' Book came to an end in December 1921. This was the statement to readers announcing the end of the magazine. It was called "Valedictory."

> Messrs. Du Bois and Dill announce with regret the discontinuance of *The Brownies' Book.* Recognizing the great need which exists for literature adapted to colored children and indeed to all children who live in a world of varied races, we have for two years made the experiment of publishing at our own expense *The Brownies' Book.*
>
> The fault has not been with our readers. We have had an unusually enthusiastic set of subscribers. But the magazine was begun just at the time of industrial depression following the war, and the fault of our suspension therefore is rather in the times which are so out of joint, than in our constituency.

In *Dusk of Dawn,* Dr. Du Bois commented on his foray into the world of publishing for children.

> In these days, 1920 and 1921, I made one effort toward which I look back with infinite satisfaction; an attempt in *The Brownies' Book* to furnish a little magazine for Negro children, in which my

efforts were ably seconded by Augustus Dill and Jessie Fauset: it was really a beautiful publication, but it did not pay its way.

In speaking of him at the memorial tribute in Ghana on September 29, 1963, Reverend William Howard Melish said, "Du Bois never took adversity as a feeling of defeat. He went from one project to another never doubting that each was good and that good came from each."

Today we all look upon *The Brownies' Book* with infinite satisfaction. It was a magnificent publication. Through it one of the greatest men of the twentieth century contributed unstintingly in an effort to restore a sense of self-esteem to the black child, our child of the sun. It was a magnificent publication which brought satisfaction to the thousands of children who knew it. For the many parents it was a small but vitally significant vehicle in assisting them to prepare their children for a place in society.

Since the publication of *The Brownies' Book* there has been nothing to compare with it. In the field of children's publications it more than holds its own. Even now, one searches in vain for a magazine to fulfill the needs of today's so-called "culturally deprived" Brownies. The spirit of *The Brownies' Book* is as undying as the ideas of those who created it.

The message was never more urgent.

Honoring Dr. Du Bois

MARTIN LUTHER KING, JR.

Tonight we assemble here to pay tribute to one of the most remarkable men of our time.

Dr. Du Bois was not only an intellectual giant exploring the frontiers of knowledge, he was in the first place a teacher. He would have wanted his life to teach us something about our tasks of emancipation.

One idea he insistently taught was that Black people have been kept in oppression and deprivation by a poisonous fog of lies that depicted them as inferior, born deficient, and deservedly doomed to servitude to the grave. So assiduously has this poison been injected into the mind of America that its disease has infected not only whites but many Negroes. So long as the lie was believed the brutality and criminality of conduct toward the Negro was easy for the conscience to bear. The twisted logic ran—if the black man was inferior he was not oppressed—his place in society was appropriate to his meager talent and intellect.

Dr. Du Bois recognized that the keystone in the arch of oppression was the myth of inferiority and he dedicated his brilliant talents to demolish it.

There could scarcely be a more suitable person for such a monumental task. First of all he was himself unsurpassed as an intellect and he was a Negro. But beyond this he was passionately proud to be black and finally he had not only genius and pride but he had the indomitable fighting spirit of the valiant.

To pursue his mission, Dr. Du Bois gave up the substantial privileges a highly educated Negro enjoyed living in the North. Though he held degrees from Harvard and the University of Berlin, though he had more academic credentials than most Americans, black or white, he moved south where a majority of Negroes then lived. He deliberately chose to share their daily abuse and humiliation. He could have offered himself to the white rulers and exacted substantial tribute for selling his genius. There were few like him, Negro or white. He could have amassed riches and honors and lived in material splendor and applause from the powerful and important men of his time. Instead, he lived part of his creative life in the South—most of it in modest means and some of it in poverty and he died in exile, praised sparingly and in many circles ignored.

But he was an exile only to the land of his birth. He died at home in Africa among his cherished ancestors and he was ignored by a pathetically ignorant America but not by history.

History cannot ignore W. E. B. Du Bois. Because history has to reflect truth and Dr. Du Bois was a tireless explorer and a gifted discoverer of social truths. His singular greatness lay in his quest for truth about his own people. There were very few scholars who concerned themselves with honest study of the black man and he sought to fill this immense void. The degree to which he succeeded discloses the great dimensions of the man.

Yet he had more than a void to fill. He had to deal with the army of white propagandists—the myth-makers of Negro history. Dr. Du Bois took them all on in battle. It would be impossible to sketch the whole range of his intellectual contributions. Back in the nineteenth century he laid out a program of a hundred years of study of problems affecting American Negroes and worked tirelessly to implement it.

Long before sociology was a science he was pioneering in the field of social study of Negro life and completed works on health, education, employment, urban conditions, and religion. This was at a time when scientific inquiry of Negro life was so unbelievably neglected that only a single university in the entire nation had such a program and it was funded with $5,000 for a year's work.

Against such odds Dr. Du Bois produced two enduring classics before the twentieth century. His *Suppression of the African Slave Trade* written in 1896 is Volume I in the Harvard Historical Studies. His study, *The Philadelphia Negro,* completed in 1899, is still used today. Illustrating the painstaking quality of his scientific method, to do this work Dr. Du Bois personally visited and interviewed five thousand people.

He soon realized that studies would never adequately be pursued nor changes realized without the mass involvement of Negroes. The scholar then became an organizer and with others founded the NAACP. At the same time he became aware that the expansion of imperialism was a threat to the emergence of Africa.

He recognized the importance of the bonds between American Negroes and the land of their ancestors and he extended his activities to African affairs. After World War I he called Pan-African Congresses in 1919, 1921, and 1923, alarming imperialists in all countries and disconcerting Negro moderates in America who were afraid of this restless, militant, black genius.

Returning to the United States from abroad he found his pioneering agitation for Negro studies was bearing fruit and a beginning was made to broaden Negro higher education. He threw himself into the task of raising the intellectual level of this work. Much later in 1940 he participated in the establishment of the first Negro scholarly publication, *Phylon*. At the same time he stimulated Negro colleges to collaborate through annual conferences to increase their effectiveness and elevate the quality of their academic studies.

But these activities, enough to be the life work for ten men, were far from the sum of his achievements. In the six years between 1935 and 1941 he produced the monumental seven-hundred-page volume on *Black Reconstruction in America,* and at the same time writing many articles and essays. *Black Reconstruction* was six years in writing but was thirty-three years in preparation. On its publication, one critic said: "It crowns the long, unselfish, and brilliant career of Dr. Du Bois. It is comparable in clarity, originality, and importance to the Beards' *Rise of American Civilization.*" The *New York Times* said, "It is beyond question the most painstaking and thorough study ever made of the Negroes' part in Reconstruction," and the *New York Herald Tribune* proclaimed it "a solid history of the period, an economic treatise, a philosophical discussion, a poem, a work of art all rolled into one."

To understand why his study of the Reconstruction was a monumental achievement it is necessary to see it in context. White historians had for a century crudely distorted the Negro's role in the Reconstruction years. It was a conscious and deliberate manipulation of history and the stakes were high. The Reconstruction was a period in which black men had a small measure of freedom of action. If, as white historians tell it, Negroes wallowed in corruption, opportunism, displayed spectacular stupidity, were wanton, evil, and ignorant, their case was made. They would have proved that freedom was dangerous in the hands of inferior beings. One generation after another of Americans were assiduously taught these falsehoods and the collective mind of America became poisoned with racism and stunted with myths.

Dr. Du Bois confronted this powerful structure of historical distortion and dismantled it. He virtually, before anyone else and more than anyone else, demolished the lies about Negroes in their most important and creative period of history. The truths he revealed are not yet the property of all Americans but they have been recorded and arm us for our contemporary battles.

In *Black Reconstruction* Dr. Du Bois dealt with the almost universally accepted concept that civilization virtually collapsed in the South during Reconstruction because Negroes had a measure of political power. Dr. Du Bois marshalled irrefutable evidence that far from collapsing, the Southern economy was recovering in these years. Within five years the cotton crop had been restored and in the succeeding five years had exceeded prewar levels. At the same time other economic activity had ascended so rapidly the rebirth of the South was almost completed.

Beyond this he restored to light the most luminous achievement of the Reconstruction—it brought free public education into existence not only for the benefit of the Negro but it opened school doors to the poor whites. He documented the substantial body of legislation that was socially so useful it was retained into the twentieth century even though the Negroes who helped to write it were brutally disenfranchised and driven from political life. He revealed that far from being the tragic era white historians described, it was the only period in which democracy existed in the South. This stunning fact was the reason the history books had to lie because to tell the truth would have acknowledged the Negroes' capacity to govern and fitness to build a finer nation in a creative relationship with poor whites.

With the completion of his book *Black Reconstruction,* despite its towering contributions, despite his advanced age, Dr. Du Bois was still not ready to accept a deserved rest in peaceful retirement. His dedication to freedom drove him on as relentlessly in his seventies as it did in his twenties. He had already encompassed three careers. Beginning as a pioneer sociologist he had become an activist to further mass organization. The activist had then transformed himself into a historian. By the middle of the twentieth century when imperialism and war arose once more to imperil humanity he became a peace leader. He served as chairman of the Peace Information Bureau and like the Rev. William Sloane Coffin and Dr. Benjamin Spock of today he found himself indicted by the Government and harried by reactionaries. Undaunted by obstacles and repression, with his characteristic fortitude he fought on. Finally in 1961, with Ghana's independence established, an opportunity opened to begin the writing of an African Encyclopedia and in his ninety-third year he emigrated to Ghana to begin new intellectual labors. In 1963 death finally came to this most remarkable man.

It is axiomatic that he will be remembered for his scholarly contributions and organizational attainments. These monuments are imperishable. But there were human qualities less immediately visible that are no less imperishable.

Dr. Du Bois was a man possessed of priceless dedication to his people. The vast accumulation of achievement and public recognition were not for him pathways to personal affluence and a diffusion of identity. Whatever else he was, with his multitude of careers and professional titles, he was first and always a black man. He used his richness of talent as a trust for his people. He saw that Negroes were robbed of so many things decisive to their existence that the theft of their history seemed only a small part of their losses. But Dr. Du Bois knew that to lose one's history is to lose one's self-understanding and with it the roots for pride. This drove him to become a historian of Negro life and the combination of his unique zeal and intellect rescued for all of us a heritage whose loss would have profoundly impoverished us.

Dr. Du Bois *the man* needs to be remembered today when despair is all too prevalent. In the years he lived and fought there was far more justification for frustration and hopelessness and yet his faith in his people never wavered. His love and faith in

Negroes permeate every sentence of his writings and every act of his life. Without these deeply rooted emotions his work would have been arid and abstract. With them his deeds were a passionate storm that swept the filth of falsehood from the pages of established history.

He symbolized in his being his pride in the black man. He did not apologize for being black and because of it, handicapped. Instead he attacked the oppressor for the crime of stunting black men. He confronted the Establishment as a model of militant manhood and integrity. He defied them and though they heaped venom and scorn on him his powerful voice was never stilled.

And yet, with all his pride and spirit he did not make a mystique out of blackness. He was proud of his people, not because their color endowed them with some vague greatness but because their concrete achievements in struggle had advanced humanity and he saw and loved progressive humanity in all its hues, black, white, yellow, red, and brown.

Above all he did not content himself with hurling invectives for emotional release and then to retire into smug passive satisfaction. History had taught him it is not enough for people to be angry—the supreme task is to organize and unite people so that their anger becomes a transforming force. It was never possible to know where the scholar Du Bois ended and the organizer Du Bois began. The two qualities in him were a single unified force.

This life style of Dr. Du Bois is the most important quality this generation of Negroes needs to emulate. The educated Negro who is not really part of us, and the angry militant who fails to organize us, have nothing in common with Dr. Du Bois. He exemplified black power in achievement and he organized black power in action. It was no abstract slogan to him.

We cannot talk of Dr. Du Bois without recognizing that he was a radical all of his life. Some people would like to ignore the fact that he was a communist in his later years. It is worth noting that Abraham Lincoln warmly welcomed the support of Karl Marx during the Civil War and corresponded with him freely. In contemporary life the English-speaking world has no difficulty with the fact that Sean O'Casey was a literary giant of the twentieth century and a communist or that Pablo Neruda is generally considered the greatest living poet though he also served in the Chilean Senate as a communist. It is time to cease muting the fact that Dr. Du Bois was a genius and chose to be a communist. Our irrational obsessive anti-communism has led us into too many quagmires to be retained as if it were a mode of scientific thinking.

In closing it would be well to remind white America of its debt to Dr. Du Bois. When they corrupted Negro history they distorted American history because Negroes are too big a part of the building of this nation to be written out of it without destroying scientific history. White America, drenched with lies about Negroes, has lived too long in a fog of ignorance. Dr. Du Bois gave them a gift of truth for which they should eternally be indebted to him.

Negroes have heavy tasks today. We were partially liberated and then re-enslaved. We have to fight again on old battlefields but our confidence is greater, our vision is clearer and our ultimate victory surer because of the contributions a militant, passionate black giant left behind him.

Dr. Du Bois has left us but he has not died. The spirit of freedom is not buried in the grave of the valiant. He will be with us when we go to Washington in April to demand our right to life, liberty, and the pursuit of happiness.

We have to go to Washington because they have declared an armistice in the war on poverty while squandering billions to expand a senseless, cruel, unjust war in Vietnam. We will go there, we will demand to be heard, and we will stay until the Administration responds. If this means forcible repression of our movement, we will confront it, for we have done this before. If this means scorn or ridicule, we will embrace it for that is what America's poor now receive. If it means jail we accept it willingly, for the millions of poor already are imprisoned by exploitation and discrimination.

Dr. Du Bois would be in the front ranks of the peace movement today. He would readily see the parallel between American support of the corrupt and despised Thieu-Ky regime and Northern support to the Southern Slavemasters in 1876. The CIA scarcely exaggerates, indeed it is surprisingly honest, when it calculates for Congress that the war in Vietnam can persist for a hundred years. People deprived of their freedom do not give up

—Negroes have been fighting more than a hundred years and even if the date of full emancipation is uncertain, what is explicitly certain is that the struggle for it will endure.

In conclusion let me say that Dr. Du Bois' greatest virtue was his committed empathy with all the oppressed and his divine dissatisfaction with all forms of injustice. Today we are still challenged to be dissatisfied. Let us be dissatisfied until every man can have food and material necessities for his body, culture and education for his mind, freedom and human dignity for his spirit. Let us be dissatisfied until rat-infested, vermin-filled slums will be a thing of a dark past and every family will have a decent sanitary house in which to live. Let us be dissatisfied until the empty stomachs of Mississippi are filled and the idle industries of Appalachia are revitalized. Let us be dissatisfied until brotherhood is no longer a meaningless word at the end of a prayer but the first order of business on every legislative agenda. Let us be dissatisfied until our brother of the Third World—Asia, Africa, and Latin America—will no longer be the victim of imperialist exploitation, but will be lifted from the long night of poverty, illiteracy, and disease. Let us be dissatisfied until this pending cosmic elegy will be transformed into a creative psalm of peace and "justice will roll down like waters from a mighty stream."

PART FOUR

DU BOIS: INTERNATIONAL MAN

Du Bois and Pan-Africa

RICHARD B. MOORE

So sang the great-grandmother of William Edward Burghardt Du Bois who in his autobiography *Dusk of Dawn* wrote wistfully: "With Africa I had only one direct cultural connection and that was the African melody which my great-grandmother Violet used to sing." This melody had been set down by the talented author in his classic book *The Souls of Black Folk* in the final chapter "The Sorrow Songs"—"these weird old songs in which the soul of the black slave spoke to man."

The song which his maternal ancestor had crooned to the child between her knees was passed on through generations thus: "The child sang it to his children, and they to their children's children, and so two hundred years it has traveled down to us and we sing it to our children, knowing as little as our fathers what the words may mean, but knowing well the meaning of its music."

What had caused this African song to possess uncommon significance is also recorded in that great and revealing book *The Souls of Black Folk,* where the youthful seer Du Bois at the very outset spoke "Of Our Spiritual Strivings." There inimitably and touchingly portrayed is the descent of the veil of prejudice and proscription, the result of that system of slavery and segregation which cruelly shut out people of African descent from full participation in the mainstream of life and culture in these United States of America.

It is precisely the recoil from this system of prejudice which directly thrust the Afroamerican back to the quest for his ancestral culture and history. Something of this evidently affected the grandfather of Du Bois on his paternal side. For this grandfather, Alexander Du Bois, who had been brought from the Bahamas in the Caribbean to Connecticut in the U.S.A., has been characterized by his illustrious grandson as a "rebel, bitter at his lot in life, resentful at being classed as a Negro and yet implacable in his attitude toward whites."

Unlike Alexander Hamilton, Alexander Du Bois allied himself through marriage with the people of African descent in America. Apparently it was his rebellious spirit which led him to migrate to Haiti some time after that nation had achieved independence as a result of the Revolution of 1791–1804. There in that free and sunny Caribbean island, where Toussaint L'Ouverture and his comrades-in-arms had routed the French colonial slavemasters, Alexander's son, Alfred I. Du Bois, the father of W. E. B. Du Bois, was born in 1825.

Shortly thereafter the Du Bois family returned to the United States where they lived in Connecticut and then in Massachusetts. In the little town of Great Barrington, Massachusetts, three years after the close of the Civil War, on February 23, 1868, a child was born who was to become one of the greatest men of letters, history, and social science of America and one of the most conscious and resolute champions of the people of Africa and their dispersed descendants.

However, it is not by physical or "racial" heredity, but by cultural processes, that African consciousness is passed on from one generation to another. This Du Bois himself clearly understood and wrote accordingly: "My African racial feeling was then purely a matter of my own later learning; my recoil from the assumptions of the whites; my experience in the South at Fisk. But it was none the less real and a large determinant of my life and character. I felt myself African by 'race' and by that token was African and an integral member of the group of dark Americans who were called Negroes."

This background of the Pan-Africanism of W. E. B. Du Bois is essential to a clear understanding of his role. It seems necessary then to explore this somewhat further. Noting how the concept of "race" had become more and more devoid of "exact definition and understanding," Dr. Du Bois explained further while discussing "The Concept of Race" in *Dusk of Dawn* as follows:

> Since then the concept of race has so changed and presented so much of contradiction that as I face Africa I ask myself: what is it between us that constitutes a tie which I can feel better than I can explain? Africa is of course my fatherland. Yet neither my father nor my father's father ever saw Africa or cared overmuch for it. My mother's folk were closer and yet their direct connection, in culture and race, became tenuous; still, my tie to Africa is strong. On this vast continent were born and lived a large portion of my direct ancestors going back a thousand years or more.
>
> But one thing is sure and that is the fact that since the fifteenth century these ancestors of mine and their other descendants have had a common history; have suffered a common disaster and have one long memory. The actual ties of heritage between the individuals of this group, vary with the ancestors that they have in common and many others: Europeans and Semites, perhaps Mongolians, certainly Indians. But the physical bond is least and the badge of color relatively unimportant save as a badge; the real essence of this kinship is its social heritage of slavery; the discrimination and insult; and this heritage binds together not simply the children of Africa, but extends through yellow Asia and into the South Seas. It is this unity that draws me to Africa.

A better understanding should thus be reached of why and how Dr. Du Bois achieved the prophetic world vision which encompassed his idea of Pan-Africa. At the turn of the century the Doctor declared: "The problem of the Twentieth Century is the problem of the color line—the relation of the darker to the lighter races of men in Asia and Africa, in America and the islands of the sea."

What had given rise to the problem of the color line was later stated, as he saw it, by Dr. Du Bois in *Dusk of Dawn*. After surveying the events of that period, the social scientist had reached this conclusion: "That history may be epitomized in one word—Empire; the domination of white Europe over black Africa and yellow Asia, through political power built on the economic control of labor, income and ideas. The echo of this industrial imperialism in America was the expulsion of black men from American democracy, their subjection to caste control and wage slavery."

First Pan-African Conference

With such insight and awareness W. E. B. Du Bois, then professor of economics and history at Atlanta University, was thus prepared to participate in the First Pan-African Conference where he began his prominent and continuing role in this great endeavor. The call for this Conference was issued by Henry Sylvester Williams, a barrister-at-law from Trinidad who had made fraternal and fruitful contacts with African students and leaders in London. Thus was the idea born of a Pan-African Conference which would "bring into closer touch with each other the peoples of African descent throughout the world."

To Bishop Alexander Walters of the African Methodist Episcopal Zion Church, president of this First Pan-African Conference, we are indebted for a summary of its proceedings. Among the thirty-two delegates who assembled in London at Westminster Hall on July 23–25, 1900, there were four representatives of African peoples: the Emperor of Ethiopia, Menelik II, delegated his aide-de-camp M. Benito Sylvain of Haiti; the Republic of Liberia sent its former attorney general, Hon. F. S. R. Johnson; from Sierra Leone came Councillor G. W. Dove; and from Ghana, then "Gold Coast," came the barrister-at-law, A. F. Ribero, Esq.

A fair representation of Afroamericans at this important initial Pan-African gathering consisted of eleven delegates, including four women, all prominent in professional and public activity. Some thirteen delegates had come from the Caribbean either directly or indirectly as sojourners in England and Scotland. The famous Afroenglish composer S. Coleridge-Taylor participated; attending also were the director of the Fisk Jubilee Singers, J. F. Loudin and his wife, then resident in England though hailing originally from the United States. Rev. Henry Box Brown of fugitive slave fame represented the community in Lower Canada.

Welcomed and its delegates feted by the Lord Bishop of London, Dr. Greighton, this First Pan-African Conference adopted and presented a Memorial to the British Government. This Memorial protested against "acts of injustice directed against Her Majesty's subjects in South Africa and other parts of her dominions." A reply was sent to the Secretary H. Sylvester Williams, assuring the Pan-African Conference that "Her Majesty's Government will not overlook the interests and welfare of the native races." It is distressing and challenging to note that today, after sixty-four years, such horrendous injustices still persist in apartheid South Africa and are even intensified.

As Chairman of the Committee on Address to the Nations of the World, Professor W. E. B. Du Bois, submitted the Address which included the following significant pronouncement: "In any case the modern world must needs remember that in this age, when the ends of the world are being brought so near together, the millions of black men in Africa, America and the islands of the sea, not to speak of the myriads elsewhere, are bound to have great influence upon the world in the future, by reason of sheer numbers and physical contact."

Duly adopted by the First Pan-African Conference, this Address was "sent to the sovereigns in whose realms are subjects of African descent." The appeal was made among others that the peoples of Africa should not be "sacrificed to the greed of gold, their liberties taken away," etc.; that the British nation should accord "the rights of responsible government to the Black Colonies of Africa and the West Indies;" that Afroamericans should be granted "the right of franchise, security of person and property," . . . Similar appeals were also made to the German Empire, the French Republic, and the Congo Free State.

The Address to the Nations of the World then concluded with the following general appeal and call to action: "Let the Nations of the World respect the integrity and independence of the free Negro states of Abyssinia (properly Ethiopia), Liberia, Haiti, etc. and let the inhabitants of these states, the independent tribes of Africa, the Negroes (people of African descent) of the West Indies and America, and the black subjects of all Nations take courage, strive ceaselessly, and fight bravely, that they may prove to the world their incontestable right to be counted among the great brotherhood of mankind."

Ironically enough this First Pan-African Conference was almost forgotten. Because of the minuscule difference in the designating terms *Conference* and *Congress,* or perhaps due to the frailty of the human mind however great, this historic first international body which pointed specifically to the unifying and liberating of all people of African origin and descent, was not even counted along with the subsequent "Pan-African Congresses."

From the vantage point of the present, however, it would now appear appropriate to recognize all these bodies as Pan-African Congresses, and to number them inclusively, beginning with this first epoch-making Congress of 1900. This has already been recognized by Colin Legum in *Pan-Africanism*. It appears that Dr. Du Bois himself moved in this direction when in writing of "The Pan-African Movement" he stated: "This meeting attracted attention, put the word 'Pan-African' in the dictionaries for the first time."

It should now be clear that whether in motivation, conception, or composition, all these Pan-African Congresses have alike expressed the same basic purpose. That aim has been stated by Dr. Du Bois in *Dusk of Dawn,* namely, to achieve "such world organization of black men as would oppose a united front to European aggression. . . . Out of this there might come, not race war and opposition, but broader cooperation with the white rulers of the world, and a chance for peaceful and accelerated development of black folk."

Growth of Pan-Africanism

While tracing the specific background and development of W. E. B. Du Bois in the Pan-African endeavor, there should be observed some other important aspects of the unfoldment of this great idea. For though mirrored in the mind of the individual,

Pan-Africanism was and is a widespread social force. The Pan-African idea grew directly out of reaction against colonialist domination and racist oppression. Its roots therefore, like its branches, are not single but manifold.

Whence the observation made by Colin Legum in his study *Pan-Africanism:* "It developed through what Dr. Shepperson described as 'a complicated Atlantic triangle of influences' between the New World, Europe and Africa." This might be viewed as the counterpart of that earlier triangle of traffic across the Atlantic which involved the exchange of New England rum, African slaves, and Caribbean molasses. Our limits here preclude any extended treatment of all these widespread influences or these manifold Pan-African roots. Nevertheless, some indication of these seems necessary and appropriate.

As might be expected, it was in Haiti, where the bonds of chattel slavery and colonialist subjugation were first burst asunder in the western hemisphere, that the Pan-African idea began to germinate. Foreshadowed even earlier, the cultural aspect of Pan-Africanism was still more definitely expressed in the epochal work of Antenor Firmin, *De l'égalité des races humaines,* 1885, later in Hannibal Price's *De la réhabilitation de la race noire,* 1900, and still later in the *Ainsi parla l'oncle* of Jean Price-Mars, 1928. Even later still the Haitian poet Jacques Roumain avowed overtly and poignantly, "Africa I have kept your memory. Africa, you are in me."

George Padmore, who also made an outstanding contribution in keeping alive and developing the Pan-African Movement, has pointed in his book *Pan-Africanism or Communism?* to several of these roots in the various Back to Africa movements. Padmore there hailed the initiative of the British Abolitionist movement led by such men as Thomas Clarkson, William Wilberforce, Granville Sharp, and the statesman William Pitt, who all fostered the settlement of Sierra Leone as a haven for people of African origin and descent.

Padmore indicated various groups who returned to Africa and settled in Sierra Leone: the original African resettlers in Granville town, and Nova Scotia settlers who came thence from the United States, the Jamaican Maroon repatriates, the restored Africans rescued by the British navy from slave ships, the thirty-eight persons transported in 1815 to Sierra Leone in his own vessel the *Traveller* by the pioneer Afroamerican shipbuilder and African repatriation leader Paul Cuffe, who declared "the travail of my soul is that Africa's inhabitants may be favored with reformation."

Noted likewise was the founding of Liberia, which was stimulated by the example of Paul Cuffe. However, colonization to Liberia was supported by Euroamerican slaveholders for a quite opposite end, namely, that of ridding themselves of the free Afroamericans whose very presence and example they felt tended to undermine their profitable "peculiar institution" of chattel slavery. Nevertheless, several Afroamerican leaders, who desired to aid in the establishment of a nation in which people of African origin and descent could rule themselves, took advantage of the opportunity thus afforded to migrate to Liberia.

Eminent among the early founders of Liberia was John B. Russwurm, originally from Jamaica, who was the first person of African descent to graduate from a university in the United States and the founder of the first periodical *Freedom's Journal* conducted by Afroamericans. Outstanding also in political and economic service to the fledgling Liberian nation were the first President, Hon. Joseph Jenkins Roberts of Virginia, and still later President Arthur Barclay and his brother Secretary of State Ernest Barclay, both of whom were brought from Barbados to Liberia by their father in 1865.

In Oklahoma there developed a powerful movement for emigration to Liberia from about 1897 to 1914. The climax was reached under the proclaimed Ashanti "Chief" Alfred C. Sam, who had failed to attract much response in New York but succeeded in the Middle West, in Kansas, and widely in Oklahoma. Chief Sam's company reported $100,000 subscribed, and purchased a steamship, but when many met death on its too fatal voyage, this Black Africa movement subsided. At about the same time there arose the "Prophetic Liberator of the Colored Race," Arthur Anderson, who had earlier contact, as Marcus Garvey later, with African nationalists abroad, particularly Duse Mohamed of the *African Times and Orient Review* in London.

The expedition to the Niger Valley, and the treaties effected by

Martin R. Delany for the settlement of Afroamericans there, came to naught with the outbreak of the Civil War in America.

But the Back to Africa movement was revived after the Reconstruction period. Reacting against prejudiced proscription and brutal Ku Klux Klan lynch terror in the South, many Afroamericans turned their eyes longingly back to their ancestral fatherland. Bishop Henry McNeal Turner of the African Methodist Episcopal Church was a prominent leader in this repatriation and hundreds signed up to go to Liberia from North and South Carolina. The Liberation Exodus and Joint Stock Company was organized; the ship *Azor* was secured at a price of $7,000 and was used to transport 274 emigrants during 1878. But the exodus was checked when the *Azor* was seized and sold. Another expedition brought some 197 emigrants to Liberia. About 1881 the *Pedro Gorino* sailed for Africa under the command of its owner Captain Harry Dean who sought "to rehabilitate Africa."

Influence of Edward Blyden

It was in Liberia that there grew to maturity Edward Wilmot Blyden, the man who appears to have been the earliest forthright advocate of the "African personality," and champion of independent nationhood, African continental unity, and cultural Pan-Africanism. An able scholar, educator, and statesman, Dr. Blyden's ancestors had been brought as slaves, either from Ghana or Togo, to St. Thomas in the Virgin Islands of the Caribbean. Migrating to the United States and failing to find the educational opportunity which he sought, Blyden sailed back to Africa specifically to Liberia in 1850.

Dr. Blyden's Inaugural Address as President of Liberia College in 1881 bespoke the great change then beginning in Africa. Among many deep insights and sage counsels, Dr. Blyden declared: "We must not suppose that the Anglo-Saxon methods are final. . . . We must study our brethren in the interior, who know better than we do the laws of growth for the race." Though Blyden often spoke in terms then current of "the Negro race," he took a firm stand "against perpetuating race antagonism." In the conclusion of his address the educator and statesman underscored the necessity for successful efforts "to build up a nation, to wrest from Nature her secrets, to lead the van of progress in this country, and to regenerate a continent."

Closely associated with Dr. Blyden in the furtherance of these ideas was the scholarly and genteel Alexander Crummell. Following years of shocking and direful mistreatment at the hands of his Christian Euroamerican brethren and bishops, and after unfolding in the more amicable and cultured climate of Cambridge University in England, the Reverend Dr. Crummell went voluntarily to Africa—Sierra Leone and Liberia. There from 1853 to 1873 Alexander Crummell labored earnestly for the regeneration of Africa. His views classically expressed in *Africa and America* were farseeing and germinal for Pan-Africa.

Similar ideas were approached by Dr. James Africanus Horton of Sierra Leone in 1865 and again during 1868 in *A Vindication of the African Race*. These ideas of Pan-African unity and regeneration blossomed as the twentieth century dawned. Africans themselves had been deeply stirred by the defeat of the imperialist Italian invaders of Ethiopia by the armies of Menelek II at Adowa in 1896. In the following year Sudanese officers rose to wrest Uganda from British rule. From Barbados and Guiana that same year there burgeoned the African Colonial Enterprise, projected by Albert Thorne for the settlement of Afrocaribbeans in central Africa. From Trinidad too there came F. E. M. Hercules building an organization to unite all people of African descent. During 1898 the confrontation of French and British imperialist armies at Fashoda in the Eastern Sudan barely missed setting off a European war, but led to the rise of a new militant Egyptian nationalism.

In West Africa during 1895 there had erupted the protest of some five thousand people at Lagos, Nigeria, against a proposed house and land tax. This struggle against British domination was carried forward rigorously from 1908 to 1948 by Herbert Macaulay, father of Nigerian nationalism. A revolt flared up likewise during 1898 in the Sierra Leone Protectorate against poll tax and corporal punishment. John Mensah Sarbah, Jacob Wilson Sey, and other leaders organized the Aborigines Rights Protection Society in 1897 in the "Gold Coast," now Ghana. Another barrister and able nationalist leader Joseph Casely Hayford prepared a successful protest against legislation which threatened to alienate African lands to the British Crown. Kings and chiefs of the Western Province also petitioned for the right to participate in legislation. Progressing in Pan-Africanism, the farseeing Casely Hayford inspired the West African National Congress in 1920 which united peoples of four colonial areas: Gambia, Sierra Leone, Gold Coast—now Ghana—and Nigeria.

In South Africa and later in central Africa indigenous Africans had broken away from the segregated Christian church and formed Ethiopian and Zionist Churches of their own. Nationalist to a degree, these Ethiopian Churches sought contact with the African Methodist Episcopal Church of the U.S.A. and Bishop H. M. Turner toured Africa in 1898 to affiliate these churches. Like the Rev. Charles S. Morris of the National Baptist Convention, Bishop Turner was said to be filled with a compelling sense of the mission of Afroamericans "to redeem their unhappy brethren in Africa."

Notable indeed was the project of the African Christian Union launched by the British missionary Joseph Booth, first in Natal during 1896 and a year later in Malawi, then "Nyasaland." This followed on a trip to the United States where Booth made contact with Afroamerican leaders among whom it is said was Dr. W. E. B. Du Bois. Set forth in twenty-one points was the striking plan for an organization which possessed the principal features that marked the movement launched by Marcus Garvey in Harlem over twenty years later, including the chief conjuring slogan AFRICA FOR THE AFRICAN! In fact Booth wrote to his daughter on April 9, 1897, rather prophetically: "There are many signs that a great work will spring from this side of the ocean also. I am lecturing on 'Africa for the Africans.' "

In the booklet *Africa for the African,* published in Baltimore, Maryland, during 1897, Joseph Booth stated his ideas fully. These involved securing capital for Industrial Missions; demanding equal rights for people of African origin; seeking the participation of "every man, woman, and child of the African race," especially those in the United States and the Caribbean; developing agricultural, manufacturing, and mining enterprises as well as means of transport; Back to Africa repatriation and training of Africans in modern techniques; guiding labor toward upliftment and commonwealth; calling upon Europeans to return lands to the Africans; publishing literature in the interest of the African "race," and pursuing the policy of Africa For The African and hastening a united African Christian Nation!

But the African Christian Union foundered on the rock of distrust of Europeans, which had resulted from the bitter experience of Africans with European conquest, plunder, forced labor, imperialist subjection, and denial of human dignity. The horrible Boer Wars against the Zulus and the depredations of Cecil Rhodes and other chartered companies in various areas had well nigh convinced all Africans that Bishop Colenso, friend and adviser of the Zulu king Cetewayo, "was the last of the race of true white man friends," and that "there was no white man living who was a safe guide for the African people."

Even John Chilembwe, Booth's African convert, servant, and loyal associate who had defended Booth and other Europeans against the charge of cannibalism leveled by Arab opponents, found it advisable to part with Booth. Chilembwe had been aided by Booth to travel to the U.S.A. and to secure education in an Afroamerican seminary at Lynchburg, Virginia. While associating with Booth in Virginia, Chilembwe had experienced hateful violence at the hands of prejudiced Euroamericans. Though preserving gratitude and friendship for Joseph Booth, John Chilembwe came to feel that his path lay rather with Afroamerican friends and supporters. Thus together with a number of these, John Chilembwe of East Africa launched the African Development Society in 1899.

With the blessing and support of the National Baptist Convention Foreign Mission Board, John Chilembwe returned during 1900 as an ordained minister to "Nyasaland," now Malawi, where he founded a mission and church at Mbombwe, Chiradzulu, in the "Shire Highlands." When in 1900 some three hundred soldiers were sent from Malawi to fight against the Ashanti of West Africa, the Rev. John Chilembwe protested vigorously. This foreshadowed Chilembwe's protest against the use of African troops in 1904 against the "Mad Mullah" in Somaliland, and his further protest against recruitment of Africans in the World War of 1914. This preceded the Rising in 1915 which Rev. John Chilembwe led and in which he perished.

At the opening of this century, then, even as Professor W. E. B. Du Bois penned the historic Address to the Nations of the First Pan-African Congress, indigenous Africans throughout the continent, and people of African descent in the Caribbean and on the American mainland, were stirring with the sentiment of nationalist and freedom-loving resistance against European colonialist aggression, degradation, and domination. But though efforts were made toward permanent organization, the Pan-African Movement subsided following the return of its founder H. Sylvester Williams to Trinidad, where some time after he died.

Nevertheless, knowledge and consciousness of Africa were ever more widely spread by Dr. Du Bois and other scholars. Outstanding among these was Dr. Carter G. Woodson who organized the Association for the Study of Negro Life and History in 1915 and later published the *Journal of Negro History,* the *Negro History Bulletin,* and numerous books including his own *The Negro in Our History* and *The African Background Outlined.* Historical scholars like Dr. William Leo Hansberry and Dr. Rayford W. Logan of Howard University, and Dr. Horace Mann Bond of Lincoln University, advanced African studies and the training of African students, among them the now famous Dr. Nnamdi Azikiwe, President of Nigeria, and Dr. Kwame Nkrumah, President of Ghana.

Emergence of Marcus Garvey

However, during the decade 1918–1928 the idea of "African redemption" and the "unity of the Negro race" was spread as never before directly and widely to the millions by Marcus Garvey through the Universal Negro Improvement Association and African Communities League and through the newspaper the *Negro World.* Born in Jamaica, Garvey had traveled to South and Central America and to London, England, where he lived during 1912–1914. There Garvey worked with the famous Egyptian nationalist of Sudanese descent Duse Mohamed. From this African scholar who edited the *African Times and Orient Review,* Garvey derived many of his ideas of African nationalism and the electrifying slogan *Africa for the Africans!*

Writing of this two-year stay in England as "the most decisive period in Garvey's life," Robert Hughes Brisbane, Jr., in "Some New Light on the Garvey Movement" reveals the following: "Garvey heard such slogans as 'India for the Indians' and 'Asia for the Asiatics' (Asians in the nonabusive and proper term). He became interested in the condition of the African Negro as a result of discussions with the followers of Chilembwe of Nyasaland and Kimbangu of the Congo." Chilembwe's association with Joseph Booth in the project of the African Christian Union for reclaiming "Africa for the Africans" has already been told. Booth's ideas were thus most likely communicated also to the active mind of Marcus Garvey.

In a prior article, "Africa Conscious Harlem," contributed to the Summer 1963 Harlem issue of *Freedomways* magazine, the present writer endeavored to trace something of the development of the Garvey movement, and of the vital contributions made by numerous co-workers, in the development of African consciousness, particularly Hubert H. Harrison. The effort there made at historical evaluation and sober judgment was misunderstood and even met with quite intemperate abuse.

It should suffice now to suggest that the summary presented in "Africa Conscious Harlem" be read again thoroughly and with an open mind if possible. This evaluation ought also to be compared with the estimate made by George Padmore in *Pan-Africanism or Communism?,* with that of C. L. R. James in *A History of Negro Revolt,* with the account given by Claude McKay in *Harlem: Negro Metropolis,* with the report made by Roi Ottley in *New World A-Coming,* with the appraisal made by Saunders Redding in *Lonesome Road,* with the biographical study by J. A. Rogers in *World's Great Men of Color,* Vol. II, and with Edmund David Cronon's biography *Black Moses.*

All these writers just mentioned agree on the plain, indisputable fact that Garvey propagated racist ideas and ranged himself alongside of the most hateful and violent enemies of the Afroamerican people, the Ku Klux Klan, the Anglo-Saxon Clubs, etc. The unfortunate and hostile attacks which Garvey made upon most Afroamerican leaders were largely due to his experience with color prejudice in Jamaica, where a certain vicious shade prejudice stemmed directly from some "brown men," but was incited in the first place by colonialist European rulers. (See page 85 of the *Philosophy and Opinions of Marcus Garvey,* Vol. II.) Such shade prejudice, however, was not then a similar factor in the American scene where the raw and regnant Anglo-Saxon white supremacists treated all persons of any known degree of African ancestry as "inferior Negroes."

On the other hand it must be recognized that Du Bois erred when he described Garvey as "ugly" and countenanced the drive to prosecute and to deport Garvey. All that need now be added in this respect are the observations which follow. The first has been made by Shepperson and Price in *Independent African:* "Du Bois and Garvey, though they were political opponents with fundamental disagreements on tactics, were, in reality, working for the same end: to raise the status of the Negro, materially and spiritually, in his own eyes, and in the eyes of the world at large." The second has been set down by George Padmore in *Pan-Africanism or Communism?* thus: "Pan-Africanism differed from Garveyism in that it was never conceived as a Back to Africa Movement, but rather as a dynamic philosophy and guide to action for Africans in Africa who were laying the foundations of national liberation organizations." The third and final observation is that made by Dr. Kwame Nkrumah, President of Ghana, on April 7, 1960, at the Positive Conference for Peace and Security in Africa: "When I speak of Africa for Africans, this should be interpreted in the light of my emphatic declaration that I do not believe in racialism and colonialism. The concept 'Africa for Africans' does not mean that other races are excluded from it. No. It only means that Africans, who naturally are the majority in Africa, shall and must govern themselves in their own countries. The fight is for the future of humanity, and it is a most important fight."

At the end of the First World War, W. E. B. Du Bois determined to revive the Pan-African Movement. Accordingly he maneuvered to get to Paris as a press correspondent in order to make a representation to the Allied Peace Conference which met in nearby Versailles. A similar effort at representation was made by William Monroe Trotter of the National Equal Rights League and editor of the *Boston Guardian*. Denied a passport by the U.S. Government, Trotter had to disguise himself as a cook on a ship to get to France.

Both Dr. Du Bois and editor Trotter were given the cold shoulder by that august international body convened to realize the great Wilsonian slogan "Make the World Safe for Democracy"—for which thousands of men of African origin and descent had fought and died. Nevertheless, the publicity secured in the press about their representations by Du Bois and by Trotter caused much concern among the Allied rulers. For while Woodrow Wilson at the Peace Conference appeared before the world as the champion of the right of self-determination, neither this spokesman of democracy, nor any of the European colonialist powers, had the slightest idea of according that selfsame right to their colonized subjects in Africa or elsewhere.

Second Pan-African Conference

Outwitting the great opposition which he encountered, Dr. Du Bois succeeded in reviving the Pan-African Movement and in holding a Second Conference in Paris, February 19–21, 1919. This Dr. Du Bois was able to accomplish through the aid of M. Blaise Diagne, African deputy from Senegal and Commissaire-Général for the recruitment of African troops. While Secretary Polk of the U.S. Government was giving assurance that no such assembly would be held, the Pan-African Congress was already in session.

The account later given by Dr. Du Bois himself is most fitting here:

> This Congress represented Africa partially. Of the fifty-seven delegates from fifteen countries, nine were African countries with twelve delegates. The other delegates came from the United States which sent sixteen, and the West Indies with twenty-one. Most of these delegates did not come to France for this meeting, but happened to be residing there, mainly for reasons connected with the war. America and all the colonial powers refused to issue special visas.
>
> The Congress specifically asked that the German colonies be turned

over to an international organization instead of being handled by various colonial powers. Out of this idea came the Mandates Commission.

It will be seen by comparison with the First Pan-African Congress of 1900 that there was an increase of representation at this Paris Congress of 1919. African representation was still smaller than that of Afroamericans, while that from the Caribbean still predominated. Resolutions adopted called for a code of laws for the international protection of Africans, for the establishment of a bureau to oversee the application of such laws for the welfare of the African people, and for the future government of Africans in accordance with principles stated more in detail in respect to land, capital, labor, education, and the state.

Seeking to build a permanent Pan-African organization, Dr. Du Bois arranged for the Third Pan-African Congress which met in three sessions in London, August 28–29, in Brussels, August 31–September 2, 1921, and in Paris, September 4, 1921. Total representation doubled with the largest representation this time, forty-one, from Africa, twenty-four from people of African descent living in Europe, and seven from the Caribbean.

The considerable drop in Caribbean representation was attributed by Dr. Du Bois to the hindering influence of the Garvey organization; likewise he felt that certain opposition also arose from being confounded with the Garvey movement and from a bald statement in the Brussels *Neptune* which falsely declared that the organizers of the Pan-African Congress were "said in the United States (to) have received remuneration from Moscow (Bolsheviki)."

Resolutions adopted in London, which contained a statement critical of the colonial regime in the Congo, were bitterly opposed in Belgium and an innocuous substitute stressing goodwill and investigation was declared adopted by M. Diagne, despite the opposition of a clear majority. Resolutions also affirmed equality of races to be "the founding stone of world and human advancement" and continued: "And of all the various criteria of which masses of men in the past have been prejudged, that of the color of the skin and the texture of the hair is surely the most adventitious and idiotic." Eight specific demands in the interest of African peoples were then particularized.

Third Pan-African Conference

This Third Pan-African Congress sent a committee headed by W. E. B. Du Bois to interview the officials of the League of Nations. A petition filed by this committee was published as an official document of the League of Nations. However, when M. Dantes Bellegarde of Haiti in the Assembly of the League of Nations condemned the ruthless bombing and massacre in May 1922 of the African Bondelschwartz of South-West Africa, which had been approved by Jan Christian Smuts, the Haitian statesman M. Bellegarde was recalled by the United States forces which then controlled Haiti. This plea of M. Bellegarde has been recognized, nevertheless, as "a courageous and impassioned appeal that even now stands as one of the models of eloquence in the Assemblies of the League."

At the Third Convention of the Universal Negro Improvement Association in 1922, Marcus Garvey appointed a delegation led by George O. Mark of Sierra Leone as Chairman and J. Adam of Haiti as Secretary to present a petition to the League of Nations. This petition asked that the former German colonies be placed under the control of the U.N.I.A. Through the cooperation of the representative of Persia—now Iran—the petition was presented to the League during October 1922. The next year when the Chairman returned to press this appeal, he was denied even an audience under a new rule which required such petitions to be presented through the imperial governments. A similar petition to the League of Nations was forwarded by Arden Bryan of Barbados, former Commissioner of the U.N.I.A., during 1923. Efforts to enlist the officers of the British Government for transmission as required were unavailing when the British Ambassador replied that his government could not support the petition.

The attempt again made to form a permanent Pan-African organization was unsuccessful when the young secretary who taught school in Paris sought to bring in profit-making schemes and delayed the calling of the next Pan-African Congress. With inadequate preparation, therefore, the Fourth Pan-African Congress met in 1923 rather weakly in London and somewhat better attended in Lisbon due to the participation there of the Liga Africana. Specific demands were set forth in eight cardinal points and the statement concluded: "In fine, we ask in all the world, that black folk be treated as men. We can see no other road to Peace and Progress. What more paradoxical figure today fronts the world than the official head of a great South African state striving blindly to build Peace and Goodwill in Europe by standing on the necks and hearts of millions of black Africans?"

Strivings toward Pan-Africa were stimulated by the meeting of delegates of African descent at the Brussels Congress of the League Against Imperialism during February 1927. Its Commission on the African Peoples of the World included the dedicated Garan Kouyatte who was slain by the Nazis while they occupied Paris; the brilliant Senegalese leader Lamine Senghor who was martyred shortly after this Congress in a Paris jail; the Vice President of the African National Congress of South Africa, J. T. Gumede, whose gift book, still among my most prized treasures, is inscribed "with the best wishes for the success of our common struggle for a better day;" the Secretary of the South African Non-European Federation, J. A. La Guma; the Ethiopian representative Mr. Makonnen; and the present writer who acted as secretary of this Commission and drafted its resolution.

This resolution on the Negro Question was adopted by the entire Congress of the League Against Imperialism. It recounted in summary the centuries old colonialist and racist oppression of peoples of African descent, called for their complete freedom and independence, and set forth specific demands in nine major points. Readily recognized by Dr. W. E. B. Du Bois as "a strong set of resolutions," an abstract was published by him in *The Crisis* magazine of July 1927. The Pan-African program thus gained the fraternal endorsement of hundreds of influential delegates from Europe and Asia. Several of these Asian leaders such as Prime Minister Jawaharlal Nehru of India, and President Sukarno of Indonesia, were to assemble again in the historic Asian-African Conference at Bandung, Indonesia, during April 1955.

Fifth Pan-African Conference

An effort to hold a Pan-African Congress in the Caribbean during 1925 was frustrated by exorbitant travel rates and the opposition of colonial powers. But during August 21–24, 1927, the Fifth Pan-African Congress met in New York with two hundred eight delegates from twenty-two states of the American Union and ten other countries. African representatives came from Ghana, then "Gold Coast," and from Sierra Leone, and Nigeria. The Resolution stressed six points, the chief being "The development of Africa for the Africans and not merely for the profit of the Europeans." The people of the West Indies were urged "to begin an earnest movement for the federation of the islands." Recognizing that "the narrow confines of the modern world entwine our interests with those of other peoples," the Resolution concluded thus:

> We desire to see freedom and real national independence in Egypt, in China and in India. We demand the cessation of the interference of the United States in the affairs of Central and South America.
>
> We thank the Soviet Government of Russia for its liberal attitude toward the colored races and for the help which it has extended to them from time to time.
>
> We urge the white workers of the world to realize that no program of labor uplift can be successfully carried through in Europe or America so long as colored labor is exploited and enslaved and deprived of all political power.

The writer well remembers this Pan-African Congress and the participation of a forthright group of young radicals including Otto E. Huiswoud of Guiana, dominated by the Dutch, and F. Eugene Corbie of British colonized Trinidad.

The ensuing effort to hold a Pan-African Congress in Africa itself at Tunis was nullified by the final refusal of the French Government to allow such an assemblage on African soil, and also by the setting in of the economic depression in the western world.

Sixth Pan-African Congress

The Pan-African idea thus remained dormant until the assembling, largely through labor union representatives, of the Sixth

Pan-African Congress, October 15–21, 1945, in the Chorlton Town Hall at Manchester, headquarters of the recently formed Pan-African Federation. Chiefly responsible for this Congress was the secretary of the Federation, the dedicated George Padmore, who like the initiator of the First Pan-African Congress of 1900, H. Sylvester Williams, hailed originally from Trinidad. Ably supporting Padmore was the devoted chairman of the Federation, Dr. Peter Milliard, who came from Guiana held as a colony under British rule.

A preliminary conference elected as joint political secretaries to prepare this Pan-African Congress George Padmore and Kwame Nkrumah, while Jomo Kenyatta was elected assistant secretary. A powerful but unheeded Open Letter was sent by this Secretariat to Prime Minister Attlee, who as leader of the British Labor Party had just taken office in England.

Elected to preside over the first, as over most of the other sessions of this Sixth Pan-African Congress at Manchester, Dr. W. E. B. Du Bois was hailed as "Father" of Pan-Africanism by George Padmore, designated chairman of the Platform Committee, and unanimously elected International President of the Pan-African Congress. The distinguished doctor now settled graciously into the role of elder statesman and "Grand Old Man of Pan-Africanism." Unquestionably all these tributes were well deserved, since W. E. B. Du Bois had rendered long and vital service in keeping alive and nurturing the Pan-African idea which was now developing into a new and higher stage.

The Pan-African Movement was indeed maturing with the emergence and participation of such African leaders as Kwame Nkrumah of Ghana, Jomo Kenyatta of Kenya, Ja-Ja Wachuku and O. Abowolo of Nigeria, Hastings K. Banda of Malawi, the Ghanian historian J. C. de Graft Johnson, and the South African writer Peter Abrahams. Impressive and moving was the participation of Gershon Nishie-Nikoi who represented 300,000 cocoa farmers of Ghana and Nigeria, and who, though bearing a petition, had been refused an audience by Secretary Hall of the British Labor Party, then in power.

Significant also at this Manchester Pan-African Congress was the attendance of J. S. Annan of the African Railway Employees

Union, of A. Soyemi Coker of the Trades Union Congress and Magnus Williams of the National Council of Nigeria and the Cameroons who also represented Dr. Nnamdi Azikiwe. Important too was the appearance of I. T. A. Wallace Johnson of the Sierra Leone Trades. Union Congress, E. Garba-Jahumpa of the Gambia Trades Union, I. Yatu of the Young Baganda, S. Rahinda of Tanganyika, Marko Hlubi of the South African National Congress, and many others.

Broadly representative of all the people; workers, farmers, students, civic leaders, and intellectuals, the Sixth Manchester Pan-African Congress of 1945 brought together some ninety-four regular delegates, twenty-six from Africa, thirty-three from the Caribbean, and thirty-five domiciled in Great Britain. Unlisted among the delegates, perhaps because *sui generis,* was the eminent Pan-Africanist Dr. William Edward Burghardt Du Bois, who seemed the sole participant from the United States. Among eleven fraternal delegates and observers were representatives from Somali, Cyprus, India, Ceylon, the Women's International League, Common Wealth, the Independent Labor Party, and the Negro Welfare Association.

The keynote of that epoch-making Manchester Pan-African Congress of 1945 was struck in its Declaration to the Colonial Workers, Farmers, and Intellectuals: "We affirm the right of all Colonial Peoples to control their own destiny. All colonies must be free from foreign imperialist control, whether political or economic." A new note of militancy was there expressed: "We say to the peoples of the Colonies that they must fight for these ends by all means at their disposal." A new spirit of urgency was explicit in the projection of "A PROGRAM OF ACTION."

Comprehensive resolutions were adopted treating of West Africa; the Congo and North Africa; East Africa; the Union of South Africa; the Protectorates of Bechuanaland, Basutoland, and Swaziland; the West Indies; Special Supplementary Resolutions presented by the delegation of the Universal Negro Improvement Association of Jamaica; also resolutions on Ethiopia, Liberia, Haiti; an additional resolution on Ethiopia; on colored seamen in Great Britain; and a resolution to the U.N.O. on South West Africa.

A Memorandum to the United Nations Organization was presented through its Secretariat by Dr. Du Bois as International President of the Pan-African Congress. This Resolution urged as "just, proper, and necessary that provision be made for the participation of designated representatives of the African colonial peoples . . . to the maximum extent possible under the present Charter of the United Nations." This petition was supported by some thirty-five of the most powerful organizations of Africans and people of African descent in the United States, the Caribbean, and Britain. Broadly representative, organizations included civic, religious, fraternal, professional, press, labor, women's, student, and youth bodies.

The program of ideas and action achieved at the Sixth Manchester Pan-African Congress has been summarized by Colin Legum in *Pan-Africanism* in nine chief points which must be still further compressed here: 1. "Africa for the Africans." 2. United States of Africa. 3. African renaissance of morale and culture. 4. African nationalism totally transcending tribalism and narrowness. 5. African regeneration of economic enterprise. 6. Government on the principle "one man one vote." 7. Nonviolent *Positive Action* unless met by forcible repression. 8. Solidarity of African and oppressed peoples everywhere. 9. Positive neutrality in power politics but "neutral in nothing that affects African interests."

Thence to Africa itself and to the various national liberation movements growing there was this program and the political drive of Pan-Africanism then transferred, while phases of its cultural propagation were still carried on in Europe and the Americas. Noteworthy among these ongoing phases of cultural Pan-Africa are the Conferences of Black Writers and Artists, the publication of books and the journal *Presence Africaine* edited by Alioune Diop in Paris since November 1947, and the development of the Society of African Culture in Paris followed by the associated American Society of African Culture.

With the final breakthrough of the Egyptian Revolution led by Colonel Gamal Abdel Nasser and with the independence of Ghana in 1957 under the leadership of Dr. Kwame Nkrumah, Pan-Africanism was in flower in its natural habitat. For these soon followed the First Conference of Independent African States in Accra, April 15–22, 1958. Thence proceeding through the various All African Peoples Conferences at Accra, 1958; Tunis, 1960; Cairo, 1961; and Governmental Conferences at Conakry, 1959; Sanniquelli, 1959; the Second Conference of Independent African States at Addis Ababa, 1960; Brazzaville, 1961; Casablanca, 1961; Monrovia, 1961; not without difficulties and setbacks but finally achieving mature stature at the Addis Ababa Summit Conference, May 22–25, 1963, Pan-Africa loomed through the Organization of African Unity as a powerful political continental force and an international factor of prime magnitude. This Organization was further consolidated at the Conference in Cairo, during 1964.

The Manchester Congress of 1945 thus marked a milestone in the development of the Pan-African Movement. President Nnamdi Azikiwe of the Republic of Nigeria in his Goodwill Message for the republication in 1963 of the *History of the Pan-African Congress* observed that this 1945 Congress "marked the turning point in Pan-Africanism from a passive to an active stage." In the ninety-fifth year of his life Dr. Du Bois wrote: "It carries messages which must not die, but should be passed on to aid Mankind and to inspire the darker races of Man to see themselves of one blood with all human beings. . . . For that was a decisive year in determining the freedom of Africa."

The President of Kenya, Jomo Kenyatta, welcomed the reprint of the report of the 1945 Manchester Pan-African Congress and declared: "The Congress was a landmark in the history of the African peoples' struggle for unity and freedom." Mrs. George Padmore in her Goodwill Message said of this decisive Pan-African Congress: "Its resolutions and resulting programmes inspired the leaders who participated in its deliberations to carry forward their endeavours in their native territories."

The Osagyefo Dr. Kwame Nkrumah, President of Ghana, in his Message revealed: "At Manchester, we knew that we were speaking for all Africa, expressing the deepest desires and determination of a mighty continent to be wholly free. The desire was very emphatically reiterated in Addis Ababa where the heads of state and Government of 32 Independent African States representing 250 million Africans, witnessed probably the most important turning point in the political and economic history of any continent."

Hearing the report in his ninety-sixth and last year of this Addis Ababa Conference from his wife Shirley Graham Du Bois, the Doctor could well visualize that great meeting of heads of African states and conceive its historical promise for a completely free, independent, and united Africa in the not too distant future. Thereafter, as the veteran spokesman for Pan-African liberation and champion of human rights relaxed his grasp upon the pen, or turned reluctantly from his dictation for the *Encyclopedia Africana,* as he prepared to lay himself down and to mingle his dust with the dust of his ancestral African forebears, he might well have heard the vibrant song which Union soldiers sang as they marched against the strongholds of the Southern slaveholding oligarchy:

For William Edward Burghardt Du Bois must have felt the certainty at the last that the struggle for freedom, which he had so ably waged, would be carried forward to final victory by ever more and stronger hands. So it does in truth go forward, as signalized on the occasion of the recent achievement of independence by the people of Zambia, in the words of the African poet A. C. Jordan:

> So Africa's hungry children shall survive
> And gain new strength to build a brighter world,
> Untrammell'd by the wiles of endless strife
> Created by the ravenous kings of gold.

The passing of a great African

BERNARD FONLON

In the shadow of Christianborg Castle, official residence of the President of Ghana, there lies a man whose passing should claim, from every conscious African, the tribute of a thought. For if the wind of change sweeping through Africa today goes down as the revolution which more than anything else put a mark on the mid-twentieth century, Dr. Du Bois, American Negro, Ghana citizen, who died at Accra on the 27th of August, 1963, at the venerable age of ninety-five years, Dr. Du Bois shall go down as the pioneer, indeed the father, of the Pan-African Movement.

Pan-Africanism, however, was but a part of his preoccupations; nothing that concerned the welfare of black folk in particular and that of the underprivileged world in general was foreign to his zeal: student, researcher, teacher, historian, sociologist, poet, novelist, political militant—he was, in every one of these capacities, first and foremost, a fighter for the freedom and the dignity of Negro people, a fighter for the rights of those, no matter what their race, who suffer wrong and oppression.

He is third of the Grand Triumviri, the three Negro leaders who tower head and shoulders above the rest in the history of the last hundred years; for, in the story of Negro leadership, when one thinks of Frederick Douglass, and of Booker Washington, one thinks almost inevitably of William Edward Burghardt Du Bois.

A dedicated soul

In order to appreciate fully Du Bois' work for the Negro people, it must be borne in mind that at the time when, as a young man, he dedicated himself to the service of his race, the Negro was just up from slavery in America, and, in Africa, the chains of servitude were being clapped on him anew: it was the era of the notorious Scramble and the Partition of Africa. And dark days lay before the black man on either side of the Atlantic. It was a time in the Negro's Via Dolorosa that called, as Du Bois put it himself, for "the strongman, the master-felt man, the honest man, the man who can forget himself;" the crying need was for leadership of exceptional caliber. And, by reason of the greatest opportunities with which he had been blessed, Du Bois felt, and naturally, that he had a mission to participate in this leadership.

Even as early as his young days in Fisk University, he was wont to assert: "I am a Negro; and I glory in the name; I am proud of the black blood that flows in my veins."

On his twenty-fifth birthday, even before his final university studies were over, he solemnly dedicated himself to the service of the Negro race:

> I am glad I am living, I rejoice as a strong man to run a race, and I am strong—is it egotism, is it assurance—or is it the silent call of the world spirit that makes me feel that I am royal and that beneath my sceptre a world of kings shall bow? The hot dark blood of that black fore-father born king of men—is beating at my heart, and I know that I am either a genius or a fool . . . this I do know: be the Truth what it may I will seek it on the pure assumption that it is worth seeking—and Heaven nor Hell, God nor Devil shall turn me from my purpose till I die. I will in this second quarter century of my life, enter the dark forest of the unknown world for which I have so many years served my apprenticeship—the chart and compass the world furnishes me I have little faith in—yet, I have none better—I will seek till I find—and die.
>
> These are my plans; to make a name in science, to make a name in literature and thus to raise my race. Or perhaps to raise a visible empire in Africa thro' England, France, or Germany.
>
> I wonder what will be the outcome? Who knows?

Today we see the outcome, and we know.

Into the arena

Back from Germany and armed with his doctorate at Harvard, it was borne in upon him that the activities through which he could best render service to the Negro were teaching in Negro universities and research into Negro problems: the education of its Talented Tenth would render the urgent double service of dispelling ignorance and providing the black community with enlightened leadership; research would give him a precise appraisal of Negro problems and provide a scientific basis for the struggle for Negro advancement. Yet he was not destined to keep at these for long.

For, although Emancipation had been proclaimed at the dawn of the eighteen-sixties, the lot of the Negro was far from happier: he was despoiled of his vote and reduced to political impotency; he was denied the protection of the law and crippled by economic disabilities; in society, his lot was the ostracism of the pariah. But as if these were not enough, white resentment at the Negro's very existence vented itself in violence and often, black-white relations were rocked and marred by bloody race riots. But the most horrifying shape that white violence took against blacks was lynching. According to accounts, some of these lynchings were so barbaric that one stands aghast how it could happen that people who proudly proclaim "IN GOD WE TRUST," could perpetrate acts of such unearthly butchery.

In the face of such savagery, no leader dedicated to the defense of his people could rest content with teaching and research in a university ivory tower: the call rang out for organization and direct agitation. And, in answer to this call, Du Bois and a few radical friends launched the Niagara Movement.

The men of the Niagara Movement, *declared their manifesto,* coming from the toil of a year's work, and pausing a moment from the earning of their daily bread, turn toward the nation and again ask in the name of ten million the privilege of a hearing. In the past year the work of the Negro-hater has flourished in the land. Step by step the defenders of the rights of American citizens have retreated. The work of stealing the black man's ballot has progressed and the fifty and more representatives of stolen votes still sit in the nation's capital. Discrimination in travel and public accommodation has so spread that some of our weaker brethren are actually afraid to thunder against color discrimination as such and are simply whispering for ordinary decencies.

Against this the Niagara Movement eternally protests. We will not be satisfied to take one jot or tittle less than our full manhood rights. We claim for ourselves every single right that belongs to a free-born American, political, civil and social; and until we get these rights we will never cease to protest and assail the ears of America. The battle we wage is not for ourselves alone, but for all true Americans. It is a fight for ideals, lest this, our common fatherland, false to its founding, become in truth the land of the "Thief and the home of the Slave"—a by-word and a hissing among the nations for its sounding pretensions and pitiful accomplishment.

Never before in the modern age has a great and civilized folk threatened to adopt so cowardly a creed in the treatment of its fellow citizens, born and bred on its soil. Stripped of verbiage and subterfuge and in its naked nastiness, the new American creed says: fear to let the black men even try to rise lest they become the equals of the white. And this is the land that professes to follow Jesus Christ. The blasphemy of such a course is only matched by its cowardice.

The Niagara Movement, however, did not achieve much more than this ringing protest. Moreover, Atlanta University, where he taught, depended on the generosity of philanthropy and because Du Bois' radicalism was stirring up resentment in philanthropic circles, he was becoming an increasing embarrassment to the university. But a chance soon came which fitted his radical mood more perfectly than the university chair. There was a lynching in Springfield in 1907 and the anger it aroused led some white liberals to join hands with some Negro leaders including Du Bois, the following year, to form the National Association for the Advancement of Colored Peoples. Thus when, in 1910, he was invited to take the editorship of *The Crisis,* the association's organ, he leapt to the occasion.

And, for years, Du Bois' superb editorial talents made *The Crisis* the focal point of the Negro struggle.

Pan-Africa

The outstanding thing about his leadership is that it embraced the whole Negro world, so much so that one can assert without fear or exaggeration that the entire struggle for the freedom of black folk, on either side of the Atlantic, rests on his shoulders. For Du Bois' devotion to Africa was intense and the attraction of Africa, to him, irresistible.

> The spell of Africa is upon me, *he exclaimed*. The ancient witchery of her medicine is burning my drowsy, dreamy blood. This is not a country, it is a world—a universe of itself and for itself, a thing Different, Immense, Menacing, Alluring. It is a great black bosom where the Spirit longs to die. It is a life so burning, so fire encircled that one bursts with terrible soul inflaming life. One longs to leap against the sun, and then calls, like some great hand of fate, of immovable Power beyond, within, around. Then comes the calm. The dreamless beat of midday stillness, at dusk, at dawn, at noon, always . . . Africa is the Spiritual Frontier of human kind.

In order to appreciate the overwhelming significance of Du Bois' services to the land of his ancestors, one needs to keep constantly in mind what the condition of Africa was, during the first three decades of this century. Imperialism was at the height of its power and few could dare to challenge it; the continent had long been reduced to submission and silence; and education, dealt out in meager doses, had not yet produced those who were destined to give authentic vent and voice to the African resentment.

Who then would speak for Africa?
Who else but those of the descendants of the African exiles who, in spite of impossible odds, in America and in the West Indies, had wrung an education from the grudging and hostile white man?

Who else, among these, was more prepared to do this than Du Bois himself?

Thus he found himself with the Pan-African Movement from its very genesis and stood steadfast by it, and nursed it tenderly until it was mature enough to be transferred to the African continent. For he participated as Secretary to the very first Pan-African Congress that was organized in London, at the dawn of the century, by a Trinidadian barrister, Henry Sylvester Williams, as a forum of protest against the aggressive policies of imperialism in Africa; on the death of Sylvester Williams, he took up the struggle and organized five further congresses between 1919 and 1945.

Unlike Marcus Garvey whose Negro Zionism had for final purpose the leading of the Negro peoples from the New World back to Africa, Du Bois sought, through the Pan-African Movement, to promote national self-determination among Africans, under African leadership, for the benefit of the Africans themselves. He saw the struggle for African independence as inextricably linked with the fight for Negro equality in the United States; for it was his African background that was being used as an excuse to keep the Negro down; self-determination in Africa would hasten real emancipation for the Negro in America. This view has since been amply vindicated by events.

When the conference at Versailles was about to be held at the close of the First World War, Du Bois felt it imperative that the voice of Africa should be heard at such a historic and far-reaching gathering. With the very able assistance of Blaise Diagne—then member for Senegal in the French Chamber of Deputies—who had the ear of Clemenceau, he organized the second Pan-African Congress to coincide with the Conference.

> We in Cameroon have a special dept of gratitude to Du Bois, because it was he who originated the idea of international trusteeship, an idea that shaped the course of our history for forty years and without which it is doubtful whether Cameroon could have survived as a political entity; there was nothing to prevent the victorious allies from dismembering the conquered territories and integrating their share purely and simply into their adjacent colonies. But led by Du Bois, the Pan-African Congress passed a resolution urging the allied powers to place the former German colonies under international supervision to be held in trust, for the inhabitants, as future self-governing territories.

There is no need here to go into the details of the Congresses that he organized between the wars; but stress must be laid on this: that the indifference which he met with on every side, and the difficulties he had to face, and the fact that he clung to the idea notwithstanding, show how deeply convinced Du Bois was that Pan-Africanism would triumph in the end.

The abdication of the Talented Tenth

I have said above what a determining part Mr. Blaise Diagne played in the success of the 1919 Congress; the NAACP too had lent its aid. But in the subsequent Congresses, both withdrew their support; the NAACP did not think it its mission to fight for the advancement of colored peoples outside the United States; and, faced with a choice between Pan-Africanism and France, Diagne chose France. This change in the attitude of his former ardent collaborator led Du Bois to sound a warning against the danger that educated leaders of black folk would take part in the robbery of their race rather than lead the masses to education and culture.

This is a danger that looms larger as time goes by. In the early years, Du Bois had championed the principle that if the highest opportunities for education were placed within the reach of the Talented Tenth, they would use their achievements to serve and lead the masses. This was what he himself had done and he seemed to think that the following of this course, by others equally blest, was rather in the nature of things. He was later to be disenchanted and to give vent to bitter disappointment.

The majority of the American Negro intelligentsia, he observed, together with the West Indian and West African leadership, showed symptoms of following in the footsteps of Western acquisitive society with its exploitation of labor, monopoly of land and its resources and with private profit for the smart and unscrupulous, in a world of poverty, disease, and ignorance, as the natural end of human culture; the Talented Tenth had become fully American in defending exploitation, imitating conspicuous expenditure and ignorance of socialism.

Resurgent Pan-Africa

A very striking thing it is indeed how far Du Bois was ahead of his time.

Despite the indifference of former friends, despite the covert hostility of imperialist powers, despite the overt antagonism of Garvey's Back-to-Africanism, despite apparent failure, the ideas of

Pan-Africanism were taking root, notwithstanding, and this, especially among the younger generation of politically-minded Negroes who, thanks to increased education between the wars and to the shock of firsthand experience abroad, had gained a new consciousness—men like the late George Padmore, Dr. Nnamdi Azikiwe, Dr. Kwame Nkrumah, Jomo Kenyatta. These were the ones destined to bring Pan-Africanism to maturity, and back to Africa.

The shake-up of the world by the Second World War and the reawakening to which it jolted the underprivileged peoples provided a moment and an atmosphere ideal for the relaunching of the Pan-African struggle. Du Bois was too deep-sighted to miss this chance. And thus the Manchester Congress was summoned in 1945, on the morrow of the War. As the old man, now seventy-seven years of age, set about, with youthful energy and excitement, preparing for the Congress, he declared that it would become the real movement for the emancipation of Africa.

And it did.

The young men who surrounded him at Manchester are today the makers of the African revolution.

No victory without socialism

Even from very early in his career as thinker and leader, Du Bois' keen-sightedness saw that the struggle for Negro equality in the New World and for independence in the Old was a struggle that could not win a thorough victory without a corresponding economic revolution. For the problem of dark-skinned peoples restive under white domination was only part of a larger problem, namely, the problem of workers weary of an economic system that gave them slavery and their masters luxury.

As far back as 1907, that is, ten years before the Russian Revolution and the advent of Communism, Du Bois came to the conclusion that socialism was the only genuine solution to the Negro problem; that socialism was the great road to progress and the hope of the world's depressed masses.

Today, every African leader of any standing, every African thinker of any depth knows that for us some measure of socialism is a must; socialism, in African unity, is our only road toward genuine independence, our only safeguard against the intrigues of the capitalist conspiracy, our only effective weapon against the might of organized reaction.

Faithful to the end

In the defense of the principles for which he stood, for which he had lived and fought a whole lifetime—equality for the American Negro, independence for his African brother, justice for labor, peace for mankind—Du Bois' spirit remained unbent to the last. In fact, in 1951, when he was eighty-three, his campaign for peace aroused the hostility of the U.S. Government and almost landed him behind prison bars. But the *grand old man,* completely unintimidated by the U.S. Government's charges, stepped up his campaign to denounce the same evils and preach the same gospel: that big business was paralyzing democracy by creating a military dictatorship; that only some form of socialism could preserve the ideals of democratic America; that nothing could stop communism but something better than Communism. No softening down, no equivocation, no compromise.

> I wanted, *he declared,* to dispel, in the minds of the government and of the public any lingering doubt as to my determination to think and speak freely on the economic foundation of the wars and frustrations of the twentieth century.

On the invitation of Dr. Nkrumah, Professor Du Bois came to spend the evening of his life in Ghana, to spend what was left of his tremendous energies on a project which he had conceived back at the beginning of the century but never found the funds to embark upon it, until the Ghana Government came to his aid, in the closing days; this project was the *Encyclopedia Africana* which he was now left with others to complete.

Here a deep-felt tribute must be paid to Osagyefo Dr. Kwame Nkrumah, for enabling the life of this great son of Africa to close in so worthy a way: nowhere could Dr. Du Bois' last days have been more fittingly spent than the continent that owes him so much; no burial more due than the honors that were rendered his passing in Accra; no soil more worthy to receive his remains than the soil of Africa. And of all African countries none was worthier than Ghana to honor, and be honored by conferring its citizenship on this eminent African; for Ghana is the one African nation where an all-out effort is being made to incarnate the ideas for which Dr. Du Bois stood and lived and strove to the end of his days.

When I ask myself what it is in the life of Dr. William Edward Burghardt Du Bois that emerges as his most outstanding achievement, I have no hesitation whatsoever as to my answer. It is that he stood fast by his principles and ideals right to the end, that his conviction about them grew stronger, that his defense of them grew more vigorous with the passing years.

What then was the secret of this unswerving consistency, this unflagging constancy, this ever-deepening radicalism? The question can be put another way. Why does so much youthful idealism end up, so often, in cynicism? Why is it that, so often, youth who begin as fervent radicals become conformists even before their young days are over? Why do so many ardent progressives end up before long in reaction? In other words, what was it in Du Bois that is lacking in the faithful who fall by the wayside?

There can be external reasons why: chill poverty that blights the promises of youth; an illiberal atmosphere that suffocates and smothers youthful aspirations. But these, though formidable, are not the deadliest foes; for, if the flame within burns strong and true, no external forces can stamp it out completely.

The spirit that perseveres to the end is sustained by a threefold force—of feeling, of will, and of mind.

Saeva indignatio

Idealism, progressivism, radicalism, revolutionary fervor cannot last except in a man with a burning thirst for justice, social justice, a man provoked to fierce, even savage indignation by man's inhumanity to man. For as certain as it is that beneath all conservatism, capitalism, imperialism, monopoly, colonialism, reaction, there lies consuming greed, just so certain is it that there can be no genuine radicalism without a deeply generous nature, a nature that is inclined to overlook personal wrong but cannot brook injury done to others by wrongful social systems. Such a nature was that of this son of Africa.

For he was an angry, angry man, Dr. Du Bois, angry against the white world's vermin and filth:

> All the dirt of London,
> All the scum of New York;
> Valiant despoilers of women
> And conquerors of unarmed men;
> Shameless breeders of bastards,
> Drunk with the greed of gold,
> Baiting their blood-stained hooks
> With cant for the souls of the simple;
> Bearing the white man's burden
> Of liquor and lust and lies!
> I hate them, Oh I
> I hate them well,
> I hate them, Christ!
> As I hate hell
> If I were God
> I'd sound their knell
> This day!

The same burning rage, though softened by grief and religious faith, pulses through the *Litany at Atlanta* that he wrote on the morrow of the race riot that shook that city in 1906.

A will of iron

There can be no lasting fidelity to principle, therefore, without a passion for justice and right. But this by itself is not enough, for there are in man other thirsts, born of greed, which, more often than not, prove far more powerful than the thirst for truth and justice. There is the attraction of wealth, the enticement of pleasure, the irresistible force of mad ambition.

For a man to have stood firm by his principles, to have fought for them from youth to the extreme of age, is proof enough of a backbone of granite.

But power of emotion and a will of iron would be but blind and passionate obstinacy, or even destructive wrongheadedness, if they are not enlightened.

Science must be the basis

There can be no genuine radical or progressive who is not at the same time endowed with keenness of mind. For, if indignation is to be a constructive force, it must be led by deep insight; problems must be clearly understood before appropriate remedies for them can be proposed. And yet, merely natural intelligence will not do; it must be intelligence deepened by study and fed with fact and principle.

Thanks to his keenness of mind, thanks to his early research and seasoned scholarship, Professor Du Bois got so clear a grasp of the Negro problem that he never had cause to abandon his course, at least in so far as fundamentals were concerned. In fact, with passing years, he is becoming more and more vindicated.

Dr. Du Bois insisted on the overwhelming importance of scientific research as an indispensable prerequisite in the struggle for Negro equality and freedom. It was imperative that the tackling of his problem be preceded by thorough and intelligent fact-finding; without the groundwork of discriminatory, cold-blooded, scientific research, judgment however shrewd could hardly be protected from the numberless possibilities of error, especially in a question that aroused such violent emotions.

The overwhelming importance of this principle in present-day African affairs cannot be overemphasized. A program for the welfare of a people cannot be improvised. Nor can a policy, however intelligent, be successful, if the machinery for carrying it out is riddled with incompetence. No action can be fruitful if it is not based on thought; and thought is airy and groundless if not based on fact; and facts can only be organized into principles by careful research. First, fact-finding and, then, a program based on the facts. Airy notions and groundless assumptions, an unwillingness to face the naked truth—these mark the surest road to failure and disaster.

A burning thirst for justice, a firm will never to treat with wrong, keen insight into the real nature of social problems—these are the hallmarks of the genuine radical, idealist, progressive.

A monument to his name

Such was this great son of Africa, this eminent Negro leader who deserves memory and honor wherever there are black men, who deserves a monument in every Negro capital.

But there can be no better way of hallowing the name of W. E. B. Du Bois, no monument to his memory more lasting than to take up the fight where he left it and to remain faithful to his principles to the end. The only genuine way whereby African leaders can honor their departed dean is to dedicate themselves anew to their task; to resolve that there shall be no compromise with reaction; that they shall strive to further an ever closer union of the African peoples; to resolve that each, in his state, shall never rest until the point is reached where no mother is afraid that her child will not be educated, where no man is anxious that he will be workless and without means of livelihood, that he will be left uncared for in times of illness, where no man is afraid that he will be neglected in his old age.

Was this not the piercing cry that rang out from his inmost soul throughout his life, the deepest desire of his heart, the single and dedicated purpose of all his striving, namely, the welfare of each and every one among black folk?

This, however, I can assert, that if the dead came back to life and William Edward Burghardt Du Bois were asked how he would be honored, how best his memory could be hallowed and perpetuated, I am sure he would confirm that there could be nothing dearer to his soul, no more enduring monument to his name than a United Socialist Africa.

PART FIVE

HIS WRITING

CREDO

At the advent of the twentieth century, Du Bois was thirty-three years of age and teaching and carrying on research at Atlanta University, a Negro institution in Georgia. Among the author's first publications was a Credo, *written in 1900, in which he tried to reconcile his religious belief with the ethics of the race problem.*

I believe in God, who made of one blood all nations that on earth do dwell. I believe that all men, black and brown and white, are brothers, varying through time and opportunity, in form and gift and feature, but differing in no essential particular, and alike in soul and the possibility of infinite development.

Especially do I believe in the Negro Race: in the beauty of its genius, the sweetness of its soul, and its strength in that meekness which shall yet inherit this turbulent earth.

I believe in Pride of race and lineage and self: in pride of self so deep as to scorn injustice to other selves; in pride of lineage so great as to despise no man's father; in pride of race so chivalrous as neither to offer bastardy to the weak nor beg wedlock of the strong, knowing that men may be brothers in Christ, even though they be not brothers in law.

I believe in Service—humble, reverent service, from the blackening of boots to the whitening of souls; for Work is Heaven, Idleness Hell, and Wage is the "Well done!" of the Master, who summoned all them that labor and are heavy laden, making no distinction between the black, sweating cotton hands of Georgia and the first families of Virginia, since all distinction not based on deed is devilish and not divine.

I believe in the Devil and his angels, who wantonly work to narrow the opportunity of struggling human beings, especially if they be black; who spit in the faces of the fallen, strike them that

Excerpt: W. E. B. Du Bois, *Darkwater* (New York: Harcourt, Brace and World, 1920).

cannot strike again, believe the worst and work to prove it, hating the image which their Maker stamped on a brother's soul.

I believe in the Prince of Peace. I believe that War is Murder. I believe that armies and navies are at bottom the tinsel and braggadocio of oppression and wrong, and I believe that the wicked conquest of weaker and darker nations by nations whiter and stronger but foreshadows the death of that strength.

I believe in Liberty for all men: the space to stretch their arms and their souls, the right to breathe and the right to vote, the freedom to choose their friends, enjoy the sunshine, and ride on the railroads, uncursed by color; thinking, dreaming, working as they will in a kingdom of beauty and love.

I believe in the Training of Children, black even as white; the leading out of little souls into the green pastures and beside the still waters, not for self nor peace, but for life lit by some large vision of beauty and goodness and truth; lest we forget, and the sons of the fathers, like Esau, for mere meat barter their birthright in a mighty nation.

Finally, I believe in Patience—patience with the weakness of the Weak and the strength of the Strong, the prejudice of the Ignorant and the ignorance of the Blind; patience with the tardy triumph of Joy and the mad chastening of Sorrow; patience with God!

Behold the land

This speech was delivered in Columbia, South Carolina, October 20, 1946, as the principal address at the closing session of the Southern Youth Legislature, sponsored by the Southern Negro Youth Congress.

The text, for all its brevity, or possibly because of it, bears all the marks of a classic statement on the South. In slightly more than two thousand words, Dr. Du Bois, with the incomparably brilliant insight which characterizes all his works, illuminates the basic nature of the social, political, and economic life of the South.

The reader will be interested in the circumstances under which the address was delivered. At the closing public session of the Southern Youth Legislature, 861 young delegates, Negro and white, crowded into Antisdel Chapel of Benedict College. They were joined by a large and sympathetic public who stood in the aisles, jammed the doors, and listened through loudspeakers outside the auditorium.

The future of American Negroes is in the South. Here three hundred and twenty-seven years ago, they began to enter what is now the United States of America; here they have made their greatest contribution to American culture; and here they have suffered the damnation of slavery, the frustration of reconstruction and the lynching of emancipation. I trust then that an organization like yours is going to regard the South as the battleground of a great crusade. Here is the magnificent climate; here is the fruitful earth under the beauty of the southern sun; and here, if anywhere on earth, is the need of the thinker, the worker, and the dreamer. This is the firing line not simply for the emancipation of the American Negro but for the emancipation of the African Negro and the Negroes of the West Indies; for the emancipation of the colored races; and for the emancipation of the white slaves of modern capitalistic monopoly.

Remember here, too, that you do not stand alone. It may seem like a failing fight when the newspapers ignore you; when every effort is made by white people in the South to count you out of citizenship and to act as though you did not exist as human beings while all the time they are profiting by your labor; gleaning wealth from your sacrifices and trying to build a nation and a civilization upon your degradation. You must remember that despite all this, you have allies and allies even in the white South. First and greatest of these possible allies are the white working classes about you. The poor whites whom you have been taught to despise and who in turn have learned to fear and hate you. This must not deter you from efforts to make them understand, because in the past in their ignorance and suffering they have been led foolishly to look upon you as the cause of most of their distress. You must remember that this attitude is hereditary from slavery and that it has been deliberately cultivated ever since emancipation.

Slowly but surely the working people of the South, white and black, must come to remember that their emancipation depends upon their mutual cooperation; upon their acquaintanceship with each other; upon their friendship; upon their social intermingling. Unless this happens each is going to be made the football to break the heads and hearts of the other.

White youth is frustrated

White youth in the South is peculiarly frustrated. There is not a single great ideal which they can express or aspire to, that does not bring them into flat contradiction with the Negro problem. The more they try to escape it, the more they land into hypocrisy, lying, and double-dealing; the more they become, what they least wish to become, the oppressors and despisers of human beings. Some of them, in larger and larger numbers, are bound to turn toward the truth and to recognize you as brothers and sisters, as fellow travelers toward the dawn.

There has always been in the South that intellectual elite who saw the Negro problem clearly. They have always lacked and some still lack the courage to stand up for what they know is right. Nevertheless they can be depended on in the long run to follow their own clear thinking and their own decent choice. Finally even the politicians must eventually recognize the trend in the world, in this country, and in the South. James Byrnes, that favorite son of this commonwealth, and Secretary of State of the United States, is today occupying an indefensible and impossible position; and if he survives in the memory of men, he must begin to help establish in his own South Carolina something of that democracy which he has been recently so loudly preaching to Russia. He is the end of a long series of men whose eternal damnation is the fact that they looked *truth* in the face and did not see it; John C. Calhoun, Wade Hampton, Ben Tillman are men whose names must ever be besmirched by the fact that they fought against freedom and democracy in a land which was founded upon democracy and freedom.

Eventually this class of men must yield to the writing in the stars. That great hypocrite, Jan Smuts, who today is talking of humanity and standing beside Byrnes for a United Nations, is at the same time oppressing the black people of Africa to an extent which makes their two countries, South Africa and the American South, the most reactionary peoples on earth. Peoples whose exploitation of the poor and helpless reaches the last degree of shame. They must in the long run yield to the forward march of civilization or die.

What does the fight mean?

If now you young people, instead of running away from the battle here in Carolina, Georgia, Alabama, Louisiana, and Mississippi, instead of seeking freedom and opportunity in Chicago and New York—which do spell opportunity—nevertheless grit your teeth and make up your minds to fight it out right here if it takes every day of your lives and the lives of your children's children; if you do this, you must in meetings like this ask yourselves what does the fight mean? How can it be carried on? What are the best tools, arms, and methods? And where does it lead?

I should be the last to insist that the uplift of mankind never calls for force and death. There are times, as both you and I know, when

> Tho' love repine and reason chafe,
> There came a voice without reply,
> 'Tis man's perdition to be safe
> When for truth he ought to die.

At the same time and even more clearly in a day like this, after the millions of mass murders that have been done in the world since 1914, we ought to be the last to believe that force is ever the final word. We cannot escape the clear fact that what is going to win in this world is reason if this ever becomes a reasonable world. The careful reasoning of the human mind backed by the facts of science is the one salvation of man. The world, if it resumes its march toward civilization, cannot ignore reason. This has been the tragedy of the South in the past; it is still its awful and unforgivable sin that it has set its face against reason and against the fact. It tried to build slavery upon freedom; it tried to build tyranny upon democracy; it tried to build mob violence on law and law on lynching and in all that despicable endeavor, the state of South Carolina has led the South for a century. It began not the Civil War—not the War between the States—but the War to Preserve Slavery; it began mob violence and lynching and today it stands in the front rank of those defying the Supreme Court on disenfranchisement.

Nevertheless reason can and will prevail; but of course it can only prevail with publicity—pitiless, blatant publicity. You have got to make the people of the United States and of the world know what is going on in the South. You have got to use every field of publicity to force the truth into their ears, and before their eyes. You have got to make it impossible for any human being to live in the South and not realize the barbarities that prevail here. You may be condemned for flamboyant methods; for calling a congress like this; for waving your grievances under the noses and in the faces of men. That makes no difference; it is your duty to do it. It is your duty to do more of this sort of thing than you have done in the past. As a result of this you are going to be called upon for sacrifice. It is no easy thing for a young black man or a young black woman to live in the South today and to plan to continue to live here; to marry and raise children; to establish a home. They are in the midst of legal caste and customary insults; they are in continuous danger of mob violence; they are mistreated by the officers of the law and they have no hearing before the courts and the churches and public opinion commensurate with the attention which they ought to receive. But that sacrifice is only the beginning of battle, you must rebuild this South.

There are enormous opportunities here for a new nation, a new economy, a new culture in a South really new and not a mere renewal of an old South of slavery, monopoly, and race hate. There is a chance for a new cooperative agriculture on renewed land owned by the state with capital furnished by the state, mechanized and coordinated with city life. There is chance for strong, virile trade unions without race discrimination, with high wage, closed shop, and decent conditions of work, to beat back and hold in check the swarm of landlords, monopolists, and profiteers who are today sucking the blood out of this land. There is chance for cooperative industry, built on the cheap power of T.V.A. and its future extensions. There is opportunity to organize and mechanize domestic service with decent hours, and high wage and dignified training.

"Behold the land"

There is a vast field for consumers' cooperation, building business on public service and not on private profit as the mainspring of industry. There is chance for a broad, sunny, healthy home life, shorn of the fear of mobs and liquor, and rescued from lying, stealing politicians, who build their deviltry on race prejudice.

Here in this South is the gateway to the colored millions of the West Indies, Central and South America. Here is the straight path to Africa, the Indies, China, and the South Seas. Here is the path to the greater, freer, truer world. It would be shame and cowardice to surrender this glorious land and its opportunities for civilization and humanity to the thugs and lynchers, the mobs and profiteers, the monopolists and gamblers who today choke its soul and steal its resources. The oil and sulphur; the coal and iron; the cotton and corn; the lumber and cattle belong to you the workers, black and white, and not to the thieves who hold them and use them to enslave you. They can be rescued and restored to the people if you have the guts to strive for the real right to vote, the right to real education, the right to happiness and health and the total abolition of the father of these scourges of mankind, *poverty.*

"Behold the beautiful land which the Lord thy God hath given thee." Behold the land, the rich and resourceful land, from which for a hundred years its best elements have been running away, its youth and hope, black and white, scurrying North because they are afraid of each other, and dare not face a future of equal, independent, upstanding human beings, in a real and not a sham democracy.

To rescue this land, in this way, calls for the *Great Sacrifice;* this is the thing that you are called upon to do because it is the right thing to do. Because you are embarked upon a great and holy crusade, the emancipation of mankind, black and white; the upbuilding of democracy; the breaking down, particularly here in the South, of forces of evil represented by race prejudice in South Carolina; by lynching in Georgia; by disfranchisement in Mississippi; by ignorance in Louisiana and by all these and monopoly of wealth in the whole South.

There could be no more splendid vocation beckoning to the youth of the twentieth century, after the flat failures of white civilization, after the flamboyant establishment of an industrial system which creates poverty and the children of poverty which are ignorance and disease and crime; after the crazy boasting of a white culture that finally ended in wars which ruined civilization in the whole world; in the midst of allied peoples who have yelled about democracy and never practiced it either in the British Empire or in the American Commonwealth or in South Carolina.

Here is the chance for young women and young men of devotion to lift again the banner of humanity and to walk toward a civilization which will be free and intelligent; which will be healthy and unafraid; and build in the world a culture led by black folk and joined by peoples of all colors and all races—without poverty, ignorance, and disease!

Once, a great German poet cried: "Selig der den Er in Sieges Glanze findet."

"Happy man whom Death shall find in Victory's splendor."

But I know a happier one: he who fights in despair and in defeat still fights. Singing with Arna Bontemps the quiet, determined philosophy of undefeatable men:

> I thought I saw an angel flying low,
> I thought I saw the flicker of a wing
> Above the mulberry trees; but not again,
> Bethesda sleeps. This ancient pool that healed
> A Host of bearded Jews does not awake.
> This pool that once the angels troubled does not move.
> No angel stirs it now, no Saviour comes
> With healing in His hands to raise the sick
> and bid the lame man leap upon the ground.
>
> The golden days are gone. Why do we wait
> So long upon the marble steps, blood
> Falling from our open wounds? and why
> Do our black faces search the empty sky?
> Is there something we have forgotten? Some precious thing
> We have lost, wandering in strange lands?
>
> There was a day, I remember now,
> I beat my breast and cried, "Wash me God,"
> Wash me with a wave of wind upon
> The barley; O quiet one, draw near, draw near!
> Walk upon the hills with lovely feet
> And in the waterfall stand and speak!

Opening speech: Conference of 'Encyclopedia Africana'

I wish first to express my sincere thanks to those of you here who have accepted the invitation of our Secretariat to participate in this Conference and thus assist us in the preparatory work which we have undertaken for the creation of an *Encyclopedia Africana.*

Had there been any doubts in your minds of the importance of African Studies, I am sure the papers and discussions of the past week have dispelled them. The wide attendance at the First International Congress of Africanists attests to the almost feverish interest throughout the world in the hitherto "Dark Continent."

It remains, therefore, for me only to lay before you the importance of an *Encyclopedia Africana* based in *Africa* and compiled by *Africans.*

You have noted from letters cited in our Information Report, the most gratifying endorsement from scholars in all sections of the world of the general aims of this work. Some of you, however, ask if an *Encyclopedia Africana* at this time is not premature. Is this not a too ambitious undertaking for African scholars to attempt? Is there enough scientifically proven information ready for publication? Our answer is that an *Encyclopedia Africana* is long overdue. Yet, it is logical that such a work had to wait for independent Africans to carry it out.

We know that there does exist much scientific knowledge of Africa which has never been brought together. We have the little known works of African scholars of the past in North Africa, in the Sudan, in Egypt. Al Azhar University and the Islamic University of Sankore made large collections; *Presence Africaine* has already brought to light much material written in the French language. We can, therefore, begin, remembering always that an Encyclopedia is never a finished or complete body of information. Research and study must be long and continuous. We can collect, organize, and publish knowledge as it emerges. The *Encyclopedia* must be seen as a living effort which will grow and change—which will expand through the years as more and more material is gathered from all parts of Africa.

It is true that scientific written records do not exist in most parts of this vast continent. But the time is *now* for beginning. The *Encyclopedia* hopes to eliminate the artificial boundaries created on this continent by colonial masters. Designations such as "British Africa," "French Africa," "Black Africa," "Islamic Africa" too often serve to keep alive differences which in large part have been imposed on Africans by outsiders. The *Encyclopedia* must have research units throughout West Africa, North Africa, East, Central, and South Africa which will gather and record information for these geographical sections of the continent. The *Encyclopedia* is concerned with Africa as a whole.

It is true that there are not now enough trained African scholars available for this gigantic task. In the early stages we have need of the technical skills in research which have been highly developed in other parts of the world. We have already asked for and to a most gratifying degree been granted the unstinted cooperation and assistance of the leading Institutes of African Studies outside Africa. Many of you who have gathered here from distant lands can, and I believe will, make valuable contributions to this undertaking. And you can assist us in finding capable African men and women who can carry the responsibilities of this work in their own country and to their people. For it is African scholars themselves who will create the ultimate *Encyclopedia Africana*.

My interest in this enterprise goes back to 1909 when I first attempted to launch an *Encyclopedia Africana* while still teaching at Atlanta University in Georgia, U.S.A. Though a number of distinguished scholars in the United States and various European countries consented to serve as sponsors, the more practical need of securing financial backing for the projected Encyclopedia was not solved and the project had to be abandoned. Again, in 1931, a group of American scholars met at Howard University and agreed upon the necessity of preparing an *Encyclopedia of the Negro*—using this term in its broadest sense. There was much organization work and research done in the preparation, but once again, the undertaking could not be carried through because money could not be secured. Educational foundations had doubts about a work of this kind being accomplished under the editorship of

Negroes. We are deeply grateful to the President of Ghana and to the Government of this independent African state for inviting us to undertake this important task here where the necessary funds for beginning this colossal work are provided. After all, this is where the work should be done—in Africa, sponsored by Africans, for Africa. *This Encyclopedia will be carried through.*

Much has happened in Africa and the world in the last twenty years. Yet, something of what I wrote in the preparatory volume of the *Encyclopedia of the Negro,* which was published in 1945, will bear repeating now:

> Present thought and action are all too often guided by old and discarded theories of race and heredity, by misleading emphasis and silence of former histories. These conceptions are passed on to younger generations of students by current textbooks, popular histories and even public discussion. Our knowledge of Africa today is not, of course, entirely complete; there are many gaps where further information and more careful study is needed; but this is the case in almost every branch of knowledge. Knowledge is never complete, and in few subjects does a time arrive when an encyclopedia is demanded because no further information is expected. Indeed, the need for an encyclopedia is greatest when a stage is reached where there is a distinct opportunity to bring together and set down a clear and orderly statement of the facts already known and agreed upon, for the sake of establishing a base for further advance and further study.

For these reasons and under these circumstances it would seem that an *Encyclopedia Africana* is of vital importance to Africa as a whole and to the world at large.

Africa and the French Revolution

If you should penetrate the campus of an American Ivy League college and challenging a senior, ask what, in his opinion, was the influence of Africa on the French Revolution, he would answer in surprise if not pity, "None." If, after due apology, you ventured to approach his teacher of "historiography," provided such sacrilege were possible, you would be told that between African slavery in America and the greatest revolution of Europe, there was of course some connection, since both took place on the same earth; but nothing causal, nothing of real importance, since Africans have no history.

Nevertheless, it is a perfectly defensible thesis of scientific history that Africans and African slavery in the West Indies were the main causes and influences of the American Revolution and of the French Revolution. And when, after long controversy and civil war, Negro slavery and serfdom were not suppressed, the United States turned from democracy to plutocracy and opened the path to colonial imperialism and made wide the way for the final world revolutions in the twentieth century.

Let us now look at the story. Columbus had a Negro pilot, and in the sixteenth century his son Diago was governor of the island of San Domingo and his slaves staged a revolt in 1522. A few years later Vasquez d'Allyon tried to settle in Virginia but his slaves revolted. From the sixteenth century on, the revolt of the black workers stolen in Africa and transported to America continued. This was proven by the fright of the planters shown by the increased severity of the laws; at the same time, their desire to pretend that the slave system for blacks was perfect and was not resented.

Early in the sixteenth century the Maroons appeared all over the West Indies. This was the name given to runaway slaves who took refuge in the mountains of Cuba, Haiti, Jamaica, and Central America. They formed their own governments and even built cities. They fought with the Spanish, the British, and the French; they made treaties which the whites broke.

Meantime, by the middle of the seventeenth century Cromwell had seized Jamaica and the French had started sugar planting on their islands. White indentured servants were imported into the West Indies and the African slave trade increased. Between 1700 and 1776, 600,000 blacks were imported to the West Indies, Central, and South America. French commerce quadrupled between 1714 and 1789. Dutch slaves revolted and gained their independence, and in Haiti a succession of black rulers in this land of mountains carried on continuous governmental organization which lasted through the eighteenth century and still exists.

San Domingo was an island of mountains rising in places six thousand feet above sea level. The San Domingo planters and the British and French bourgeoisie were the new owners of some of the richest property in the world. Of these three the most important in 1790 were the planters of San Domingo. The island was beautiful. The climate was favorable, and crops grew the year round. The planters lived luxuriously, and spent their vacations or old age in Paris. In France they formed a powerful political force as their counterparts did in England. French women from the gutter as well as the middle class came to the colony. French aristocracy came to rebuild their shattered fortunes. They took Negro concubines. Colonial cities were centers of dirt, gambling, and debauchery. In 1789, of seven thousand mulatto women in San Domingo, five thousand were either prostitutes or mistresses. Failures from all countries flocked to San Domingo. No white person was a servant or did any work that he could get a Negro to do for him. The owners lived in barbaric luxury and the island produced more sugar, coffee, chocolate, indigo, timber, and spices than all the rest of the West Indies put together. As early as 1685 Louis XIV had issued a Code Noir which made wives and children of Frenchmen free. By the beginning of the eighteenth century mulattoes began to accumulate property and educate their children in France. Their children began to return by 1763 and tried as freemen to take part in public affairs.

Meantime, the British were profiting by the slave trade and building up their mercantile system of colonial trade.

The French regarded the colonies as existing for the profit of France. Colonies must buy all manufactured goods in France and could sell their produce only to France. The goods must be transported in French ships. Sugar must be refined in France. In 1664 France gave the rights of trade with San Domingo to a private company. The colonists refused and the governor had to ease restrictions. This happened again in 1722. There was another insurrection, the governor was imprisoned, and the privileges of the company modified. The colonists thought of separating from France. Long before 1789 the French bourgeoisie was the most powerful force in France and the slave trade in the colonies, the basis of its power. The fortunes created at Bordeaux and at Nantes by the slave trade gave the bourgeoisie the pride that demanded "liberty." In 1666, 108 ships went from Nantes to Africa with 37,430 slaves valued at 37 million dollars and giving the owners from 15 to 20 per cent on their money. In 1700 Nantes was sending 50 ships a year to the West Indies with food, clothing, and machinery. Nearly all the industries developed in France were based on the slave trade or the trade with America. Bordeaux grew rich by 1750 with 16 factories refining sugar. San Domingo was the special center of the Marseilles trade. A dozen other great towns refined sugar. Hides and cotton came from the West Indies. Two to six million Frenchmen depended for their livelihood upon colonial trade. In 1789 San Domingo received in its ports more ships than Marseilles. France used for the San Domingo trade 750 vessels employing 24,000 soldiers. In 1774 the colonies owed France 200 million and by 1789 between 3 and 5 million. The British eyed San Domingo with alarm after the independence of America. San Domingo doubled its production between 1783 and 1789.

The British slave trade became an increasing source of profit and their monopoly of colonial trade a matter of increasing importance. When, therefore, the American colonists tried to extricate themselves from British power they struck first at the slave trade. Already the Negro workers were beginning to take part in the struggle. Crispus Attucks led a mob in Boston and Daniel Webster said that the severance of America from the British empire dated from his death. The day of his death was a national American holiday for nearly a quarter of a century.

In 1776 Jefferson emphasized the slave trade as America's grievance against Great Britain. The American Revolution stopped the trade. In 1774, the Second Article of the Continental Association said, "that we will neither import nor purchase slaves imported after the first day of December next, after which we will wholly discontinue the slave trade." This all agreed would stop slavery. As the war progressed Negroes took part. General Nathaniel Green writes, "The natural state of the country appears to me to consist more in the blacks than in the whites." American Negroes fought for freedom, perhaps a larger proportion of them than among whites. In the early battles of the revolutionary war Negro soldiers fought side by side with the whites. It was feared that their presence might encourage slaves in the South to accept the offer of freedom given by the British governor, Dunmore, of Virginia, and for a while Washington was induced to refuse colored enlistments. But this he soon gave up. Negroes fought throughout the revolutionary war, mostly on the side of the Americans, but some on the side of the British. And Negro slavery was certainly one of the strongest arguments for the American Revolution. After America gained its freedom in 1783 it was felt in France and America that slavery in America was at an end.

The French Revolution has been written so largely from the white point of view that the part which the blacks played in this drama has been either forgotten or unknown.

A revolution is a transfer of power from the top aristocracy of a nation to lower and lower classes. Very often all the work and demand of an aristocracy is interpreted as transfer of power to the masses of people. This is usually untrue. Magna Carta was not a democratic movement. It was a successful attempt of the higher British aristocracy to wrest power from the king. The writ of *habeas corpus* did not mean that the working masses escaped unjust imprisonment; it was for the benefit of the rich middle class. And so in France the fall of the Bastille was a victory for unjustly treated aristocrats.

The freedom which France demanded in 1787 was freedom to build their current prosperity on the products of slave labor supported by a slave trade from Africa. Profits from this source were at their highest and French migrants were rushing to San Domingo to get rich. About this time the colored bastards whom the

Code Noir had declared to be free and Negroes who had either earned or bought their freedom began to demand French citizenship, and French theorists and dreamers backed them as Friends.

In 1788, France exported to French San Domingo 21 million dollars in flour, wine, and manufactures, with 580 vessels in this trade and 98 in the African trade, and 29,500 slaves were brought to San Domingo from Africa.

In 1789, the West Indian colony of San Domingo supplied two-thirds of the overseas trade to France and was the greatest individual market for the European slave trade. It was an integral part of the economic life of the age, the pride of France, and the envy of every imperialist nation. The whole structure rested on the labor of the half million black slaves.

San Domingo was now incomparably the finest colony in the world and its possibilities were limitless. But without slaves San Domingo was doomed. The British colonies had enough slaves from all their trade and the British bourgeoisie who had no other West Indian interests set up a howl for the abolition of the slave trade. The rising British industrial bourgeoisie turned toward free trade and the exploitation of India and called the West Indies, "sterile rocks."

Adam Smith and Arthur Young condemned slave labor. India, after the loss of America, became a source of sugar. The production of cotton in India doubled in a few years. Indian free labor cost only a penny a day. There were hoards of gold, silver, and jewels.

In 1786 Wilberforce began the anti-slave trade campaign. Pitt egged him on. Liberals in France, including the great names of the revolution, formed a society, the Friends of the Negro, aimed at the abolition of slavery.

In the Estates General which met in 1789 the French aristocracy gave up many of their rights and formed a Constituent Assembly under the domination of the upper middle classes. They for three years made this bourgeoisie equal in power to the former aristocrats. Thus equality which came in France was equality for the property owners and not for the working, starving masses. For a year the mass of workers began to put forward their demands in the Legislative Assembly and then finally for three years came real revolution. The monarchy was abolished. A Committee of

Public Safety was established and pure democracy which allowed the masses to vote was proposed but not ratified. The king was killed and the parties fought for power. A reign of terror ensued which by 1794 was killing 354 people a month until suddenly came Thermidor. Robespierre himself was killed. The power of the Paris Commune with its extreme democracy was stopped. Babeuf, the serf, was executed. But the people were starving and there must be a change. In which direction would the change go, to a further devolution of power to the workers? Certainly not, said the respectable people. They turned to Bonaparte who had just married the granddaughter of a Negro and finished an Italian campaign. They brought him back from his wild Egyptian venture and the coup d'etat of the 18th Brumaire which ended in the empire. This is the story we are told and Africa touches it nowhere, save that we say that the terror in France was copied in Haiti and that Napoleon gave Louisiana to America.

This is not the complete story. Let us go over the details again: when the revolution broke out in France in 1787 San Domingo was the source of the greatest accumulation of wealth. San Domingo had more than three-quarter million slaves. The cities of France were flourishing with the slave trade. The French who were gaining equality with the former aristocrats were basing this equality on the profits of the slave trade and on crops grown by black slaves. From the very beginning two parties appeared in France: the moral philosophers and the social theorists, demanding freedom of the slaves. On the other hand, the planters demanded recognition as citizens and the exclusion of the poor whites and the mulattoes.

The planters supported the monarchy against the revolution. The poor whites supported the revolution against the king but opposed the mulattoes. The mulattoes sought alliance with either or both groups of whites. In 1789 the mulattoes sent Raymond and Ogé to Paris with six million pounds in gold and a promise of this and one-fifth of the property which the mulattoes owned in San Domingo to pay the French public debt. These delegates were received by the Constituent Assembly, and the Assembly thus recognized the citizenship of free Negroes. The planters were opposed as were also the manufacturers and merchants of the great French cities. The Constituent Assembly voted by large majority not to interfere with the internal government of the colonies and refused to abolish the slave trade. But on March 18, 1790, the Amis des Noirs secured a vote declaring free Negroes citizens. Planters in Martinique, Guadeloupe, and San Domingo all decreed that the law recognizing the right to vote applied only to white persons. The planters and poor whites fought each other, but both were against the Negroes.

The planters of San Domingo by secret manipulation placed six of their number in the Constituent Assembly. When representatives of the free Negroes and mulattoes appeared in Paris to demand hearing they were received and backed by the organization called the Friends of Negroes. The Declaration of the Rights of Man was adopted.

Ogé returned to America with British money, landing secretly in north San Domingo. He collected three hundred men. He was attacked and took refuge in the Spanish part of the island; the governor surrendered him. Ogé and Chavannes were sentenced while alive to have their arms, legs, and spines broken and then be exposed to the sun. This was done in the presence of the northern provincial assembly gathered in state.

War started between the planters and the free Negroes. The planters, reinforced by poor whites from France pouring in to make money from slavery, numbered 40,000. The free Negroes and mulattoes were about 26,000. And, despite the supporting votes of the National Convention, the war was going against them.

Then the unexpected happened. The bolder slaves had formed bands of Maroons in the mountains and before 1700 became dangerous. Over 1,000 Maroons are reported in 1720, 3,000 in 1751.

By 1750 their greatest chief was Macandel. He planned a rebellion but was captured and burned alive. The planters were determined that nothing would interfere with their methods and the slave system. A half million black Africans long self-trained in the mountains of Haiti on August 22, 1791, in a midnight thunderstorm, attacked. Thiers tells us: "In an instant twelve hundred coffee and two hundred sugar plantations were in flames; the buildings, the machinery, the farmhouses, were reduced to ashes; and the unfortunate proprietors were hunted down, murdered, or thrown into the flames, by the infuriated Negroes. The horrors of a servile war universally appeared. The unchained African signalized his ingenuity by the discovery of new methods and unheard-of modes of torture."

They killed, raped, and murdered. They destroyed property. The smoke of the fires blotted out the sun for days. The richest colony of France lay in ruins. The world shuddered. The slaveholders were frightened to death. But only gradually on slow sailing ships, loaded with lies, did the truth about what was happening reach France. Only after months did it realize that the foundations of its wealth and prosperity had disappeared. It was this and not any demands from the masses of French workers or of European philanthropists that turned the reaction of Thermidor into a reality and in time brought the counterrevolution of the 18th Brumaire.

The Terror did not spread from France to Haiti in 1793. Already in 1791 it came to France from Haiti. It was Africa in America and Africans led by Toussaint L'Ouverture who struck the French Revolution after it had given freedom to propertyholders, and faced it with chaos. They plunged into anarchy, tempered by murder, until the reaction of Thermidor restored property to power.

The revolt was all the more startling because while it had been in the fears and imagination of the colonists for two hundred years, it was always undreamed of as an actual occurrence. There had been numberless revolts, which had spread terror to whites all over the West Indies, Central America, and the mainland of the United States; but once they were quickly suppressed, their details and facts minimized, the records destroyed and the memory forgotten.

In San Domingo itself the dangers of slave revolts was not unknown. For years runaway slaves had hidden in the mountains, especially in the northeastern part of the island. There were serious slave revolts in 1679, 1691, and 1718, and in the middle of the eighteenth century a Negro, Macandel, carried out systematic poisoning which created a panic.

In Europe the organization of the lowest classes of workers and servants, peasants, and laborers to gain political power and property was rare and cannot be compared to the corresponding organizations of the African slaves in the West Indies and South America. Many European revolts which are pictured as risings of the masses are nothing of the sort. The Protest revolution had no sympathy with the peasants and Martin Luther kicked them in the teeth when they revolted. There were revolts of the suffering masses in Hungary, France, and England but they were small compared with the concerted, long-continued rebellion of the black Maroons. While the blacks of San Domingo were in wild rebellion France faced two paths: one was that of Babeuf who came up from the bottom of modern class organization, the servant class; he saw the masses starving, he felt their misery and he sang the dirge of the dying. He struggled for a commune of the workers; equality not of property owners but of those who gave property its value. He prayed and struggled for his Paris commune, but the mounting power of the property owners pushed and beat him back until he died. He died on the scaffold in 1796 but he arose from the dead in 1848 and again in 1871 in France; in 1917 in Russia; in 1939 in China and in 1961 in Cuba.

France, repudiating Babeuf, in its unconscious frenzy, took refuge in the reaction of Thermidor, after abolishing monarchy, killing the king, and murdering their leaders. Thermidor was the rule of the property-holders displacing the aristocrats. But in San Domingo, horror faced Toussaint and his rebels. Toussaint revered the king, his chieftain; he believed in discipline and authority. He deserted impious France and led his legions to the service of Charles IV of Spain. Slowly he and his successors in after years developed his ancient tribal communalism in San Domingo. Beyond these political provisions, he turned attention toward the economic; the island was divided into districts with inspectors who were to see that the freedmen returned to their work. A fifth part of the produce of each estate was to go to the workers. Commercial arrangements were made with the United States and England. He immediately issued a manifesto to all Negroes and mulattoes. "I am Toussaint L'Ouverture; my name is perhaps known to you. I have undertaken to avenge your wrongs. It is my desire that liberty and equality shall reign in San Domingo! I am striving to this end. Come and unite with us, brothers, and fight with us for the same cause."

Through the prowess of Toussaint, the Spanish pushed the French farther and farther back and in a short time secured possession of nearly the whole north of the island and a part of the south. The French commission found itself in a tight place and tried to extricate itself in June 1793, by offering to free all slaves who would enroll in the army. In August they went even further and proclaimed universal emancipation in San Domingo, and this action was confirmed by the French National Convention, February 4, 1794.

The first proclamation had no influence upon Toussaint. As a Spanish general, he refused to recognize the authority of the French. But when the English invaded San Domingo, the aspect of things changed. They landed in September and soon had captured that city with its heavy artillery and two million dollars' worth of shipping in its harbor. Toussaint knew the British as slave traders, and he now suspected that Spain wanted vengeance on France rather than freedom for the slaves. When, therefore, the French government affirmed universal emancipation early in 1794, he returned to French allegiance to the open delight of the commission. They said, "Remember that distinctions of color are no more!"

The blacks under Toussaint now proceeded to restore San Domingo to France. The mere magic of his name did much without fighting. In April Toussaint left the Spanish army; in May the French flag was flying at Gonaives. From now on Toussaint was known as L'Ouverture, the Savior. Gradually the whole northern part of the island was in his possession. As Sonthonax wrote in his diary, "These Negroes perform miracles of bravery."

In after years, the successors of Toussaint, Dessalines and Christophe, developed communalism and made the Haitian state independent and owner of its land and crops; but the surrounding world whirled away: it monopolized wealth in private hands, organized military power in their hand and France, the United States, and Britain forced Haiti to become the victim of their stooge who rules Haiti today. Still high in its mountains roll the tom-toms of ancient Africa and its dreams.

People who achieved equality in the French Revolution had neither liberty nor brotherhood for the black slaves of Haiti who were dying for the glory of France. For two years a National Convention was in control, which abolished the monarchy and vainly planned an equalitarian democracy. They tried to free the slaves, their own reaction could not survive slavery and live.

Meantime, separated by a vast ocean, with news traveling by slow sailing vessels, and couriers loaded with lies, France and San Domingo led for a long period almost separate lives, neither knowing exactly what was occurring in the other. The French commissioners representing the state arrived in San Domingo. They joined the mulattoes and free Negroes and revoked the abolition of the slavery of the blacks. Toussaint, leader of the blacks, went over to the Spaniards and the French planters appealed to the British.

The governor of the colony helplessly called on the revolting Negroes to surrender. In answer Toussaint wrote: "Sir,—We have never thought of failing in the duty and respect which we owe to the representative of the person of the King, nor even to any of his servants whatever; we have proofs of the fact in our hands; but do you, who are a just man as well as a general, pay us a visit; behold this land which we have watered with our sweat or rather, with our blood,—those edifices which we have raised, and that in the hope of a just reward! Have we obtained it? The King —the whole world—has bewailed our lot, and broken our chains; while in our part, we, humble victims, were ready for anything, not wishing to abandon our masters. What do we say? We are mistaken; those, who next to God, should have proved our fathers, have been tyrants, monsters unworthy of the fruits of our labours: and do you, brave general, desire that as sheep we should throw ourselves into the jaws of the wolf? No! it is too late. God, who fights for the innocent is our guide; he will never abandon us. Accordingly, this is our motto—*Death or Victory!*"

Thus while the slaves arranged themselves with the king as symbolic head of the state, the new colonial assembly, August 24,

1791, instead of appealing to France, begged protection, especially for their property, from England: "Fire lays waste our possessions, the hands of our Negroes in arms are already dyed with the blood of our brethren. Very prompt assistance is necessary to save the wreck of our fortunes—already half-destroyed; and confined within the towns, we look for your aid."

The British after five years were sick of their attempt to conquer Haiti. By September 30, 1796, out of the whole number of white troops, British and foreign, who had landed in Haiti since 1795, at least 15,000 men, only 3,000 were left alive. April 22, 1798, the British Commander Maitland evacuated all towns in Haiti except Mole St. Nicholas. He had only about a thousand troops alive.

The brilliant success of Toussaint not only aroused the envy of the mulattoes, but the suspicion of France. The commissioner, Sonthonax,* who had returned from San Domingo, reported to the new government in the Directory in France, the facts concerning Toussaint, and they thought it best to send a governor who would curb his power. Hédouville, the new governor, arrived April 20, 1798, and proposed to take charge of the negotiations with the English; but Maitland, the English commander, was only too glad to affront France by dealing directly and exclusively with Toussaint and to attempt to gain for England by flattery and bribery what he could not take by force. After five years of fighting, the loss of thirty thousand men, and the expenditure of one hundred million dollars, he offered to surrender.

On October 1, 1798, Toussaint entered Mole St. Nicholas as conqueror. The white troops saluted him. He was dined in the public square, on a silver service which was afterwards presented to him in the name of the king of England. A treaty was signed by which the English gave up the island, recognized Haiti as independent, and entered into a commercial agreement. Then they

* The Frenchman, Sonthonax, was a true representative of the revolution. "With the blacks his name was already a talisman, and in an insurrection which took place in the revolutionary center, Port-de-Paix, where whites were massacred, the laborers had risen to cries, 'long live Sonthonax.'" C. R. L. James, *The Black Jacobins* (London: Secker and Warburg, 1938), p. 146.

tried secretly to induce Toussaint to declare himself king, but he refused.

Paris between March 1793 and July 1794 passed through one of the supreme epochs of political history. In these few months of their nearest approach to power the masses did not forget the blacks. They felt toward them as brothers, and the old slave-owners whom they knew to be supporters of the counterrevolution, they hated as if Frenchmen themselves had suffered under the whip. There were many so moved by the sufferings of the slaves that they had long ceased to drink coffee, thinking of it as drenched with blood and sweat of men turned into brutes.

This was the France to which, in January 1794, three deputies sent by San Domingo to the Convention arrived. Bellay, a Negro slave, who had purchased his freedom, Mills, a mulatto, and Dufay, a white man. On February 3 they attended their first session. What happened there was quite unpremeditated.

The Chairman of the Committee on Decrees addressed the Convention, "Citizens, your Committee on Decrees has verified the credentials of the deputies from San Domingo. It finds them in order, and I move that they be admitted to their places in the Convention." Camboulas rose. "Since 1789 the aristocracy of birth and the aristocracy of religion have been destroyed; but the aristocracy of the skin still remains. That too is now at its last gasp, and equality has been consecrated. A black man, a yellow man, are about to join this Convention in the name of the free citizens of San Domingo." The three deputies of San Domingo entered the hall. The black face of Bellay and the yellow face of Mills excited long and repeated bursts of applause.

Lacroix (of Eure-et-Loire) followed. "The Assembly has been anxious to have within it some of those men of color who have suffered oppression for so many years. Today it has two of them. I demand that their introduction be marked by the President's fraternal embrace."

Next day, Bellay, the Negro, delivered a long and fiery oration, pledging the blacks to the cause of the revolution and asking the Convention to declare slavery abolished. It was fitting that a Negro and ex-slave should make the speech which introduced one of the most important legislative acts ever passed by any political assembly. No one spoke after Bellay. Instead Levasseur (of Sarthe) moved: "When drawing up the constitution of the French people we paid no attention to the unhappy Negroes. Posterity will bear us a great reproach for that. Let us repair the wrong—let us proclaim the liberty of the Negroes. Mr. President, do not suffer the Convention to dishonor itself by a discussion." The Assembly rose in acclamation. The two deputies of color appeared on the tribune and embraced while the applause rolled round the hall from members and visitors. Lacroix led the mulatto and the Negro to the President who gave them the presidential kiss, when the applause started again.

Cambon, a deputy, drew the attention of the House to an incident which had taken place among the spectators.

"A citizeness of color who regularly attends the sittings of the Convention has just felt so keen a joy at seeing us give liberty to all her brethren that she has fainted (applause). I demand that this fact be mentioned in the minutes, and that this citizeness be admitted to the sitting and receive at least this much recognition of her civic virtues." The motion was carried and the woman walked to the front bench of the amphitheatre and sat to the left of the President, drying her tears amidst another burst of cheering.

Lacroix, who had spoken the day before, then proposed the draft of the decree. "I demand that the Minister of Marine be instructed to despatch at once advices to the Colonies to give them the happy news of their freedom, and I propose the following decree: The national Convention declares slavery abolished in all the colonies. In consequence it declares that all men, without distinction of color, domiciled in the colonies, are French citizens, and enjoy all the rights assured under the Constitution."

During this time, the leaders of French industry continued their protests outside the National Convention.

"There is no longer any ship-building in our ports, still less any construction of boats. The manufactories are deserted and the shops even are closed. Thus, thanks to your sublime decrees, every day is a holiday for the workers. We can count more than three hundred thousand in our different towns who have no other occupation than, arms folded, to talk about the news of the day, of the Rights of Man, and of the Constitution."

On June 5, the day after the celebrations of the king's birthday and the capture of Port-au-Prince, the English commanders at St. Kitts heard that seven French ships had escaped the British fleet and landed at Guadeloupe. In command was Victor Hugues, a mulatto, "one of the great personalities of the French Revolution to whom nothing was impossible," taken from his post as public prosecutor in Rochefort and sent to the West Indies. Hugues brought only 1,500 men, but he brought also the Convention's message to the blacks. There was no black army in the Windward Islands as in San Domingo. He had to make one out of raw slaves. But he gave them the revolutionary message and dressed them in the colors of the Republic. The black army fell on the victorious British, began to drive them out of the French colonies, then carried the war into the British islands.

Toussaint got the news of the decree sometime in May. The fate of the French in San Domingo was hanging by a thread, but now that the decree of Sonthonax was ratified in France, Toussaint did not hesitate a moment but at once told Laveaux that he was willing to join him. Laveaux, overjoyed, accepted the offer and agreed to make him a brigadier-general, and Toussaint responded with a vigor and audacity that left all San Domingo gasping. He sent to the destitute Laveaux some good ammunition from the Spanish stores. Then he persuaded those of his followers who were with him to change over, and all agreed—French soldiers, ex-slaves of the rank and file and all his officers, blacks, and white royalists who had deserted the Republic to join him. "His demeanor at Mass was so devout that D'Hermona watching him communicate one day commented that God if he came to earth could not visit a purer spirit than Toussaint L'Ouverture."

The Directory which ruled from 1794 to 1799 turned to Napoleon who hated blacks. Nevertheless, he married the granddaughter of a Negro, Josephine, who was a leader of current French society. On the other hand, he dismissed General Dumas from his army solely because of his color. Napoleon was rising to prominence. He conducted a brilliant campaign in Italy and then from the foot of the Pyramids looked toward India, but the

British blocked him until unemployment in England brought the Peace of Amiens.

The French planters appealed to Napoleon. He took their side, saying: "The liberty of blacks is an insult to Europe." But Toussaint was powerful. Napoleon had to flatter and cajole him. After consultation with French bankers, Napoleon planned an American empire based on African slavery. He lured Toussaint to France and killed him. He gathered a vast army under his brother-in-law, Le Clerc, who sailed for San Domingo in 1801. He took 5 squadrons with 80 vessels and 21,000 troops. The Africans and the fever conquered this army and left Dessalines and Christophe, successors of Toussaint, masters of Haiti.

Napoleon was unable to start colonial imperialism in America. That was accomplished in later years when American democracy restored African slavery in the cotton kingdom.

But the world hailed Toussaint, he was one of the great men of his time. He made an extraordinary impression upon those who knew him personally or studied his life, whether they were friends or enemies. August Comte included him with Washington, Plato, Buddha, and Charlemagne as worthy to replace all the calendar saints. Morvins, biographer of Napoleon, calls him "a man of genius." Beauchamp refers to him as "one of the most extraordinary men of a period when so many extraordinary men appeared on the scene." Lamartine wrote a drama with Toussaint as his hero. Harriet Martineau wrote a novel on his life. Whittier wrote about him. Sir Spencer St. John, consular agent in Haiti, called him "the one grand figure of a cruel war." Rainsford, a British officer, refers to him as "that only great man." Chateaubriand charges that Bonaparte not only murdered, but imitated him.

A French planter said, "God in his terrestrial globe did not commune with a purer spirit." Wendell Phillips said, "You think me a fanatic, for you read history, not with your eyes, but with your prejudices. But fifty years hence, when Truth gets a hearing, the Muse of history will put Phocion for the Greek, Brutus for the Roman, Hampden for the English, Lafayette for France; choose Washington as the bright, consummate flower of our earliest civilization; and then, dipping her pen in the sunlight, will write in the clear blue, above them all, the name of the soldier, the statesman, the martyr, Toussaint L'Ouverture." Wordsworth sang:

> There's not a breathing of the common wind
> That will forget thee: thou hast great allies;
> Thy friends are exultations, agonies,
> And love, and Man's unconquerable mind.

In 1802 and 1803 nearly forty thousand French soldiers died of war and fever. Le Clerc himself died in November 1803. Rochambeau succeeded to his command and was promised soldiers by Napoleon; but already in May 1803, Great Britain started new war with France and communication between France and San Domingo was impossible. The black insurgents held the land; the British held the sea. In November 1803, Rochambeau surrendered and white authority died in San Domingo forever.

The effect of all this was far-reaching. Napoleon gave up his dream of American empire and sold Louisiana for a song. As De Wit Talmadge said: "Thus, all of Montana and the Dakotas, and most of Colorado and Minnesota, and all of Washington and Oregon states, came to us as the indirect work of a despised Negro. Praise, if you will, the work of a Robert Livingstone or a Jefferson, but today let us not forget our debt to Toussaint L'Ouverture, who was indirectly the means of America's expansion by the Louisiana Purchase of 1803."

References

C. R. L. James, *The Black Jacobins* (London: Secker and Warburg, 1938).
W. E. B. Du Bois, *Black Folk, Then and Now* (New York: Henry Holt, 1939).
Herbert Aptheker, *American Negro Slave Revolts* (New York: Columbia University Press, 1943).

The United States and the Negro

In 1861 the legal status of the American Negro was something like this: the Chief Justice of the Supreme Court, in an *obiter dictum,* had just said that, historically, the Negro had "no rights which a white man was bound to respect." Neither a horse, nor Frederick Douglass, could get an American passport for travel. Mules and men were sold at auction in Southern cities; and, while Bob Toomb's threat to auction slaves on Bunker Hill was unpopular, the act would not have been illegal. White Americans shuddered at miscegenation, yet in 1861 there were two million colored women who had no right to refuse sexual intercourse with their white owners. That these masters exercised this right was shown by 588,000 mulattoes in 1860. Kidnapping of free Negroes in the North had been made easy by the Fugitive Slave Law. All agreed that the Constitution recognized slavery as a legal institution and that the government was bound to protect it. Abolitionists were considered as contemptible for consorting with impossible radicals and recognizing Negroes as equals. Lincoln had been elected President because the South and Border split on the slave trade; Lincoln was looked upon, not as the enemy of slavery, but as opposed to its expansion. He did not want slavery to come into competition with the free Northern white workers, and the workers hated Negroes as much as slavery. Lincoln did not believe that the Negro could be integrated into the nation. He would protect slavery in the South, but he would not encourage its expansion into the North. Lincoln undoubtedly did not like slavery, but he was no champion of freedom for Negroes.

In the nation as a whole, no considerable number of citizens objected to slavery or would fight for Negro freedom. When the war opened, everybody, North and South, declared it to be a "white man's war," that is, fought by whites for objects which whites had. The wishes of Negroes were not to be taken into account. Slavery was to be protected. Northern generals went out of their way to return fugitive slaves to their masters with apologies; and, on the other hand, when General Fremont tried to free slaves in his area, he was promptly slapped down.

On the other hand, there were certain difficulties that arose. What about the slave who served his master as a servant or laborer, and helped him drive back the Northern armies? And, especially, what about the slave who ran away and took refuge in the Northern armies? The single slave might be returned; but, when the slaves poured by the thousands into the Northern armies, Butler was right in considering them "contraband of war," that is, property owned by the enemy which the Union Army should at least sequester, if not use themselves.

The enthusiasm of the North for the war was not to be counted on. After all, what was the North fighting for? Certainly not to free Negroes, also, not to subdue the South. The Northern laborer, especially the foreign-born, the civil servant, farmer, and small merchant, had no taste for going South for murder and destruction. The well-to-do bought their way out of the draft, which did not endear them to the laborers nor increase their general popularity. As the draft began to pinch the poor, they turned on the Negroes, who were not drafted, and who were willing to take the jobs of those whites who were. They hanged Negroes to lampposts in New York, and mobbed them in Cincinnati, and declared that they were not going to fight for "niggers."

This was a serious matter, especially, as many of the Negroes were willing to fight for themselves. Their leaders were begging to bear arms, but the government was adamant: no Negro soldiers. Moreover, Lincoln laughed. "If we put arms into their hands," he said, "next day they would be in the hands of our enemies." Then, again, things happened whether we would or no. Down in South Carolina, for instance, we had driven a wedge into the Southern armies. We needed soldiers to guard our gains, but the War Department had no soldiers to spare. The draft was failing. So General Hunter put guns in the hands of freed slaves, drilled them in their use, and told them to shoot intruders. Congress boiled with rage. But Hunter answered: "What else could I do? . . . I am not arming slaves, but, since there are no white troops, I have put guns in the hands of free blacks to guard what we have gained." Congress burst into laughter, and the first colored regiment was sworn into the army. That was but a beginning. Systematically, wherever the Northern armies appeared, the slaves stopped work and joined them. The generals pretended to be greatly annoyed. Here were thousands of mouths to feed, space had to be provided, and sickness cared for. They usually forgot to mention that here were invading armies whose problems of cooking, cleaning, hard labor, and menial service, were being furnished free, and in abundance, without search or wage, to armies invading a strange and hostile land. More than this, every inch of the land, every tree and river, every person and town, was known intimately to this writhing mass of people who did this work willingly, because they thought it was their own salvation. What would Alexander and Caesar have said; what would Frederick the Great and Napoleon have done, if God had sent them a gift like this?

The Federal government, for the most part, laughed, jeered, and complained. They told funny stories about the "darkeys" as they ate their biscuit and sent them on as spies. Then, too, the South was having difficulties. There was no "solid South." The South was a small group of rich and near rich slave-owners and landowners. The majority of poor whites had nothing, neither land nor employment, and were now asked to fight for slavery, when they hated the slaves, who got the work and food that belonged to them. Also, they hated the masters who got everything; and they began to desert from the Southern armies. Then, too, the plight of the elegant slave-owner before the world was not happy. England, after fostering the slave trade for a century, found it wise and more profitable to free the seized African and stop the African slave trade to America. France had carried on a revolution for freedom, equality, and brotherhood, but did not propose to include among her brothers the black slaves of Haiti. So the slaves killed the French and ran them off the island. Now, Britain and France needed the cotton raised in the southern United States. The South tried to appease them. It promised not to revive the slave trade, at least, not at once. But Frederick Douglass, talking in England and Ireland, told the factory workers how the black slaves were suffering, and the British workers refused to recognize the slave South.

On the other hand, the northern United States, refusing still to fight for abolition, nevertheless, began to use Negroes as troops and workers and spies, and explained that they were working for the "Union," and by Union they meant control of slavery's cotton crop and its sale to France and Britain at the highest possible price. Otherwise, the South, itself, would sell the crop abroad, and the Northern factories would close. Here a curious contradiction was seen as the war went on. The Northern armies cut the South in two, but they did it only by using the teeming Negro slaves of the Mississippi Valley. They marched from Atlanta to the sea, but only with the help of the black throngs of Georgia who cleared the path and stole the food for them. The grateful Northern armies, when they reached the sea, gave the Negroes land, but the Federal government, when it later gained full control, took this land away and gave it back to its former slave-holding owners. The Negroes sang in the sea-swept darkness, "Nobody knows the trouble I've seen." General Howard wept.

The war reeled on. Black men were used as shock troops and slaughtered by the thousands to make way for victorious white feet. In the end, 300,000 Negroes were used as servants, stevedores, and spies. There were 200,000 armed Negro troops, and in the background, peering from the sidelines, were three million more Negroes, ready to fight for freedom. No wonder freedom came.

The Southern leaders were frightened. If black soldiers continued to be drafted and fought as they had fought at Fort Wagner, Port Hudson, and Petersburg, then the North with its supplies, and ships, and the hesitation of Europe, would beat the South to its knees. The South tried every expedient, even seeking to enlist the slaves on their side; and, failing, surrendered.

Meantime, the North had had a vision, not the whole North, but the North of thinkers, dreamers, abolitionists, and free Negroes. *Uncle Tom's Cabin* had done its work. "John Brown's Body" was a-mouldering in the grave, and the eyes of poets had seen the "Coming of the Lord." At last, then, there was a reason for this senseless war, and that was the freeing of the slaves. Lincoln came to a decision. He would try to make the border states agree to a gradual emancipation; and he would challenge the recalcitrant South with immediate freedom of the labor which was supporting it.

It was a wise brave word which Karl Marx and his First International Workingmen's Association sent Lincoln in 1864:

> When an oligarchy of 300,000 slaveholders dared to inscribe for the first time in the annals of the world "Slavery" on the banner of armed revolt, when on the very spots where hardly a century ago the idea of one great Democratic Republic had first sprung up, whence the first declaration of the rights of man was issued, and the first impulse given to the European Revolution of the eighteenth century, when on those very spots counter-revolution, with systematic thoroughness, gloried in rescinding "the ideas entertained at the time of the formation of the old Constitution" and maintained "slavery to be a beneficial institution," indeed, the only solution of the great problem of the "relation of capital to labor," and cynically proclaimed property in man "the cornerstone of the new edifice"—then the working classes of Europe understood at once, even before the fanatic partisanship of the upper classes, for the Confederate gentry had given its dismal warnings, that the slaveholders' rebellion was to sound the tocsin for a general holy war of property against labor, and that for the men of labor, with their hopes for the future, even their past conquests were at stake in that tremendous conflict on the other side of the Atlantic. . . . They consider it an earnest sign of the epoch to come that it fell to the lot of Abraham Lincoln, the single-minded son of the working class, to lead his country through the matchless struggles for the rescue of the enchained race and the reconstruction of a social world.

The Emancipation Proclamation of 1863 sounded like more than it was. Negroes were not "henceforward and forever free." But Emancipation certainly began. The abolitionists gave up. Since the Negro was free what more was there to be done? The *Liberator* stopped publication. Lincoln saw a way out. He proposed a further step toward complete emancipation by enfranchising the elite of the Negro mass; the rich, the educated, the soldiers;

small in number, but encouraging in prospect. The South bluntly refused.

Then, after Lincoln's death, came a poor white from Tennessee, who, after being cajoled by the former masters, agreed to hurry them back in the saddle with full control over their former slaves. A series of Black Codes were adopted which made the nation gasp. Stevens and Sumner came forth with plans which made sense, but they could not command a majority in Congress. Stevens said: give the Negro a Freedman's Bureau, give each slave forty acres and a mule, and give them special legal protection. Sumner said and reiterated: give them the vote, nothing else is democracy; the Negro must have the vote.

Meantime, the mass of Northerners were neither in favor of freedom for Negroes nor votes for freedmen, and least of all, for any distribution of capital among them. What the conventional North saw, and the farmers and the factory builders, was the South walking back into Congress, threatening to lower the tariff, to attack the monopoly of gold, and to bring down prices. On top of this, they saw the spawn of war, thieves and grafters, like Tweed, start on a rampage of public theft. Industry and reform got together, and the conquered slave aristocracy got their ear. They made many of them believe that the theft and graft which was sweeping the North, was also rampant in the South because of the emancipated slaves. This was untrue, and everybody who really studied the situation knew it was untrue. Schurz and Trowbridge and others who looked at the South saw the truth. It was the educated free Negro of the North, working hand and glove with the freed Negro leader of the South, who, together, tried desperately to rescue the South from the accumulated disasters of war. The Negroes wanted free popular education. It was their talisman, their star of hope. Probably never in the world have so many oppressed people tried in every possible way to educate themselves.

The best conscience of the North rose to help them. The 8th Crusade of School Marms sent an endless column of teachers into the South. The white South reviled them, and spat upon them. When it could it drove them out and killed them. But they, the Negro politicians and the Negro masses, established the first system of free, popular education which the South ever saw, and they welcomed to the door of the school room, white and black, men, women, and children, rich and poor. Beyond that, they took over the social uplift which the South had left to the slave plantations and the whim of the slave barons. They established a system of hospitals which still exists. They built decent jails, poorhouses. They began to build orphanages and insane asylums. But the landholders refused to pay the increased taxation and felt justified in stealing and cheating governments carried on by the help of their former slaves. To these were added "carpetbaggers" who were lured South by the high price of cotton and cheap labor. The thieves and grafters came, and the white South pretended to see no difference between the uplifter and robber; but they quickly made friends with the railroad manipulators and "financiers" and the white carpetbaggers, shook hands with the Negro leaders; and, in the end, when land had been stolen and debts piled up for railroads, Negroes were blamed for the financial disaster that fell on the nation in 1873; and freedmen suffered for all the disaster that followed in the South.

The few Negro leaders did, for the most part, a splendid job. Even the slave South praised men like Cardoza of South Carolina, Dunn of Louisiana, Lynch of Mississippi, and Gibbs of Florida. These men led reform in South Carolina. They led reform in Louisiana. They fought graft in Florida and Alabama. But, instead of getting the sympathy and cooperation of the Northern leaders of reform, they got obloquy and contempt or concerted oblivion; while Northern industry and religion and the Southern aristocracy blamed every misfortune which came from the attempt to abolish slavery in the United States upon the slaves who were freed.

It was a contemptible transaction. Because, after all, it was the Negro, and the Negro alone, who restored the Union after the violence of 1861 to 1864. Indeed, who else but the Negro could have restored the Union? The mass of the Southern white population were too poor and ignorant to be of use, and they had no leaders. Their leaders had become slave-owners and their ambition was to destroy the Negro whom they hated and feared. On the other hand, the Negroes had leaders. The best of the house servants, the educated free Negro from the North, and the white

Northern teachers and missionaries. The enfranchisement, then, of the Negroes, was not an act of grace on the part of the North; it was the only thing they could do. If the Southern freedmen, with their leadership, could carry on the functions of the state, they could, if protected by military force and legal guardianship, restore the Southern states to their seats in Congress on such conditions as the victors laid down. This was done; and, instead of the anarchy and failure which the white South expected and the North was prepared to see, the South staggered to its feet; and what the leaders of the whites feared, was not the failure of these freedmen's governments, but their increasing success. They, therefore, offered the North, and especially its business leaders, a compromise. They would accept tariffs on imports, which soon reached the highest in the nation's history; they would let the national war debt be paid in monopolized gold; they would drop the demand for payment of the Southern war debt and for emancipated slaves. One thing they insisted on was the complete control of labor and the disfranchisement of the freedmen, and that they easily got from a complacent North, now on the way to immense wealth and power. Calmly, the North withdrew military protection, winked at the mob violence of the Ku Klux Klan, and promised to let the freedmen be disfranchised with only token opposition. They even gave up control and oversight of Southern voting for federal officials. This will destroy democracy, said some. Others answered: democracy is already dead.

Lynching and mob law now swept the South, and, of course, could not be allowed to continue. By 1880 the leaders of the nation began to look about to see how far they could get the Negroes themselves to assent to a caste condition in the United States based on color and race. They found, at last, such a leader in Booker Washington. Not that Washington believed in caste, not that Washington wanted anything less than other Negro leaders; but that he assented to compromise because he saw no other way. He was willing to let the whites believe that Negroes did not want social equality or the right to vote or education for the higher professions, but ask only for whatever the whites offered, and would be patient and quiet under a caste system. Industry poured millions into their propaganda; and, as a result, came disfranchisement and color caste. There followed the Niagara Movement of Negroes in 1905 and the establishment of the NAACP in 1909. The Southern states and some of the Northern states passed laws forbidding intermarriage, limiting employment, establishing ghettos, discriminating in transportation, and taking away the vote of most of the Negroes in the United States. It was an impossible condition to which no people, if they were really human, would consent. The NAACP was established by radical whites, reinforced by an increasing number of thinking Negroes, and it finally made a frontal attack upon lynching and mob law which brought the nation to its feet.

After all, a civilized nation could not continue publicly to murder one Negro each week without giving him a trial. It looked as if the chief industry of white women in the South was that of being raped by burly Negroes. The white women themselves, at last, protested, and an anti-lynching law was nearly forced through Congress, but finally failed.

Then the front of attack changed. Trusts appeared and organized wealth disguised in corporations began to take over control of the nation. They seized the West Indies, Central, and South America. They consorted with imperial Europe. When imperial colonialism drove Europe to war, the United States found it could make money by following. The First World War came and posed the fundamental question of Negro citizenship. The Supreme Court, after years of hesitation, sustained it. But the Negro was allowed to go into war as a stevedore, rather than as a soldier, and was treated with every indignity. After this war came wild speculation and severe depression. Franklin Roosevelt, with Harry Hopkins, began to socialize the nation, in order to beat back the power of the trusts and industrial monopolies. They did not wholly succeed; but they began just as the unexpected Second World War burst on civilization.

In this Second World War the Negro was registered in the ranks of the army and the navy and in the air corps, and their success only made clearer their caste condition in the nation. This, in the succeeding cold war, became so threatening a phenomenon that the Supreme Court in 1954 declared race discrimination, especially in schools, unconstitutional. The former slave South was furious, but was soon appeased by the assurance that the decree would not be enforced. The South could use "deliberate speed" which meant do little or nothing. That, again, aroused the Negroes. It led to bus strikes like that in Montgomery, and to student sit-ins, where the Negroes began to assert rights which had never been taken from them by law, but only yielded to in custom. This still goes on.

The world regards us with amazement: we are leading the "Free World." We champion "Democracy" and for this we stage Little Rock, drive Negroes from the polls, chase black students with bloodhounds, and throttle free speech. On top of this Africa arises and our FBI trains a "Peace Corps" to guide it.

Editing 'The Crisis'

From the time I entered High School at Great Barrington, Massachusetts, in 1880, I have had the itch to edit something. The first fruition was a school paper, in manuscript, called the *High School Howler,* edited by me and illustrated by Art Benham, who could draw caricatures. It had as I remember but one issue.

My next effort was while I was a student at Fisk University and I became, first, exchange editor and then editor of the *Fisk Herald,* during my junior and senior years, 1887–1888.

The next adventure was the monthly called *The Moon,* which was published by Harry Pace and Edward Simon in Memphis and edited by me in Atlanta in 1906. From 1907 to 1910, I was joint editor of a miniature magazine, published monthly in Washington, D.C. My co-laborers were H. M. Hershaw and F. H. M. Murray.

In 1910, I came to New York as Director of Publications and Research in the NAACP. The idea was that I should continue the kind of research into the Negro problem that I had been carrying on in Atlanta and that eventually I should become Secretary of the NAACP. But I did not want to raise money, and there were no funds for research; so that from the first, I urged that we have a monthly organ.

This seemed necessary because the chief Negro weekly *The New York Age* was then owned by friends of Mr. Washington, and the Tuskegee organization had tight hold of most of the rest of the Negro press. The result was that the NAACP got a pretty raw deal from the colored press and none at all from the white papers.

In addition to that the Negro press was at the time mainly organs of opinion and not gatherers of news.

I had the idea that a small publication would be read which stressed the facts and minimized editorial opinion, but made it clear and strong; and also published the opinion of others.

There were many on the board of directors who did not agree with me. I remember Albert Pilsbury, former Attorney General of Massachusetts, wrote to me and said: If you have not already determined to publish a magazine, for heaven's sake drop the idea.

The number of publications now is as many as the "plagues of Egypt!" But I was firm, and back of me stood William English Walling, Paul Kennedy, Charles Edward Russell, and John E. Mulholland and other members of the board.

But there again the matter of money was difficult. It was hard enough to raise the salaries of our two executive officers, and certainly we had no capital for investment in a periodical. I was persistent and two persons helped me: Mary Maclean, an English woman who was a writer on the *New York Times* and a loyal and efficient friend; and Robert N. Wood, a printer who was head of the Negro Tammany organization at that time.

Wood knew about printing and I knew nothing. He advised me, helped me to plan the magazine, and took the risk of getting me credit for paper and printing. The Board agreed that it would be responsible for debts up to but not exceeding $50.00 a month. It has always been a matter of pride to me that I never asked for that $50.00.

Finally after what seemed to me interminable delays on various accounts, the first number of *The Crisis* appeared in November 1910. It had sixteen 5 x 8 pages, with a cover which carried one little woodcut of a Negro child; as one of my critics facetiously said: "It is a shame to take the ten cents which this issue costs."

First because of the news which it contained, in four pages of "Along the Color Line;" then because of some blazing editorials which continually got us into hot water with friends and foes; and because of the pictures of Negroes which we carried in increasing number and often in color, *The Crisis* succeeded.

We condensed more news about Negroes and their problems in a month than most colored papers before this had published in a year. Then we had four pages of editorials, which talked turkey. The articles were at first short and negligible but gradually increased in number, length, and importance; but we were never able to pay contributors. Pictures of colored people were an innovation; and at that time it was the rule of most white papers never to publish a picture of a colored person except as a criminal and the colored papers published mostly pictures of celebrities who sometimes paid for the honor. In general the Negro race was just a little afraid to see itself in plain ink.

The circulation growth of *The Crisis* was extraordinary, even to us who believed in it. From a monthly net paid circulation of 9,000 copies in 1911, it jumped to 75,000 copies in 1918, and from an income of $6,500 to an income of $57,000. In January 1916, *The Crisis* became entirely self-supporting, paying all items of its cost including publicity, light, heat, rent, etc., and the salaries of an editor and business manager and nine clerks. It circulated in every state in the union, in all the insular possessions, and in most foreign countries including Africa.

We doubled the size of the tiny first issue in December 1910. We increased the number of pictures, trying two-color jobs on the cover in 1911 and three colors in 1912, 1917–1918. Our special education and children's numbers began in 1914. From time to time we issued special numbers on localities like Chicago and New Orleans; on "Votes for Women" and the pageant "Star of Ethiopia."

During this period two persons were indispensable in the conduct of *The Crisis:* Mary Maclean, editorial assistant, who died in harness and worked without pay; and Augustus Dill, business manager, who organized a model office. In November 1919, Jessie Fauset became literary editor and gave us inestimable help for seven years. Mattie Allison and Lottie Jarvis as secretaries, and Hazel Branch as head of the clerical staff, helped make an ideal family. Frank Turner was our bookkeeper from 1910 until the NAACP took him over in 1922.

We reached a circulation of 100,000 in 1919, following my revelation of the attitude of American army officers toward the Negroes in France. I shall never forget the circumstances of that scoop. I was in the office of Blaise Diagne in the spring of 1919. Diagne was a tall, thin, black Senegalese, French Under-Secretary of State for Colonies, and during the war, French Commissioner in West Africa, outranking the Colonial Governor. Diagne saved France by the black shock troops which he brought from Africa and threw against German artillery. They held the Germans until the Allies could get ready for them.

Diagne was consequently a great man and it was his word which induced Prime Minister Clemenceau to let the First Pan-African Congress meet in Paris against the advice of the Americans. Diagne did not like white Americans.

"Did you see," he stormed, "what the American Mission told the French about the way Negroes should be treated?" Then he showed me the official document. I read it and sat very still. Then I said, as carelessly as possible, "Would it be possible to obtain a copy of this?" "Take that," said Diagne.

Having the precious document, the problem was what to do with it. I dare not carry it nor trust it to the mails. But a white friend who was sailing home offered to take anything I wished to send. I handed him the document sealed, neglecting to say what dynamite was in it. *The Crisis* office and NAACP officials read it and dropped it until I returned. I published it in May 1919. The Post Office promptly held *The Crisis* up in the mails. But it proved too hot for them; if the Government held it that would be acknowledging its authorship. They let it go. We sold 100,000 copies!

Our income in 1920 was $77,000; that was our high-water mark. Then began a slump which brought the circulation down to 35,000 copies in 1924 and a cash income of $46,000.

The causes of this were clear and strike every modern periodical: the reading public is not used to paying for the cost of the periodicals which they read; often they do not pay even for the cost of the paper used in the edition. Advertisers pay for most of the costs and advertisers buy space in periodicals which circulate widely among well-to-do persons able to buy the wares offered. *The Crisis* was known to circulate among Negro workers of low income. Moreover it antagonized many white powerful interests; it had been denounced in Congress and many respectable Negroes were afraid to be seen reading it. Mississippi passed laws against it and some of our agents were driven from home.

We got some advertising, especially from Negro businesses; some advertisers we refused because we did not like the wares they offered or suspected fraud. The "Big" advertisers remained aloof; some looked us over, but nearly all fell back on the rule not to patronize "propaganda" periodicals. Besides they did not believe the Negro market worth entering.

Our only recourse was to raise our price of subscription. In December 1919 we raised our price to a dollar and a half for a year and fifteen cents a copy; also we increased our size to sixty-four pages and cover. This might have extricated us if the prices of everything else had not gone up, while wages went down. The depression which burst on the nation in 1929, started among Negro workers as early as 1926. It struck the workers of the Negro race long before the country in general dreamed of it. I remember bringing the matter to the attention of the president of the board of directors, but he said "the country is unusually prosperous!" Nevertheless, I retorted, the Negro worker is losing old jobs and not getting new ones.

There was a wider underlying cause: How far was *The Crisis* an organ of opinion and propaganda; and of whose opinion and just what propaganda? Or how far was it an organ of an association catering to its immediate plans and needs? The two objects and methods were not incompatible with each other in the earlier days of beginnings. Indeed from 1910 to 1925 or later *The Crisis* was the predominant partner, with income and circulation larger than the income and membership of the NAACP. For just this reason the NAACP became known outside its membership, and with the energetic work of Shillady, Johnson, and White, the membership and income increased and the question of the future relation of *The Crisis* and the NAACP had to be settled. Their complete separation was proposed; or if the income of *The Crisis* continued to fall, the subsidy of *The Crisis* by the NAACP; or further attempts to prolong the present relations and increase *The Crisis* income and circulation.

From 1925 to 1934, the latter method was tried. Various efforts were made to increase *The Crisis* circulation, by change of form and content. Considerable success ensued, but the depression which now fell heavier on the nation, convinced me that *The Crisis* could not be made to pay again for a long period and that meantime the only way to keep it alive was by subsidy from the NAACP. For this reason in 1934, I gave up my position as editor and publisher of *The Crisis* and went back to teaching and writing at Atlanta University.

In the nature of the case, there is a clear distinction between an organ of an organization and a literary magazine. They have different objects and functions. The one is mainly a series of reports and records of organizational technicalities and news notes of methods and routine notices. All large organizations need such a publication. But it is never self-supporting nor widely read. So far as it tries to be literary and artistic, it misses its main function and is too narrow to achieve any other.

On the other hand, a literary and news journal must be free and uncontrolled; in no other way can it be virile, creative, and individual. While it must follow an ideal, and one of which one or more organizations approve, yet its right to deviate in particulars must be granted, else it misses its function of provoking thought, stimulating argument, and attracting readers. For many years the NAACP gave me such freedom and the public repaid them and me by wide support. But when public support lagged and the NAACP must furnish a large part of the supporting funds, it would have called for more faith than any organization was likely to have in one man, to leave me still in untrammeled control. And as for me, I had no interest in a conventional organ; I must be free lance or nothing.

Against, therefore, the strong pleas of close friends like Joel Spingarn; and against the openly expressed wish of the whole board, which did not wholly agree with me, but were willing to yield much to retain me, I resigned. And I resigned completely and not in part. I was not only editor and head of a department which was separate from that of the Executive Secretary, with my own office and staff and separate bank account; I was also one of the incorporators of the NAACP and member of the board of directors since its beginning. Its officials from the first had come to consideration and election on my recommendation. I was a member of the Spingarn Medal Committee, and chief speaker at every annual conference. It was fair to say that the policy of the NAACP from 1910 to 1934 was largely of my making.

I would not have been honest therefore with my successors to have resigned in part and hung on to remnants of my former power. I went out completely. I think some sighed in relief. But many were genuinely sorry. Among the latter was myself. For I was leaving my dream and brainchild; my garden of hope and highway to high emprise. But I was sixty-five; my life work was practically done. I looked forward to a few final years of thought, advice, and remembrance, beneath the trees and on the hills beside the graves and with the friends where first my real life work had begun in 1897.

The African roots of war

"Semper novi quid ex Africa," cried the Roman proconsul; and he voiced the verdict of forty centuries. Yet there are those who would write world history and leave out this most marvelous of continents. Particularly today most men assume that Africa lies far afield from the centers of our burning social problems, and especially from our present problem of world war.

Yet in a very real sense Africa is a prime cause of this terrible overturning of civilization which we have lived to see; and these words seek to show how in the dark continent are hidden the roots, not simply of war today but of the menace of wars tomorrow.

Always Africa is giving us something new or some metempsychosis of a world-old thing. On its black bosom arose one of the earliest, if not the earliest, of self-protecting civilizations, and grew so mightily that it still furnishes superlatives to thinking and speaking men. Out of its darker and more remote forest fastnesses, came, if we may credit many recent scientists, the first welding of iron, and we know that agriculture and trade flourished there when Europe was a wilderness.

Nearly every human empire that has arisen in the world, material and spiritual, has found some of its greatest crises on this continent of Africa, from Greece to Great Britain. As Mommsen says, "It was through Africa that Christianity became the religion of the world." In Africa the last flood of Germanic invasions spent itself within hearing of the last gasp of Byzantium, and it was again through Africa that Islam came to play its great role of conqueror and civilizer.

With the Renaissance and the widened world of modern thought, Africa came no less suddenly with her new old gift. Shakespeare's Ancient Pistol cries,

> A foutre for the world, and worldings base!
> I speak of Africa, and golden joys.

He echoes a legend of gold from the days of Punt and Ophir to those of Ghana, the Gold Coast, and the Rand. This thought had sent the world's greed scurrying down the hot, mysterious coasts of Africa to the Good Hope of gain, until for the first time a real world commerce was born, albeit it started as a commerce mainly in the bodies and souls of men.

So much for the past; and now, today: the Berlin Conference to apportion the rising riches of Africa among the white peoples met on the fifteenth day of November, 1884. Eleven days earlier, three Germans left Zanzibar (whither they had gone secretly disguised as mechanics), and before the Berlin Conference had finished its deliberations they had annexed to Germany an area over half as large again as the whole German Empire in Europe. Only in its dramatic suddenness was this undisguised robbery of the land of seven million natives different from the methods by which Great Britain and France got four million square miles each, Portugal three quarters of a million, and Italy and Spain smaller but substantial areas.

The methods by which this continent has been stolen have been contemptible and dishonest beyond expression. Lying treaties, rivers of rum, murder, assassination, mutilation, rape, and torture have marked the progress of Englishman, German, Frenchman, and Belgian on the dark continent. The only way in which the world has been able to endure the horrible tale is by deliberately stopping its ears and changing the subject of conversation while the deviltry went on.

It all began, singularly enough, like the present war, with Belgium. Many of us remember Stanley's great solution of the puzzle of Central Africa when he traced the mighty Congo sixteen hundred miles from Nyangwe to the sea. Suddenly the world knew that here lay the key to the riches of Central Africa. It stirred uneasily, but Leopold of Belgium was first on his feet, and the result was the Congo Free State—God save the mark! But the Congo Free State, with all its magniloquent heralding of Peace, Christianity, and Commerce, degenerating into murder, mutilation, and downright robbery, differed only in degree and concentration from the tale of all Africa in this rape of a continent already furiously mangled by the slave trade. That sinister traffic, on which the British Empire and the American Republic were largely built, cost black Africa no less than 100,000,000 souls, the wreckage of its political and social life, and left the continent in precisely that state of helplessness which invites aggression and exploitation. "Color" became in the world's thought synonymous with inferiority, "Negro" lost its capitalization, and Africa was another name for bestiality and barbarism.

Thus the world began to invest in color prejudice. The "Color Line" began to pay dividends. For indeed, while the exploration of the valley of the Congo was the occasion of the scramble for Africa, the cause lay deeper. The Franco-Prussian War turned the eyes of those who sought power and dominion away from Europe. Already England was in Africa, cleaning away the debris of the slave trade and half consciously groping toward the new Imperialism. France, humiliated and impoverished, looked toward a new northern African empire sweeping from the Atlantic to the Red Sea. More slowly Germany began to see the dawning of a new day, and, shut out from America by the Monroe Doctrine, looked to Asia and Africa for colonies. Portugal sought anew to make good her claim to her ancient African realm; and thus a continent where Europe claimed but a tenth of the land in 1875 was in twenty-five more years practically absorbed.

Why was this? What was the new call for dominion? It must have been strong, for consider a moment the desperate flames of war that have shot up in Africa in the last quarter of a century: France and England at Fashoda, Italy at Adua, Italy and Turkey in Tripoli, England and Portugal at Delagoa Bay, England, Germany, and the Dutch in South Africa, France and Spain in Morocco, Germany and France in Agadir, and the world at Algeciras.

The answer to this riddle we shall find in the economic changes in Europe. Remember what the nineteenth and twentieth centuries have meant to organized industry in European civilization. Slowly the divine right of the few to determine economic income and distribute the goods and services of the world has been questioned and curtailed. We called the process Revolution in the eighteenth century, advancing Democracy in the nineteenth, and Socialization of Wealth in the twentieth. But whatever we call it, the movement is the same: the dipping of more and grimier hands into the wealth-bag of the nation, until today only the ultrastubborn fail to see that democracy in determining income is the next inevitable step to democracy in political power.

With the waning of the possibility of the Big Fortune, gathered by starvation wage and boundless exploitation of one's weaker and poorer fellows at home, arose more magnificently the dream of exploitation abroad. Always, of course, the individual merchant had at his own risk and in his own way tapped the riches of foreign lands. Later, special trading monopolies had entered the field and founded empires overseas. Soon, however, the mass of merchants at home demanded a share in this golden stream; and finally, in the twentieth century, the laborer at home is demanding and beginning to receive a part of his share.

The theory of this new democratic despotism has not been clearly formulated. Most philosophers see the ship of state launched on the broad, irresistible tide of democracy, with only delaying eddies here and there; others, looking closer, are more disturbed. Are we, they ask, reverting to aristocracy and despotism—the rule of might? They cry out and then rub their eyes, for surely they cannot fail to see strengthening democracy all about them?

It is this paradox which has confounded philanthropists, curiously betrayed the Socialists, and reconciled the Imperialists and captains of industry to any amount of "Democracy." It is this paradox which allows in America the most rapid advance of democracy to go hand in hand in its very centers with increased aristocracy and hatred toward darker races, and which excuses and defends an inhumanity that does not shrink from the public burning of human beings.

Yet the paradox is easily explained: the white workingman has been asked to share the spoil of exploiting "chinks and niggers." It is no longer simply the merchant prince, or the aristocratic monopoly, or even the employing class, that is exploiting the world: it is the nation, a new democratic nation composed of united capital and labor. The laborers are not yet getting, to be sure, as large a share as they want or will get, and there are still at the bottom large and restless excluded classes. But the laborer's equity is recognized, and his just share is a matter of time, intelligence, and skillful negotiation.

Such nations it is that rule the modern world. Their national bond is no mere sentimental patriotism, loyalty, or ancestor-worship. It is increased wealth, power, and luxury for all classes on a scale the world never saw before. Never before was the average citizen of England, France, and Germany so rich, with such splendid prospects of greater riches.

Whence comes this new wealth and on what does its accumulation depend? It comes primarily from the darker nations of the world—Asia and Africa, South and Central America, the West Indies, and the islands of the South Seas. There are still, we may well believe, many parts of white countries like Russia and North America, not to mention Europe itself, where the older exploitation still holds. But the knell has sounded faint and far, even there. In the lands of darker folk, however, no knell has sounded. Chinese, East Indians, Negroes, and South American Indians are by common consent for governance by white folk and economic subjection to them. To the furtherance of this highly profitable economic dictum has been brought every available resource of science and religion. Thus arises the astonishing doctrine of the natural inferiority of most men to the few, and the interpretation of "Christian brotherhood" as meaning anything that one of the "brothers" may at any time want it to mean.

Like all world-schemes, however, this one is not quite complete. First of all, yellow Japan has apparently escaped the cordon of this color bar. This is disconcerting and dangerous to white hegemony. If, of course, Japan would join heart and soul with the whites against the rest of the yellows, browns, and blacks, well and good. There are even good-natured attempts to prove the Japanese "Aryan," provided they act "white." But blood is thick, and there are signs that Japan does not dream of a world governed mainly by white men. This is the "Yellow Peril," and it may be necessary, as the German Emperor and many white Americans think, to start a world crusade against this presumptuous nation which demands "white" treatment.

Then, too, the Chinese have recently shown unexpected signs of independence and autonomy, which may possibly make it necessary to take them into account a few decades hence. As a result, the problem in Asia has resolved itself into a race for "spheres" of economic "influence," each provided with a more or less "open door" for business opportunity. This reduces the danger of open clash between European nations, and gives the yellow folk such chance for desperate unarmed resistance as was shown by China's repulse of the Six Nations of Bankers. There is still hope among some whites that conservative North China and the radical South may in time come to blows and allow actual white dominion.

One thing, however, is certain: Africa is prostrate. There at least are few signs of self-consciousness that need at present be heeded. To be sure, Abyssinia must be wheedled, and in America and the West Indies Negroes have attempted futile steps toward freedom; but such steps have been pretty effectually stopped (save through the breech of "miscegenation"), although the ten million Negroes in the United States need, to many men's minds, careful watching and ruthless repression.

Thus the white European mind has worked, and worked the more feverishly because Africa is the Land of the Twentieth Century. The world knows something of the gold and diamonds of South Africa, the cocoa of Angola and Nigeria, the rubber and ivory of the Congo, and the palm oil of the West Coast. But does the ordinary citizen realize the extraordinary economic advances of Africa and, too, of black Africa, in recent years? E. T. Morel, who knows his Africa better than most white men, has shown us how the export of palm oil from West Africa has grown from 283 tons in 1800, to 80,000 tons in 1913, which together with by-products is worth today $60,000,000 annually. He shows how native Gold Coast labor, unsupervised, has come to head the cocoa-producing countries of the world with an export of 89,000,000 pounds (weight *not* money) annually. He shows how the cotton crop of Uganda has risen from 3,000 bales in 1909 to 50,000 bales in 1914; and he says that France and Belgium are no more remarkable in the cultivation of their land than the Negro province of Kano. The trade of Abyssinia amounts to only $10,000,000 a year, but it is its infinite possibility of growth that is making the nations crowd to Addis Ababa. All these things are but beginnings; "but tropical Africa and its peoples are being brought more irrevocably each year into the vortex of the economic influences that sway the western world." There can be no doubt of the economic possibilities of

Africa in the near future. There are not only the well-known and traditional products, but boundless chances in a hundred different directions, and above all, there is a throng of human beings who, could they once be reduced to the docility and steadiness of Chinese coolies or of seventeenth- and eighteenth-century European laborers, would furnish to their masters a spoil exceeding the gold-haunted dreams of the most modern of imperialists.

This, then, is the real secret of that desperate struggle for Africa which began in 1877 and is now culminating. Economic dominion outside Africa has, of course, played its part, and we were on the verge of the partition of Asia when Asiatic shrewdness warded it off. America was saved from direct political dominion by the Monroe Doctrine. Thus, more and more, the imperialists have concentrated on Africa.

The greater the concentration the more deadly the rivalry. From Fashoda to Agadir, repeatedly the spark has been applied to the European magazine and a general conflagration narrowly averted. We speak of the Balkans as the storm-center of Europe and the cause of war, but this is mere habit. The Balkans are convenient for occasions, but the ownership of materials and men in the darker world is the real prize that is setting the nations of Europe at each other's throats today.

The present world war is, then, the result of jealousies engendered by the recent rise of armed national associations of labor and capital whose aim is the exploitation of the wealth of the world mainly outside the European circle of nations. These associations, grown jealous and suspicious at the division of the spoils of trade-empire, are fighting to enlarge their respective shares; they look for expansion, not in Europe but in Asia, and particularly in Africa. "We want no inch of French territory," said Germany to England, but Germany was "unable to give" similar assurances as to France in Africa.

The difficulties of this imperial movement are internal as well as external. Successful aggression in economic expansion calls for a close union between capital and labor at home. Now the rising demands of the white laborer, not simply for wages but for conditions of work and a voice in the conduct of industry, make industrial peace difficult. The workingmen have been appeased by all sorts of essays in state socialism, on the one hand, and on the other hand by public threats of competition by colored labor. By threatening to send English capital to China and Mexico, by threatening to hire Negro laborers in America, as well as by old-age pensions and accident insurance, we gain industrial peace at home at the mightier cost of war abroad.

In addition to these national war-engendering jealousies there is a more subtle movement arising from the attempt to unite labor and capital in worldwide free-booting. Democracy in economic organization, while an acknowledged ideal, is today working itself out by admitting to a share in the spoils of capital only the aristocracy of labor—the more intelligent and shrewder and cannier workingmen. The ignorant, unskilled, and restless still form a large, threatening, and, to a growing extent, revolutionary group in advanced countries.

The resultant jealousies and bitter hatreds tend continually to fester along the color line. We must fight the Chinese, the laborer argues, or the Chinese will take our bread and butter. We must keep Negroes in their places, or Negroes will take our jobs. All over the world there leaps to articulate speech and ready action that singular assumption that if white men do not throttle colored men, then China, India, and Africa will do to Europe what Europe has done and seeks to do to them.

On the other hand, in the minds of yellow, brown, and black men the brutal truth is clearing: a white man is privileged to go to any land where advantage beckons and behave as he pleases; the black or colored man is being more and more confined to those parts of the world where life for climatic, historical, economic, and political reasons is most difficult to live and most easily dominated by Europe for Europe's gain.

What, then, are we to do, who desire peace and the civilization of all men? Hitherto the peace movement has confined itself chiefly to figures about the cost of war and platitudes on humanity. What do nations care about the cost of war, if by spending a few hundred millions in steel and gunpowder they can gain a thousand millions in diamonds and cocoa? How can love of humanity appeal as a motive to nations whose love of luxury is built on the inhuman exploitation of human beings, and who, especially in recent years, have been taught to regard these human beings as inhuman? I appealed to the last meeting of peace societies in St. Louis, saying, "Should you not discuss racial prejudice as a prime cause of war?" The secretary was sorry but was unwilling to introduce controversial matters!

We, then, who want peace, must remove the real causes of war. We have extended gradually our conception of democracy beyond our social class to all social classes in our nation; we have gone further and extended our democratic ideals not simply to all classes of our own nation, but to those of other nations of our blood and lineage—to what we call "European" civilization. If we want real peace and lasting culture, however, we must go further. We must extend the democratic ideal to the yellow, brown, and black peoples.

To say this, is to evoke on the faces of modern men a look of blank hopelessness. Impossible! we are told, and for so many reasons—scientific, social, and what not—that argument is useless. But let us not conclude too quickly. Suppose we have to choose between this unspeakably inhuman outrage on decency and intelligence and religion which we call the World War and the attempt to treat black men as human, sentient, responsible beings? We have sold them as cattle. We are working them as beasts of burden. We shall not drive war from this world until we treat them as free and equal citizens in a world democracy of all races and nations. Impossible? Democracy is a method of doing the impossible. It is the only method yet discovered of making the education and development of all men a matter of all men's desperate desire. It is putting firearms in the hands of a child with the object of compelling the child's neighbors to teach him, not only the real and legitimate uses of a dangerous tool but the uses of himself in all things. Are there other and less costly ways of accomplishing this? There may be in some better world. But for a world just emerging from the rough chains of an almost universal poverty, and faced by the temptation of luxury and indulgence through the enslaving of defenseless men, there is but one adequate method of salvation—the giving of democratic weapons of self-defense to the defenseless.

Nor need we quibble over those ideas—wealth, education, and

political power—soil which we have so forested with claim and counterclaim that we see nothing for the woods.

What the primitive peoples of Africa and the world need and must have if war is to be abolished is perfectly clear:—

First: land. Today Africa is being enslaved by the theft of her land and natural resources. A century ago black men owned all but a morsel of South Africa. The Dutch and England came, and today 1,250,000 white own 264,000,000 acres, leaving only 21,000,000 acres for 4,500,000 natives. Finally, to make assurance doubly sure, the Union of South Africa has refused natives even the right to *buy* land. This is a deliberate attempt to force the Negroes to work on farms and in mines and kitchens for low wages. All over Africa has gone this shameless monopolizing of land and natural resources to force poverty on the masses and reduce them to the "dumb-driven-cattle" stage of labor activity.

Secondly: we must train native races in modern civilization. This can be done. Modern methods of educating children, honestly and effectively applied, would make modern, civilized nations out of the vast majority of human beings on earth today. This we have seldom tried. For the most part Europe is straining every nerve to make over yellow, brown, and black men into docile beasts of burden, and only an irrepressible few are allowed to escape and seek (usually abroad) the education of modern men.

Lastly, the principle of home rule must extend to groups, nations, and races. The ruling of one people for another people's whim or gain must stop. This kind of despotism has been in later days more and more skillfully disguised. But the brute fact remains: the white man is ruling black Africa for the white man's gain, and just as far as possible he is doing the same to colored races elsewhere. Can such a situation bring peace? Will any amount of European concord or disarmament settle this injustice?

Political power today is but the weapon to force economic power. Tomorrow, it may give us spiritual vision and artistic sensibility. Today, it gives us or tries to give us bread and butter, and those classes or nations or races who are without it starve, and starvation is the weapon of the white world to reduce them to slavery.

We are calling for European concord today; but at the utmost European concord will mean satisfaction with, or acquiescence in, a given division of the spoils of world dominion. After all, European disarmament cannot go below the necessity of defending the aggressions of the whites against the blacks and browns and yellows. From this will arise three perpetual dangers of war. First, renewed jealousy at any division of colonies or spheres of influence agreed upon, if at any future time the present division comes to seem unfair. Who cared for Africa in the early nineteenth century? Let England have the scraps left from the golden feast of the slave trade. But in the twentieth century? The end was war. These scraps looked too tempting to Germany. Secondly, war will come from the revolutionary revolt of the lowest workers. The greater the international jealousies, the greater the corresponding costs of armament and the more difficult to fulfill the promises of industrial democracy in advanced countries. Finally, the colored peoples will not always submit passively to foreign domination. To some this is a lightly tossed truism. When a people deserve liberty they fight for it and get it, say such philosophers; thus making war a regular, necessary step to liberty. Colored people are familiar with this complacent judgment. They endure the contemptuous treatment meted out by whites to those not "strong" enough to be free. These nations and races, composing as they do a vast majority of humanity, are going to endure this treatment just as long as they must and not a moment longer. Then they are going to fight and the War of the Color Line will outdo in savage inhumanity any war this world has yet seen. For colored folk have much to remember and they will not forget.

But is this inevitable? Must we sit helpless before this awful prospect? While we are planning, as a result of the present holocaust, the disarmament of Europe and a European international world-police, must the rest of the world be left naked to the inevitable horror of war, especially when we know that it is directly in this outer circle of races, and not in the inner European household, that the real causes of present European fighting are to be found?

Our duty is clear. Racial slander must go. Racial prejudice will follow. Steadfast faith in humanity must come. The domination of one people by another without the other's consent, be the subject people black or white, must stop. The doctrine of forcible economic expansion over subject peoples must go. Religious hypocrisy must stop. "Bloodthirsty" Mwanga of Uganda killed an English bishop because they feared that his coming meant English domination. It did mean English domination, and the world and the bishop knew it, and yet the world was "horrified!" Such missionary hypocrisy must go. With clean hands and honest hearts we must front high Heaven and beg peace in our time.

In this great work who can help us? In the Orient, the awakened Japanese and the awakening leaders of New China; in India and Egypt, the young men trained in Europe and European ideals, who now form the stuff that revolution is born of. But in Africa? Who better than the twenty-five million grandchildren of the European slave trade, spread through the Americas and now writhing desperately for freedom and a place in the world? And of these millions first of all the ten million black folk of the United States, now a problem, then a world salvation.

Twenty centuries before the Christ a great cloud swept over sea and settled on Africa, darkening and well-nigh blotting out the culture of the land of Egypt. For half a thousand years it rested there until a black woman, Queen Nefertari, "the most venerated figure in Egyptian history," rose to the throne of the Pharaohs and redeemed the world and her people. Twenty centuries after Christ, black Africa, prostrate, raped, and shamed, lies at the feet of the conquering Philistines of Europe. Beyond the awful sea a black woman is weeping and waiting with her sons on her breast. What shall the end be? The world-old and fearful things, War and Wealth, Murder and Luxury? Or shall it be a new thing—a new peace and new democracy of all races: a great humanity of equal men? "Semper novi quid ex Africa!"

Selected poems

FOREWORD

We have here the eloquent expressions of a sensitive fighter poet who for three-quarters of a century struggled against the waves of oppression, misery, and woe which engulfed his people. There is evidence of bitterness and bewilderment and frustration in these lines, but there is also understanding, hope, vision, and irresistible pride of race.

Above all this, is the indomitable spirit of W. E. B. Du Bois, who was glad of the opportunity to spend the evening of his day working in free and independent Ghana to advance the dignity of his race.

KWAME NKRUMAH

EXPOSITION

This group of poems will come as a surprise to the present generation of African writers. They are apt to think of Du Bois as a legendary figure: the "Father of Pan-Africanism," the militant organizer in the struggle for justice, equality, and dignity, a pioneer sociologist and economist, one of the earliest prophets and exponents of socialism, the intellectual giant among Afro-Americans.

Before the words *negritude* or *Negrismo* were coined, Du Bois was singing:

> I am the Smoke King.
> I am black.
> I am darkening with song,
> I am hearkening to wrong;
> I will be black as blackness can,
> The blacker the mantle the mightier the man.

But Du Bois wrote in awful isolation; an isolation at first imposed because of his color and later wholeheartedly embraced. Before the end of the nineteenth century, having acquired the best of the white world's education—Harvard University in the United States and the University of Berlin in Germany—Du Bois knew the fallacy of that education unless he discovered for himself the world of black men. By 1895 he had written his resolution to use that education for one purpose—to liberate his people. In his Forethought to *The Souls of Black Folk,* published in 1903, he writes:

> Leaving then, the white world, I have slipped within the Veil, raising it that you may view faintly its deeper recesses, the passion of its human sorrow, the struggle of its greater souls. . . . I, who speak here am bone of the bone and flesh of the flesh of them that live within the Veil.

Du Bois followed no school of writing nor did he bring into being a movement among writers. Much later Claude McKay, Countee Cullen, and the early Langston Hughes all acknowledge their debt to Du Bois, yet they speak more specifically of his ideas, ideals, and vision than of his style in writing. For Du Bois' style is always highly personal and is neither constant nor consistent. Prose and verse flow and blend until frequently they become indistinguishable. His lines are often complex and unconventional. His words well up out of the turbulent waters in which he struggles.

Eugene O'Neill wrote of him:

> Ranking as he does among the foremost writers of true importance in this country, one selfishly wishes sometimes (as a writer oneself) that he could devote all his time to the accomplishment of that fine and moving prose which distinguishes his books. But at the same time one realizes, self-reproachfully, that with Dr. Du Bois it is a cause—an ideal—that overcomes the personal egoism of the artist.

His poems, therefore, are not written as lyrical entities, but they must be seen as passionate outcries which demand the beat of rhythm, the cadence of song, and the flow of deep waters. He demands justice from God and from man, moving in time from the humble petitioner who implores God to the confident adult who, shouldering his responsibilities says: "Courage, God! I come!" He was a poet in exile. "I was a little boy, at home with strangers," he begins his "Ghana Calls" and one hears the mournful longing in the rich, somber melody of his "Riddle of the Sphinx:"

> Dark daughter of the lotus leaves that watch the Southern sea,
> Wan spirit of a prisoned soul a-panting to be free!

But very often he employs the scornful whiplash. His fist beats a hard, staccato of protest in:

> I hate them, Oh!
> I hate them well,
> I hate them, Christ,
> As I hate hell!
> If I were God,
> I'd sound their knell
> This day!

I hesitated to include "A Litany at Atlanta" in this collection. It was written on scraps of paper in a "Jim Crow" car on a train, by an anxious father, hurrying back to his family in Atlanta, Georgia, where one of the worst race riots ever experienced in America was sweeping over the city. It is a prayer of agony, bewilderment, and pain. Perhaps it is not a poem. But these lines, written in 1901, have been published and republished in more languages and in more parts of the world than anything else Du Bois has written during his fruitful lifetime. It would be missed.

The University of Ghana planned this publication of the first selected collection of his poems as a tribute to him in the evening of his life. He was deeply appreciative and enjoyed going over the manuscript as I typed up pages. It was his idea that the date when each poem was published should be noted. He commented whimsically. "Over the long span of years I have changed my mind many times, but truth remains the same."

Night fell for him. But his pursuit of truth remains with us—unchanged.

SHIRLEY GRAHAM

WAR

Hail and Hail again
Uncounted Dead of all the Wars of all the World!
Outnumbering the living
Millions to one.
Hail and farewell!

Brood of blood-clotted babies
Birthed in bitter pain,
Sired of Old Man Murder,
Mothered by the harlot, Gain!
Nursed in the crippled brains of senile Senators
On the mined gold of venal Congressmen.
Trained by Generals, tricked in tawdry tinsel,
Singing to martial music, trumpeting to drum:
March, March, Robots, March!
Kill, kill, ever kill!
  Come Deaf, Blind, Dumb!
  Die, die, always die!
  Rot, rot, ta-ra-ra- rot!

Scream, O silent Dead,
Into whose sad and sightless faces
I stand and stare.
I feel what you felt
When Assyria quenched the first fine flame of Egypt;
I see what you saw when Greeks buried Greece beneath the Parthenon;
I hear what you heard when Rome tore down her towers and fell her endless fall.
I know what you know as America murders Asia
As Africa is pain and shame
And Europe rushes down to Hell
Shrieking with candle, book, and bell.
I weep the tears you can no longer weep
For you are dead and Death is black
And I am black

And Blacks are red with all the blood
That Whites have shed.
If cowards die let brave men live
To face the sky.
Let all be one and one vast will
Cry: Stop, Halt, Hold!
Awake O Witless, drear and dread
Awake O Mothers of the dead
Save the World!

Save the children and their dreams
Save the color and the sound
Save the form of faiths unfound

Save Civilization, soul and sod,
Save the tattered shreds of God!
War is murder, murder hate
And suicide, stupidity
Incorporate.

In Battle for Peace, 1952

THE SONG OF THE SMOKE

I am the smoke king,
I am black.
I am swinging in the sky.
I am ringing worlds on high:
I am the thought of the throbbing mills,
I am the soul of the soul toil kills,
I am the ripple of trading rills,

Up I'm curling from the sod,
I am whirling home to God.
I am the smoke king,
I am black.

I am the smoke king,
I am black.
I am wreathing broken hearts,
I am sheathing devils' darts;
Dark inspiration of iron times,
Wedding the toil of toiling climes
Shedding the blood of bloodless crimes,

Down I lower in the blue,
Up I tower toward the true,
I am the smoke king,
I am black.

I am the smoke king,
I am black.

I am darkening with song,
I am hearkening to wrong;
I will be black as blackness can,
The blacker the mantle the mightier the man,
My purpl'ing midnights no day dawn may ban.
I am carving God in night,
I am painting hell in white.

I am the smoke king,
I am black.

I am the smoke king,
I am black.

I am cursing ruddy morn,
I am nursing hearts unborn;
Souls unto me are as mists in the night,
I whiten my blackmen, I beckon my white,
What's the hue of a hide to a man in his might!
Hail, then, grilly, grimy hands,

Sweet Christ, pity toiling lands!
Hail to the smoke king,
Hail to the black!

The Horizon, 1899

A LITANY AT ATLANTA

O Silent God, Thou whose voice afar in mist and mystery hath left our ears an-hungered in these fearful days—

Hear us, good Lord;

Listen to us, Thy children: our faces dark with doubt are made a mockery in Thy Sanctuary. With uplifted hands we front Thy Heaven, O God, crying:

We beseech Thee to hear us, good Lord;

We are not better than our fellows, Lord; we are but weak and human men. When our devils do deviltry, curse Thou the doer and the deed—curse them as we curse them, do to them all and more than ever they have done to innocence and weakness, to womanhood and home.

Have mercy upon us, miserable sinners;

And yet, whose is the deeper guilt? Who made these devils? Who nursed them in crime and fed them on injustice? Who ravished and debauched their mothers and their grandmothers? Who bought and sold their crime and waxed fat and rich on public iniquity?

Knowest, good God!

Is this Thy Justice, O Father, that guile be easier than innocence and the innocent be crucified for the guilt of the untouched guilty?

Justice, O Judge of men;

Wherefore do we pray? Is not the God of the Fathers dead? Have not seers seen in Heaven's halls Thine hearsed and lifeless form stark amidst the black and rolling smoke of sin, where all along bow bitter forms of endless dead?

Awake, Thou that sleepest!

Thou are not dead, but flown afar, up hills of endless light through blazing corridors of suns, where worlds do swing of good and gentle men, of women strong and free—far from the cozenage, black hypocrisy, and chaste prostitution of this shameful speck of dust!

Turn again, O Lord; leave us not to perish in our sin!

From lust of body and lust of blood,—

Great God, deliver us!

From lust of power and lust of gold,—

Great God, deliver us!

From the leagued lying of despot and of brute,—
Great God, deliver us!

A city lay in travail, God our Lord, and from her loins sprang twin Murder and Black Hate. Red was the midnight; clang, crack, and cry of death and fury filled the air and trembled underneath the stars where church spires pointed silently to Thee. And all this was to sate the greed of greedy men who hide behind the veil of vengeance.

Bend us Thine ear, O Lord!

In the pale, still morning we looked upon the dead. We stopped our ears and held our leaping hands, but they—did they not wag their heads and leer and cry with bloody jaws: *Cease from Crime!* The word was mockery, for thus they train a hundred crimes while we do cure one.

Turn again our captivity, O Lord!

Behold this maimed and broken thing, dear God; it was an humble black man, who toiled and sweat to save a bit from the pittance paid him. They told him: *Work and Rise.* He worked. Did this man sin? Nay, but someone told how someone said another did—one whom he had never seen nor known. Yet for that man's crime this man lieth maimed and murdered, his wife naked to shame, his children to poverty and evil.

Hear us, O heavenly Father!

Doth not this justice of hell stink in Thy nostrils, O God? How long shall the mounting flood of innocent blood roar in Thine ears and pound in our hearts for vengeance? Pile the pale frenzy of blood-crazed brutes, who do such deeds, high on Thine Altar, Jehovah Jirah, and burn it in hell forever and forever!

Forgive us, good Lord; we know not what we say!

Bewildered we are and passion-tossed, mad with the madness of a mobbed and mocked and murdered people; straining at the arm-posts of Thy throne, we raise our shackled hands and charge Thee, God, by the bones of our stolen fathers, by the tears of our dead mothers, by the very blood of Thy crucified Christ: What meaneth this? Tell us the plan; give us the sign!

Keep not Thou silent, O God!

Sit not longer blind, Lord God, deaf to our prayer and dumb to our dumb suffering. Surely Thou, too, art not white, O Lord, a pale, bloodless, heartless thing!

Ah, Christ of all the Pities!

Forgive the thought! Forgive these wild, blasphemous words. Thou art still the God of our black fathers and in Thy Soul's Soul sit some soft darkenings of the evening, some shadowings of the velvet night.

But whisper—speak—call, great God, for Thy silence is white terror to our hearts! The way, O God, show us the way and point us the path!

Whither? North is greed and South is blood; within the coward, and without the liar. Whither? To death?

Amen, Welcome, dark sleep!

Whither? To life? But not this life, dear God, not this. Let the cup pass from us, tempt us not beyond our strength, for there is that clamoring and clawing within, to whose voice we would not listen, yet shudder lest we might—and it is red. Ah! God! It is red and awful shape.

Selah!

In yonder East trembles a star.

Vengeance is Mine; I will repay, saith the Lord!

Thy Will, O Lord, be done!

Kyrie Eleison!

Lord, we have done these pleading, wavering words,

We beseech Thee to hear us, good Lord!

We bow our heads and hearken soft to the sobbing of women and little children,

We beseech Thee to hear us, good Lord!

Our voices sink in silence and in night.

Hear us, good Lord,

In night, O God of a godless land!

Amen!

In silence, O Silent God.

Selah!

SUEZ

Young Egypt rose and seized her ditch
And said: "What's mine is mine!"
Old Europe sneered and cried: "The bitch
Must learn again to whine!"

The British lion up and roared
But used his nether end
Which raised a stink and made men shrink
As world peace seemed to rend.

Dull Dulles rushed about the world,
His pockets full of gold.
Ike sadly left his game of golf
And talked as he was told:

"Lord God! Send Peace and Plenty down
And keep on drafting men.
Send billions east and so at least
No income tax shall end."

Adlai essays with polished phrase
To say the same thing less
And prove without a shade of doubt
Both parties made this mess.

The campaign's done and Ike has won,
We spent ten millions for the fun.
Meantime it would be well to note
How many million did not vote.

Young Israel raised a mighty cry:
"Shall Pharaoh ride anew?"
But Nasser grimly pointed West,
"They mixed this witches' brew!"

Big Three are shouting long and loud;
United Nations boil;
Big Business raves: "Drop on these waves
A million tons of oil!"

With whites withdrawn, the traffic runs
As it has run before.
But white folk fumed and pointed out
Red pilots from the shore.

Old Britain would be great again
With war on Earth, bad will to men!
But France would civilize the dead
And make the black Sahara red.

Greed splits the West and hatreds swell
To rebuild race and color pride,
Where Moses and Mohammed died
And Jesus Christ was crucified.

Israel as the West betrays
Its murdered, mocked, and damned,
Becomes the shock troops of two knaves
Who steal the dark man's land.

Beware, white world, that great black hand
Which Nasser's power waves
Grasps hard the concentrated hate
Of myriad million slaves.

The Soviets in blood and tears
Have made their socialism strong
The West quite frantic in its fears
Has tried to stamp it to the ground.

This cannot be, it's but the sight
Of private capital's said plight.
Fear makes America feel free
To buy revolt in Hungary.

For eastward trumpets sing the song,
The rising sun calls loud and long.
All Africa lifts high its head,
And sees all Asia burning Red!

Mainstream, December, 1956

GHANA CALLS

TO OSAGYEFO KWAME NKRUMAH

I was a little boy, at home with strangers.
I liked my playmates, and knew well,
Whence all their parents came;
From England, Scotland, royal France
From Germany and oft by chance
The humble Emerald Isle.

But my brown skin and close-curled hair
Was alien, and how it grew, none knew:
Few tried to say, some dropped a wondering word or stray;
Some laughed and stared.

And then it came: I dreamed.
I placed together all I knew
All hints and slurs together drew.
I dreamed.

I made one picture of what nothing seemed
I shuddered in dumb terror
In silence screamed,
For now it seemed this I had dreamed;

How up from Hell, a land had leaped
A wretched land, all scorched and seamed
Covered with ashes, chained with pain
Streaming with blood, in horror lain
Its very air a shriek of death
And agony of hurt.

Anon I woke, but in one corner of my soul
I stayed asleep.
Forget I could not,
But never would I remember

That hell-hoist ghost
Of slavery and woe.

I lived and grew, I worked and hoped
I planned and wandered, gripped and coped
With every doubt but one that slept
Yet clamored to awaken.

I became old; old, worn and gray;
Along my hard and weary way
Rolled war and pestilence, war again;
I looked on Poverty and foul Disease
I walked with Death and yet I knew
There stirred a doubt: Were all dreams true?
And what in truth was Africa?

One cloud-swept day a Seer appeared,
All closed and veiled as me he hailed
And bid me make three journeys to the world
Seeking all through their lengthened links
The endless Riddle of the Sphinx.

I went to Moscow; Ignorance grown wise taught me Wisdom;
I went to Peking: Poverty grown rich
Showed me the wealth of Work
I came to Accra.

Here at last, I looked back on my Dream;
I heard the Voice that loosed
The Long-locked dungeons of my soul
I sensed that Africa had come
Not up from Hell, but from the sum of Heaven's glory.

I lifted up mine eyes to Ghana
And swept the hills with high Hosanna
Above the sun my sight took flight
Till from that pinnacle of light

I saw dropped down this earth of crimson, green and gold
Roaring with color, drums and song.

Happy with dreams and deeds worth more than doing
Around me velvet faces loomed
Burnt by the kiss of everlasting suns
Under great stars of midnight glory
Trees danced, and foliage sang;

The lilies hallelujah rang
Where robed with rule on Golden Stool
The gold-crowned Priests with duty done
Pour high libations to the sun
And danced to gods.

Red blood flowed rare 'neath close-clung hair
While subtle perfume filled the air
And whirls and whirls of tiny curls
Crowned heads.

Yet Ghana shows its might and power
Not in its color nor its flower
But in its wondrous breadth of soul
Its Joy of Life
Its selfless role
Of giving.

School and clinic, home and hall
Road and garden bloom and call
Socialism blossoms bold
On Communism centuries old.

I lifted my last voice and cried
I cried to heaven as I died:
O turn me to the Golden Horde
Summon all western nations
Toward the Rising Sun.

From reeking West whose day is done,
  Who stink and stagger in their dung
  Toward Africa, China, India's strand
  Where Kenya and Himalaya stand
  And Nile and Yang-tze roll:
  Turn every yearning face of man.

Come with us, dark America:
  The scum of Europe battened here
  And drowned a dream
  Made fetid swamp a refuge seem:

Enslaved the Black and killed the Red
  And armed the Rich to loot the Dead;
  Worshipped the whores of Hollywood
  Where once the Virgin Mary stood
  and lynched the Christ.

Awake, awake, O sleeping world
  Honor the sun;
  Worship the stars, those vaster suns
  Who rule the night
  Where black is bright
  And all unselfish work is right
  And Greed is sin.

And Africa leads on
  Pan Africa!

Freedomways, Winter, 1962

ALMIGHTY DEATH

Softly, quite softly—
For I hear, above the murmur of the sea,
Faint and far-fallen footsteps, as of One
Who comes from out beyond the endless ends of Time,
With voice that downward looms thro' singing stars;
Its subtle sound I see thro' these long-darkened eyes,
I hear the light He bringeth on his hands—
Almighty Death!
Softly, oh, softly, lest He pass me by,
And that unquivering Light toward which my Longing soul
And tortured body through these years have writhed,
Fade to the dun darkness of my days.

Softly, full softly, let me rise and greet
The strong, low luting of that long-awaited call;
Swiftly be all my good and going gone,
And this vast veil and vanquished vigor of my soul
Seek somehow otherwhere its rest and goal,
Where endless spaces stretch,
Where endless time doth moan,
Where endless light doth pour
Thro' the black kingdoms of eternal death.

Then haply I may see what things I have not seen,
Then I may know what things I have not known;
Then may I do my dreams.
Farewell! No sound of idle mourning let there be
To shudder this full silence—save the voice
Of children—little children, white and black,
Whispering the deeds I tried to do for them;
While I at last unguided and alone
Pass softly, full softly.

The Crisis, November, 1911

Letter to Gus Hall

To Gus Hall,
Communist Party of the U.S.A.
New York, New York.

On this first day of October, 1961, I am applying for admission to membership in the Communist Party of the United States. I have been long and slow in coming to this conclusion, but at last my mind is settled.

In college I heard the name of Karl Marx, but read none of his works, nor heard them explained. At the University of Berlin, I heard much of those thinkers who had definitively answered the theories of Marx, but again we did not study what Marx himself had said. Nevertheless, I attended meetings of the Socialist Party and considered myself a socialist.

On my return to America, I taught and studied for sixteen years. I explored the theory of socialism and studied the organized social life of American Negroes; but still I neither read or heard much of Marxism. Then I came to New York as an official of the new NAACP and editor of *The Crisis* Magazine. The NAACP was capitalist-oriented and expected support from rich philanthropists.

But it had a strong socialist element in its leadership in persons like Mary Ovington, William English Walling, and Charles Edward Russell. Following their advice, I joined the Socialist Party in 1911. I knew then nothing of practical socialist politics and in the campaign of 1912, I found myself unwilling to vote the Socialist ticket, but advised Negroes to vote for Wilson. This was contrary to Socialist Party rules and consequently I resigned from the Socialist Party.

For the next twenty years I tried to develop a political way of life for myself and my people. I attacked the Democrats and Republicans for monopoly and disfranchisement of Negroes; I attacked the Socialists for trying to segregate Southern Negro members; I praised the racial attitudes of the Communists, but opposed their tactics in the case of the Scottsboro boys and their advocacy of a Negro state. At the same time I began to study Karl Marx and the communists; I read *Das Kapital* and other communist literature; I hailed the Russian Revolution of 1917, but was puzzled at the contradictory news from Russia.

Finally in 1926, I began a new effort: I visited communist lands. I went to the Soviet Union in 1926, 1936, 1949, and 1959; I saw the nation develop. I visited East Germany, Czechoslovakia, and Poland. I spent ten weeks in China, traveling all over the land. Then, this summer, I rested a month in Rumania.

I was early convinced that socialism was an excellent way of life, but I thought it might be reached by various methods. For Russia I was convinced she had chosen the only way open to her at the time. I saw Scandinavia choosing a different method, half-way between socialism and capitalism. In the United States I saw Consumers Cooperation as a path from capitalism to socialism, while England, France, and Germany developed in the same direction in their own way. After the depression and the Second World War, I was disillusioned. The Progressive movement in the United States failed. The cold war started. Capitalism called communism a crime.

Today I have reached a firm conclusion:

Capitalism cannot reform itself; it is doomed to self-destruction. No universal selfishness can bring social good to all.

Communism—the effort to give all men what they need and to ask of each the best they can contribute—this is the only way of human life. It is a difficult and hard end to reach—it has and will make mistakes, but today it marches triumphantly on in education and science, in home and food, with increased freedom of thought and deliverance from dogma. In the end communism will triumph. I want to help to bring that day.

The path of the American Communist Party is clear: It will provide the United States with a real Third Party and thus restore democracy to this land. It will call for:

1. Public ownership of natural resources and of all capital.
2. Public control of transportation and communications.

3. Abolition of poverty and limitation of personal income.
4. No exploitation of labor.
5. Social medicine, with hospitalization and care of the old.
6. Free education for all.
7. Training for jobs and jobs for all.
8. Discipline for growth and reform.
9. Freedom under law.
10. No dogmatic religion.

These aims are not crimes. They are practiced increasingly over the world. No nation can call itself free which does not allow its citizens to work for these ends.

W. E. B. DU BOIS

GUS HALL'S REPLY

Dear Dr. Du Bois:

In reply to your letter of October 1st in which you made application for membership in the Communist Party of the United States allow me to relate the following:

I read it before our National Board on October 13th, where it was greeted with the highest enthusiasm and responded to with many heartfelt testimonials to the titanic labors which you have performed over a glorious span of sixty years of dedicated services and leadership in the cause of human progress, peace, science, and culture.

Already in 1906 in your historic Address to the Country of the Niagara Movement, you had perceived the main line of development of our century, and wrote these prophetic words:

"The morning breaks over the hills. Courage, brothers! The battle for humanity is not lost or losing. The Slav is rising in his might, the yellow minions are testing liberty, the black Africans are writhing toward the light, and everywhere the laborer is opening the gates of Opportunity and Peace."

And so it has come, and is coming to pass. And knowledgeable people everywhere are mindful of the fact that your selfless labors and mighty works have been a powerful contribution to the dawn of our new epoch, the epoch of the final triumph of man over all manner of oppression, discrimination and exploitation.

You (the first Negro to receive the Doctor of Philosophy degree from Harvard University, in 1895) are the acknowledged Dean of American letters and most eminent living American scholar.

As editor, sociologist, historian, novelist, poet, publicist, lecturer, and organizer, you have made enduring contributions. Your life is a monumental example of achievement for all Americans.

For fifty years you have been a tireless champion of the national liberation of the African peoples and new Africa's wise counselor and "elder statesman."

For more than sixty years you have been the foremost philosopher, theoretician, and practical organizer of the glorious Negro people's freedom struggle.

You have authored numerous books, each of which is a weapon against colonialism, racism, and imperialism, and for the victory of the cause of peace, freedom, and the brotherhood of peoples.

You have raised your voice powerfully and incessantly against war machinations, for world peace and disarmament, for friendship with the socialist countries and coexistence between the two world social systems.

Your act of joining the Communist Party at this time not only expresses that recognition of the new world reality, of the great turn of the people of the world toward socialism for the solution of mankind's need for peace, brotherhood, and well-being, but it constitutes an invitation and a challenge to men and women of science and culture, to creative thinkers of all countries, to the Negro masses and their outstanding leaders both here and abroad, to avail themselves of the social science of Marxism-Leninism and the fraternity of the Communist Parties to give new wings to their cause and their works.

You have chosen to join our Party precisely at the time when with brazen effrontery to the trends of the times, the most backward ultrareactionary forces in our country's national life have temporarily dragooned the Supreme Court's majority into upholding the most flagrantly unconstitutional thought-control laws

—the McCarran Act and Smith Act, designed to muzzle free speech, ban freedom of association, persecute Communists, and suppress our Party.

This is symbolic of the personal courage and heroic exercise of social responsibility which have characterized your service and leadership to the people's cause throughout your long life.

In joining the Communist Party, you have made that association which was clearly indicated by the very logic of your life.

Dear Dr. Du Bois, welcome into the membership of our Party! The title of Party Member is an honorable and worthy title worn with pride by the most dedicated and farseeing, the best sons and daughters of the workers and peoples of all lands in the first ranks of struggle for mankind's happy future.

With comradely greetings,
Gus Hall

A selected bibliography of the published writings of W. E. B. Du Bois

ERNEST KAISER

INTRODUCTION

Graduate students in the field of library science have compiled bibliographies of the works of Langston Hughes, Countee Cullen, and James Weldon Johnson as their theses projects. Copies of these theses are in the Schomburg Collection in New York City. The Fisk University Library staff published a bibliography of Charles S. Johnson's writings in 1947 and a much more definitive bibliography of Johnson's published writings by George L. Gardiner of the Fisk University staff in 1960. The Student Council of the College of Liberal Arts, Howard University, brought out a bibliography of E. Franklin Frazier's works just before his death in 1962. The Graduate School at Howard University published a pretty good bibliography of the writings of Alain Locke in *The New Negro: Thirty Years Afterward* (1955) after Locke's death in 1954.

M. D. Sprague's early "Richard Wright, a Bibliography" appeared in *Bulletin of Bibliography* for September–December 1953. Michel Fabre and Edward Margolies published a valuable, comprehensive bibliography of Richard Wright in *Bulletin of Bibliography and Magazine Notes* (January–April 1965). This has been reprinted in Constance Webb's *Richard Wright: A Biography* (1968) and in *Negro Digest* (January 1969). There is a "Selected Bibliography" in Robert Bone's *Richard Wright* (1969) in the University of Minnesota Pamphlets on American Writers series, the first black writer to be included in this series of almost 100 American creative writers and critics. (The Columbia University Essays on Modern Writers series has yet to include a black writer.) Jackson R. Bryor's 14-page "Richard Wright: A Selected

Checklist of Criticism" was also published in *Wisconsin Studies in Contemporary Literature* (Fall 1960).

The *Bulletin of Bibliography* carried two listings of James Baldwin's writings in the 1960s. Paul Laurence Dunbar bibliographies can be found in the *Bibliography of American Literature* (1957) and in biographies of Dunbar by Benjamin Brawley and Virginia Cunningham. The District of Columbia Historical Records Survey published a *Calendar of the Writings of Frederick Douglass* in 1940 when the Douglass papers were in the Frederick Douglass Memorial Home, Anacostia, D.C. They are now stored by the National Park Service in Washington and are in danger of destruction. Philip S. Foner's four volumes of *The Life and Writings of Frederick Douglass* are a fairly definitive listing of Douglass' work. Jessie P. Guzman, then of the Tuskegee Institute Department of Records and Research, published a classified bibliography of George Washington Carver in 1953. Daniel T. Williams, Coordinator of the Departmental Libraries and Tuskegee Archives on Negro Life and History, brought out *The Perilous Road of Marcus M. Garvey: A Bibliography* in 1969. Kraus Reprint Company will soon publish *Eight Negro Bibliographies* edited by Williams and prepared over the years by the Tuskegee Institute Library and Research staff. These are on Garvey, lynchings (with data), B. T. Washington, M. L. King, Jr., the Black Muslims, James H. Meredith and the University of Mississippi, the southern students' protest movement and the freedom rides. Richard Newman compiled in August 1969 the 20-page *Black Power: A Bibliography* for Boston University and Community Change, Inc. There are also E. Kaiser's "Recent Literature on Black Liberation Struggles and the Ghetto Crisis: A Bibliographical Survey" (*Science and Society,* Spring 1969) and his "The Literature of Harlem" in *Harlem: A Community in Transition* (1964) edited by John H. Clarke. Also Jean B. Hutson's "Harlem: A Cultural History: Selected Bibliography" (*The Metropolitan Museum of Art Bulletin,* January 1969).

Langston Hughes' long, 45-year writing career is second only to that of Du Bois, and his bibliography is also second in length only to the writings of Du Bois. Hughes' works are covered in Thermon B. O'Daniel's "A Langston Hughes Bibliography" (*CLA*

Bulletin, Vol. VII, No. 2, 1951); in the five-page, selected bibliography of material by and about Hughes in James A. Emanuel's book *Langston Hughes* (1967) in Twayne's United States Authors Series; in Ernest Kaiser's "Selected Bibliography of the Published Writings of Langston Hughes" (*Freedomways,* Spring 1968); and in Donald C. Dickinson's book *A Bio-bibliography of Langston Hughes, 1902–1967* (1967). Emanuel's book on Hughes and Harold R. Collins' book on the African writer *Amos Tutuola* (1969) in Twayne's World Authors Series are the only books on Black American, Black Caribbean, or African writers in these two series that include more than 100 writers. There are rumors that Claude McKay and one other black writer are being considered for inclusion in the series. Oxford University Press has recently started a college series of short biographies of outstanding black Africans and Afro-Americans under the editorship of Hollis R. Lynch, a black historian.

But while many magazine articles, chapters in books, bachelor and master's theses, and two full-length biographies or studies of his work (doctoral dissertations) have been written or published about the towering intellectual W. E. B. Du Bois, no one, until quite recently, has attempted the mammoth job of compiling a bibliography of the voluminous writings of this man which extend over a period of 75 to 80 years. Elliott M. Rudwick's seven-page listing of the Du Bois works which he consulted in the writing of his book *W. E. B. Du Bois: A Study in Minority Group Leadership* (1960, 1968) was a beginning. The tremendous work of Paul Partington of Whittier, California, in attempting, in the early 1960s, a complete bibliography of Du Bois came next. There are some inevitable omissions in this great and pioneering project, and Herbert Aptheker is attempting with help to complete this work for publication as a definitive bibliography of Du Bois. Aptheker is also preparing several volumes of Du Bois' letters and papers for publication by two publishing houses.

Finally, the Padmore Research Library on African Affairs in Accra, Ghana, published as No. 4 (April 1964) in its bibliography series, *Dr. W. E. B. Du Bois, 1868–1963: A Bibliography.* This bibliography is marred by many unavoidable errors since the work was done in Ghana away from most of the Du Bois writings. But this first widely published, 45-page Du Bois bibliography is important, containing books and pamphlets written by him, books and magazines edited or written in part, magazine articles by Du Bois, and in addition, books and magazine articles about Du Bois.

The selected bibliography which follows has benefited from the research of these bibliographers and scholars who have already dug up and studied the Du Bois material. It has also gone a little beyond them to include some new things. It includes the many current reprints of old, hard-to-find books by Du Bois. The writings are arranged chronologically, as in the Partington and Padmore Research Library bibliographies, to show the development, changes, or consistency in Du Bois' thinking. They do not include, among other things, his weekly newspaper columns in the *New York Amsterdam News* and the *Pittsburgh Courier* in the 1930s and in the *People's Voice* in the 1940s or his series of articles on Africa in the *Chicago Defender* in 1945.

BOOKS, PAMPHLETS, AND MAGAZINES (FOUNDED AND EDITED BY HIM)

1. *The Suppression of the African Slave Trade to the United States of America, 1638–1870* (Harvard Historical Series, I). New York: Longmans, Green and Co., 1896; 335 pp. New York: Social Science Press, 1954; 339 pp. New York: Russell and Russell (Atheneum Press), 1965. New York: Schocken Books, 1969; 335 pp. Baton Rouge: Louisiana State University Press, 1970; 335 pp.
2. *The Conservation of Races* (American Negro Academy, Occasional Papers, II). Washington, D.C.: The Academy, 1897; 15 pp. In *Occasional Papers of the American Negro Academy,* Nos. 1–22. New York: Arno Press, 1970.
3. *The Philadelphia Negro: A Social Study.* Together with a special report on domestic service by Isabel Eaton (Publications of the University of Pennsylvania, Series in Political Economy and Public Law, 45). Philadelphia: published for the University of Pennsylvania, 1899; 520 pp. New York: Schocken Books, 1967; xliv; 520 pp.
4. *A Memorial to the Legislature of Georgia on the Hardwick Bill* by Du Bois and others. A printed folder, 1899. In the Du Bois papers. (Against the Disfranchisement Bill.)

5. Atlanta University Studies on the American Negro:
   a. *Social and Physical Condition of Negroes in Cities* (Atlanta University Publications, II). Atlanta, Ga.: Atlanta University Press, 1897; 72, 14 pp.
   b. *Some Efforts of American Negroes for Their Own Social Betterment.* Atlanta, Ga.: Atlanta University Press, 1898; 66 pp.
   c. *The Negro in Business.* Atlanta, Ga.: Atlanta University Press, 1899; 77 pp.
   d. *The College-Bred Negro* (Atlanta University Publications, V). Atlanta, Ga.: Atlanta University Press, 1900; 115 pp. Second edition, 1902; 32 pp.
   e. *A Select Bibliography of the American Negro: for General Readers.* Atlanta, Ga.: Atlanta University Press, 1901; 11 pp.
   f. *The Negro Common School* (Atlanta University Publications, VI). Atlanta, Ga.: Atlanta University Press, 1901; 120 pp.
   g. *The Negro Artisan* (Atlanta University Publications, VII). Atlanta, Ga.: Atlanta University Press, 1902; 192 pp.
   h. *The Negro Church* (Atlanta University Publications, VIII). Atlanta, Ga.: Atlanta University Press, 1903; 212 pp.
   i. *Some Notes on the Negroes in New York City* (Atlanta University Conference Special Report). January 1903; 5 pp.
   j. *Some Notes on Negro Crime, Particularly in Georgia* (Atlanta University Publications, IX). Atlanta, Ga.: Atlanta University Press, 1904; 68 pp.
   k. *A Select Bibliography of the Negro American* (Atlanta University Publications, X). Third Edition. Atlanta, Ga.: Atlanta University Press, 1905; 71 pp.
   l. *The Health and Physique of the Negro American* (Atlanta University Publications, XI). Atlanta, Ga.: Atlanta University Press, 1906; 112 pp.
   m. *Economic Cooperation Among Negro Americans* (Atlanta University Publications, XII). Atlanta, Ga.: Atlanta University Press, 1907; 184 pp.
   n. *The Negro American Family* (Atlanta University Publications, XIII). Atlanta, Ga.: Atlanta University Press, 1908; 156 pp. New York: Negro Universities Press, 1969; 156 pp. New York: New American Library, 1969; 156 pp.
   o. *Efforts for Social Betterment Among Negro Americans* (Atlanta University Publications, XIV). Atlanta, Ga.: Atlanta University Press, 1910; 136 pp.
   p. *The College-Bred Negro American* (Atlanta University Pub-

lications, XV). Atlanta, Ga.: Atlanta University Press, 1911; 104 pp.

q. *The Common School and the Negro American* (Atlanta University Publications, XVI). Atlanta, Ga.: Atlanta University Press, 1912; 140 pp.

r. *The Negro American Artisan* (Atlanta University Publications, XVII). Atlanta, Ga.: Atlanta University Press, 1913; 144 pp.

s. *Morals and Manners Among Negro Americans* (Atlanta University Publications, XVIII). Atlanta, Ga.: Atlanta University Press, 1915; 136 pp.

6. *The Atlanta University Publications,* 2 vols. New York: Arno Press, 1968, 1970.
7. *The Souls of Black Folk: Essays and Sketches.* Chicago, Ill.: A. C. McClurg & Co., 1903, 265 pp. (This book has gone through more than 20 American editions involving five publishers, including the 50th anniversary edition of 1953 and the two different paperback editions of 1961 and 1969. Longmans in London brought out a cloth edition in 1965 with an introduction by C. L. R. James. *Souls* is also included in the 1965 paperback *Three Negro Classics,* with an introduction by John Hope Franklin.)
8. *The Moon Illustrated Weekly.* Memphis, Tenn.: 1906.
9. *The Horizon: A Journal of the Color Line.* Washington, D.C.: 1907–1910.
10. *John Brown.* Philadelphia, Pa.: George W. Jacobs & Co., 1909; 406 pp. New York: International Publishers, 1962; 414 pp. Centennial Edition.
11. *The Crisis: A Record of the Darker Races.* New York: 1910–1934. *Crisis,* 1910–1940. New York: Negro Universities Press, 1969. *The Crisis,* 1910–1960. New York: Arno Press, 1970.
12. *Race Prejudice* (Address delivered to the Republican Club, New York, March 5, 1910). New York: The Republican Club, 1910?; 8 pp.
13. *The Quest of the Silver Fleece: A Novel.* Chicago, Ill.: A. C. McClurg & Co., 1911; 434 pp.
14. *The Social Evolution of the Black South.* Washington, D.C.: The American Negro Monograph Co., 1911; 12 pp. (American Negro Monographs, Vol. I, No. 4.)
15. *The Star of Ethiopia* (pageant) *A History of the Negro Race.* New York: Produced for the 50th anniversary of the Emancipation Proclamation in New York City and Washington, D.C., in 1913;

repeated in Philadelphia in 1916 and in Los Angeles in 1924. (Photographs of pageant also in *The Crisis,* Vol. 11, December 1915.)

16. *The Negro.* New York: Henry Holt & Co., 1915; 254 pp. London: Williams & Norgate, 1916; 254 pp. (Home University Library of Modern Knowledge, No. 91.)
17. *Darkwater: the Twentieth Century Completion of Uncle Tom's Cabin.* Washington, D.C.: A. Jenkins Co., 1920; 276 pp. New York: Harcourt, Brace, 1920; 276 pp. (Another edition subtitled *Voices from Within the Veil*) New York: Schocken Books, 1969; x; 276 pp.)
18. *The Brownies' Book.* 2 vols. New York: 1920–21. (A monthly magazine for Negro children.)
19. *The Gift of Black Folk: Negroes in the Making of America.* Boston, Mass.: The Stratford Co., 1924; 349 pp.
20. *The Amenia Conference: An Historic Negro Gathering.* Amenia, N.Y.: Troutbeck Press, 1925; 18 pp. (pamphlet).
21. *Dark Princess: A Romance.* New York: Harcourt, Brace, 1928; 311 pp.
22. *Shall the Negro be Encouraged to Seek Cultural Equality?* (A debate with Lothrop Stoddard [negative], March 17, 1929). Chicago, Ill.: Chicago Forum, 1929; 24 pp.
23. *Africa, Its Geography, People and Products.* Girard, Kans.: Haldeman-Julius Publications, 1930; 63 pp. (booklet).
24. *Africa—Its Place in Modern History.* Girard, Kans.: Haldeman-Julius Publications, 1930; 63 pp. (booklet).
25. *Black Reconstruction in America, 1860–1880.* New York: Harcourt, Brace, 1935; 746 pp. Philadelphia, Pa.: A. Saifer, 1952? New York: Russell & Russell (Atheneum Press), 1962. New York: Meridian Books, Inc., 1964; 746 pp. New York: Atheneum Publishers, 1969; 746 pp.
26. *What the Negro Has Done for the United States and Texas.* Texas Centennial Commission. U.S. Dept. of Commerce, 1936; 10 pp.
27. *A Pageant in Seven Decades, 1868–1938.* Atlanta, Ga.: Atlanta University, 1938; 44 pp.
28. *The Revelation of Saint Orgne the Damned* (Commencement, 1938, Fisk University, Nashville, Tenn.). Nashville, Tenn.: Hemphill Press; 16 pp.
29. *Black Folk, Then and Now: An Essay in the History and Sociology of the Negro Race.* New York: Henry Holt & Co., 1939; 401 pp.

30. *Dusk of Dawn: An Essay Toward an Autobiography of a Race Concept.* New York: Harcourt, Brace & Co., 1940; 334 pp. New York: Schocken Books, 1968; viii; 334 pp.
31. *Phylon: The Atlanta University Review of Race and Culture.* Atlanta, Ga., 1940–44. *Phylon,* 1940–1967. New York: Kraus Reprint Co., 1970? (This journal is still being published.)
32. *Encyclopedia of the Negro: Preparatory Volume.* With reference lists and reports. New York: The Phelps-Stokes Fund, Inc., 1945; 207 pp. Revised edition: 1946; 215 pp.
33. *Color and Democracy: Colonies and Peace.* New York: Harcourt, Brace and Co., 1945; 143 pp.
34. *Appeal to the World.* New York: National Association for the Advancement of Colored People, 1947; 94 pp. (Petition to the United Nations by the NAACP for redress of grievances of and discrimination against U.S. Negroes.)
35. *The World and Africa: An Inquiry into the Part which Africa has played in World History.* New York: The Viking Press, 1947; 276 pp. New York: International Publishers, 1965; 352 pp. (An enlarged edition with new writings on Africa by Du Bois, 1955–1961.)
36. *I Speak for Peace* (pamphlet). (Statement on his candidacy for the U.S. Senate on the American Labor Party ticket, September 24, 1950 in New York City.) 4 pp.
37. *I Take my Stand for Peace* (pamphlet). New York: Masses and Mainstream, Publisher, 1951; 15 pp. (Also "I Take my Stand"; *Masses and Mainstream,* Vol. 4, pp. 10–16, April 1951.)
38. *In Battle for Peace: The Story of my 83rd Birthday. With comment by Shirley Graham.* New York: Masses and Mainstream, Publisher, 1952; 192 pp.
39. *The Story of Benjamin Franklin.* Vienna, Austria: Secretariat of The World Council of Peace, 1956; 39 pp.
40. *The Black Flame—A Trilogy: The Ordeal of Mansart, Mansart Builds a School, and Worlds of Color.* New York: Mainstream, Publisher, 1957, 1959, 1961; 316, 367, 349 pp. (Historical novels.)
41. *Ames Noires, Essais et Nouvelles* (French translation of 50th Anniversary edition [1953] of *The Souls of Black Folk*). Paris, France: Presence Africaine, 1959; 232 pp.
42. *W. E. B. Du Bois: A Recorded Autobiography.* New York: Folkways Records, Inc., 1961?
43. *Information Report (for Cooperation Toward an Encyclopedia Africana).* Accra, Ghana: 1962–63.

44. *An ABC of Color: Selections from over a Half Century of the Writings of W. E. B. Du Bois.* Berlin, German Democratic Republic: Seven Seas Publishers, 1963; 214 pp. New York: International Publishers, 1970; 216 pp.
45. *Socialism Today—On China and Russia* (pamphlet). Chicago, Ill.: Af-Am Books, 1964?; 8 pp.
46. *Africa—Battle Against Colonialism, Imperialism and Racism* (pamphlet). Chicago, Ill.: Af-Am Books, 1964?
47. *The Immortal Child—Background on Crises in Education* (pamphlet). Chicago, Ill.: Af-Am Books, 1964?
48. *The Damnation of Women—Predictions on Fatherless and Dependent Children* (pamphlet). Chicago, Ill.: Af-Am Books, 1964?
49. *Selected Poems.* Accra, Ghana: Ghana Universities Press, 1964?; 42 pp. (Du Bois' poems and prose poems published soon after his death in August 1963. Foreword by Kwame Nkrumah. Exposition by Shirley Graham.)
50. *The Autobiography of W. E. B. Du Bois: A Soliloquy on Viewing my Life from the Last Decade of its First Century.* New York: International Publishers, 1968; 448 pp.

CHAPTERS IN BOOKS

1. "The Enforcement of the Slave-Trade Laws" in *Annual Report of the American Historical Association for the Year 1891* (52nd Congress, 1st Session, Senate Miscellaneous Document, 173). Washington, D.C.: 1892; pp. 161–174.
2. "Careers Open to College-Bred Negroes" in *Two Addresses* delivered by alumni of Fisk University, Anniversary Exercises, June 1898. Nashville, Tenn.: Fisk University, 1898?
3. "The Freedmen's Bureau" (1901) in *An Anthology of American Negro Literature,* edited by V. F. Calverton. New York: The Modern Library, 1929; pp. 277–298. (A reprint of "the problem of the twentieth century is the problem of the color line" essay published in *Atlantic Monthly* [1901] and *The Souls of Black Folk* [1903]).
4. "Of the Wings of Atlanta" in *Reading for Writing,* edited by Ivan E. Taylor and J. Saunders Redding. New York: Ronald Press, 1952; pp. 50–54 (in *Souls of Black Folk* [1903]).
5. "My Early Relations with Booker T. Washington" and "Of Mr. Booker T. Washington and Others" (1903) in *Booker T. Wash-*

ington and His Critics, edited by Hugh Hawkins. Boston, Mass.: D. C. Heath, 1962; pp. 27–32 and 33–40 (in *Souls of Black Folk*).

6. "The Souls of Black Folk" (1903) in *The Democratic Spirit,* edited by Bernard Smith. New York: A. A. Knopf, 1941; pp. 591–99.
7. "The Souls of Black Folk" (1903) in *Voices in Dissent: An Anthology of Individualist Thought in the United States,* edited by Arthur A. Ekirch, Jr. New York: Citadel Press, 1964; pp. 195–204.
8. "The Talented Tenth" in *The Negro Problem* by Booker T. Washington, W. E. B. Du Bois, et al. New York: James Pott & Co., 1903; pp. 31–75. (Also in *Souls of Black Folk.*)
9. "The Negro Farmer" in *Negroes in the United States* (Department of Commerce and Labor, Bureau of the Census, Bulletin, V. 8). Washington, D.C.: 1904; pp. 69–98.
10. "The Negro in America" in *The Encyclopedia Americana,* edited by Frederick Converse Beach. New York, Vol. 11, 1904.
11. "Atlanta University" in *From Servitude to Service,* by Kelly Miller et al. Boston, Mass.: American Unitarian Association, 1905; pp. 153–197.
12. "The Negro Farmer" in United States Twelfth Census, *Special Reports: Supplementary Analysis and Derivative Tables.* Washington, D.C.: 1906; pp. 511–579.
13. "Niagara Address of 1906" in *A Documentary History of the Negro People in the United States,* edited by Herbert Aptheker. New York: The Citadel Press, 1951; pp. 907–910. Paperback edition, 1964. Cloth edition, 1969.
14. "A Litany at Atlanta" (1906) in *The Negro Caravan,* edited by Sterling Brown et al. New York: Dryden Press, 1941; pp. 321–324. New York: Arno Press, 1969.
15. "The Economic Revolution in the South" and "Religion in the South" in *The Negro in the South: His Economic Progress in Relation to His Moral and Religious Development,* by Booker T. Washington and W. E. B. Du Bois. Philadelphia, Pa.: George W. Jacobs & Co., 1907; pp. 79–122 and pp. 125–191.
16. "The Riddle of the Sphinx" (a chapter of his biography of John Brown [1909] in *A John Brown Reader,* edited by Louis Ruchames). New York: Abelard-Schuman, 1959; pp. 339–347.
17. "Politics and Industry" and "The Evolution of the Race Problem" in *Proceedings of the National Negro Conference.* New York, May

31, June 1, 1909. New York: National Negro Conference, 1909; pp. 79–88 and 142–158.

18. "The Negro Race in the United States of America" in *Papers on Inter-Racial Problems,* edited by G. Spiller. London: P. S. King and Son. Boston: The World's Peace Foundation, 1911; pp. 348–64. (Paper read at the First Universal Races Congress, University of London, July 26–29, 1911.)
19. "Documentary Review of 1911 NAACP Conference" in *The National Association for the Advancement of Colored People: A Case Study in Pressure Groups,* by Warren D. St. James. New York: Exposition Press, 1958; pp. 168–171 (written soon after the 1911 Conference).
20. "African Culture" (from *The Negro,* 1915) in *Primer for White Folks,* edited by Bucklin Moon. New York: Doubleday Doran, 1945; pp. 1–22.
21. "The Future of Africa" in *Africa in the World Democracy* (pamphlet) (Addresses delivered at the annual meeting of the NAACP.) New York, 1919.
22. "Résolutions du Deuxième Congrès Pan-Africain, 1921" in *La Question des Noirs aux États-Unis* by Franck Louis Schoell. Paris: Payot, 1923; pp. 268–281.
23. "Georgia: Invisible Empire State" in *These United States: A Symposium,* edited by Ernest H. Gruening. New York: Boni and Liveright, 1923–24; pp. 322–345.
24. "The Negro Mind Reaches Out" in *The New Negro,* edited by Alain Locke. New York: A. & C. Boni, 1925; pp. 385–414. New York: Atheneum Press, 1968. New York: Arno Press, 1968.
25. "Worlds of Color:" in *The Foreign Affairs Reader,* edited by Hamilton Fish Armstrong. New York: Published for the Council on Foreign Relations by Harper, 1947; pp. 77–102 (published originally in *Foreign Affairs,* Vol. 3; pp. 423–44, April 1925).
26. "What Is Civilization?—The Answer of Africa" in *What Is Civilization?,* edited by Maurice Maeterlinck et al. New York: Duffield, 1926; pp. 41–57.
27. "The Negro Citizen" in *The Negro in American Civilization,* edited by Charles S. Johnson. New York: Henry Holt and Co., 1930; pp. 463–70.
28. "Black America" in *America as Americans See It,* edited by F. J. Ringel. New York: Harcourt, Brace and Co., 1932; pp. 139–155.
29. "The Black Proletariat in South Carolina" (1935) in *Reconstruc-*

tion in the South, edited by Edwin C. Rozwenc. Boston, Mass.: D. C. Heath, 1952; pp. 62–83.

30. "That Outer, Whiter World of Harvard" (of about 1890) (from *Dusk of Dawn* [1940]) in *The Harvard Book: Selections from Three Centuries,* edited by William Bentinck-Smith. Cambridge, Mass.: Harvard University Press, 1953; pp. 226–30.
31. "My Evolving Program for Negro Freedom" in *What the Negro Wants,* edited by Rayford W. Logan. Chapel Hill, N.C.: University of North Carolina Press, 1944; pp. 31–70.
32. "A Voyage to Liberia" in *The American Looks at the World,* edited by Carlos H. Baker. New York: Harcourt, Brace and Co., 1944; pp. 159–165.
33. "The Black Man and Albert Schweitzer" in *The Albert Schweitzer Jubilee Book,* edited by A. A. Roback. Cambridge, Mass.: Sci-Art, 1945; pp. 119–129.
34. "The Pan-African Movement" in *Colonial and . . . Coloured Unity: A Programme of Action. History of the Pan-African Congress,* edited by George Padmore. Manchester, England: Pan-African Federation, 1945, 1963; pp. 13–26.
35. "Three Centuries of Discrimination Against the Negro" in *Race Prejudice and Discrimination: Readings in Intergroup Relations in the United States,* edited by Arnold M. Rose. New York: A. A. Knopf, 1951; pp. 17–25 (condensed introduction to *Appeal to the World,* 1947).
36. "A Program of Emancipation for Colonial Peoples" in *Trust and Non-Self-Governing Territories,* edited by Merze Tate. Washington, D.C.: Howard University Press, 1948; pp. 96–104. (Howard University Studies in the Social Sciences, V. 6, No. 1.)
37. "The Nature of Intellectual Freedom" in *Speaking of Peace,* edited by Daniel S. Gillmor. An edited report of the Cultural and Scientific Conference for World Peace, New York, March 25–27, 1949, under the auspices of National Council of the Arts, Sciences, and Professions. New York: National Council of the Arts, Sciences, and Professions, 1949; pp. 78–79.
38. "The Negro and Socialism" in *Toward a Socialist America: A Symposium of Essays* edited by Helen L. Alfred. New York: Peace Publications, 1958; pp. 179–191.
39. "200 Years of Segregated Schools" in *Jewish Life Anthology, 1946–1956,* edited by Louis Harap. New York: Jewish Life Magazine, 1956; pp. 201–206.

ARTICLES

1. "The Enforcement of the Slave-Trade Laws," *The Independent,* Vol. 44?; pp. 10–11, January 7, 1892.
2. "Strivings of the Negro People," *Atlantic Monthly,* Vol. 80; pp. 194–198, August 1897.
3. "The Study of Negro Problems," *Annals of the American Academy of Political and Social Science,* Vol. 11; pp. 1–23, January 1898.
4. "The Negroes of Farmville, Virginia; A Social Study," *U.S. Department of Labor Bulletin* No. 14; 38 pp. January 1898.
5. "The Negro in the Black Belt: Some Social Sketches," *U.S. Department of Labor Bulletin* No. 22; pp. 408, 412–415, September? 1899.
6. "Two Negro Conventions," *The Independent,* Vol. 51; pp. 2425–27, Sept. 7, 1899.
7. "The Suffrage Fight in Georgia," *The Independent,* Vol. 60; pp. 3226–28, Nov. 30, 1899.
8. "The Religion of the American Negro," *The New World,* Vol. 9; pp. 614–625, Dec. 1900.
9. "The Freedmen's Bureau," *Atlantic Monthly,* Vol. 87; pp. 354–365, March 1901. (Also chapter 2, "Of the Dawn of Freedom" in *Souls of Black Folk.*)
10. "The Negro as He Really Is," *World's Work,* Vol. 2; pp. 848–866, June 1901.
11. "The Negro Landholder of Georgia," *U.S. Department of Labor Bulletin* No. 35; pp. 647–777, July 1901.
12. "The Relation of the Negroes to the Whites in the South" (in *America's Race Problems* number), *Annals of the American Academy of Political and Social Science,* Vol. 18; pp. 121–133, July 1901.
13. "The Evolution of Negro Leadership," *The Dial,* Vol. 31; pp. 53–55, July 1, 1901.
14. "The Spawn of Slavery: The Convict Lease System in the South," *Missionary Review of the World,* Vol. 24; pp. 737–745, Oct. 1901.
15. "The Freedmen and Their Sons," *The Independent,* Vol. 53; p. 2709, Nov. 14, 1901.
16. "The Problem of Housing the Negro," *Southern Workman,* Vol. 30; pp. 390–395, 486–493, 535–542, 601–604, 688–693; July, Sept., Oct., Nov., Dec. 1901, Vol. 31; pp. 65–72, Feb. 1902.

17. "The Black North; A Social Study" (a series), *New York Times Magazine Supplement,* Nov. 17, 24, Dec. 1, 8, 15, 1901.
18. "The Work of Negro Women in Society," *Spelman Messenger,* Vol. 18; pp. 1–3, Feb. 1902.
19. "Of Booker T. Washington and Others," *Guardian,* July 27, 1902. (Also chapter 3 in *The Souls of Black Folk.*)
20. "Possibilities of the Negro: the Advance Guard of the Race," *Booklovers Magazine,* Vol. 2; pp. 2–15, July 1903.
21. "The Future of the Negro Race in America," *The East and the West* (London), Vol. 2; pp. 4–19, Jan. 1904.
22. "The Negro Problem from the Negro Point of View (Part V): The Parting of the Ways," *World Today,* Vol. 6; pp. 521–523, April 1904.
23. "The Development of a People," *The International Journal of Ethics,* Vol. 14; pp. 291–311, April 1904.
24. "Credo," *The Independent,* Vol. 57; p. 787, Oct. 6, 1904. *Jet,* Vol. 24, pp. 46–47, Sept. 12, 1963.
25. "The Beginning of Slavery," *Voice of the Negro,* Vol. 2; pp. 104–106, Feb. 1905.
26. "The Beginning of Emancipation," *Voice of the Negro,* Vol. 2; pp. 397–400, June 1905.
27. "The Negro South and North," *Bibliotheca Sacra,* pp. 499–513, July 1905.
28. "The Niagara Movement," *Voice of the Negro,* Vol. 2; pp. 619–622, Sept. 1905. (Principles and resolutions of the Niagara Movement and other articles by Du Bois are reprinted in *Negro Social and Political Thought, 1850–1920: Representative Texts* [1966], edited by Howard Brotz.)
29. "The Black Vote of Philadelphia" (in *The Negro in the Cities of the North* number), *Charities* (later *The Survey*), Vol. 15; pp. 31–35, Oct. 7, 1905.
30. "The Growth of the Niagara Movement," *Voice of the Negro,* Vol. 3; pp. 43–45, January 1906.
31. "The Economic Future of the Negro," *Publications of the American Economic Association,* 3rd series, Vol. 7; pp. 219–234, Feb. 1906.
32. "A Litany at Atlanta," *The Independent,* Vol. 61; pp. 856–858, Oct. 1906.
33. "Socialist of the Path," *Horizon,* Vol. 1; p. 7, Feb. 1907.
34. "Negro and Socialists," *Horizon,* Vol. 1; pp. 7–8, Feb. 1907.
35. "Africa," *Horizon,* Vol. 1; pp. 5–7, June 1907.

36. "Niagara," *Horizon,* Vol. 2, pp. 4–6, Sept. 1907.
37. "The Burden of Black Women," *Horizon,* Vol. 2; pp. 3–5, Nov. 1907.
38. "Niagara Movement," *Horizon,* Vol. 4; pp. 1–3, Sept. 1908.
39. "Fifty Years Among the Black Folk," *New York Times,* Vol. 6, Dec. 12, 1909.
40. "The Economic Aspects of Race Prejudice," *Editorial Review,* Vol. 2; pp. 488–493, May 1910.
41. "Reconstruction and Its Benefits," *American Historical Review,* Vol. 15; pp. 781–799, July 1910. Reprinted in *Black History: A Reappraisal* (1968), edited by Melvin Drimmer.
42. "The Souls of White Folk," *The Independent,* Vol. 69; pp. 339–342, Aug. 18, 1910.
43. "The Marrying of Black Folk," *The Independent,* Vol. 69; pp. 812–813, Oct. 13, 1910.
44. "Forty Years of Freedom," *Missionary Review of the World,* Vol. 34; pp. 460–461, June 1911.
45. "Social Effects of Emancipation," *The Survey;* Vol. 31; pp. 572+, Feb. 1, 1913.
46. "The Negro in Literature and Art" (in *The Negro's Progress in Fifty Years* number), *Annals of the American Academy of Political and Social Science;* pp. 233–237, Sept. 1913.
47. "The Immediate Program of the American Negro," *The Crisis,* Vol. 9; pp. 310–312, April 1915.
48. "The African Roots of War," *Atlantic Monthly,* Vol. 115; pp. 707–714, May 1915. Reprinted in *Freedomways,* Vol. 8, No. 1; pp. 12–22, Winter 1968.
49. "Of the Culture of White Folk," *The Journal of Race Development,* Vol. 7; pp. 434–447, Apr. 1917.
50. "The Passing of Jim Crow," *The Independent,* Vol. 91; pp. 53–54, 1917.
51. "The Negro's Fatherland," *The Survey,* Vol. 39; p. 141, Nov. 1917.
52. "The Pan-African Congress," *The Crisis,* Vol. 17; Apr. 1919.
53. "On Being Black," *New Republic,* Vol. 21; pp. 338–341, Feb. 18, 1920.
54. "Honey, A Story," *The Brownies' Book,* Vol. 1, No. 8; pp. 227–32, Aug. 1920.
55. "Eternal Africa," *Nation,* Vol. 111; pp. 350–52, Sept. 25, 1920.
56. "The Object of the Pan-African Congress," *African World,* p. 99, 1921–22.

57. "A Second Journey to Pan-Africa," *New Republic,* Vol. 29; pp. 39–42, Dec. 7, 1921.
58. "The South and a Third Party," *New Republic,* Vol. 33; pp. 138–141, Jan. 3, 1923.
59. "Back to Africa," *The Century Magazine,* Vol. 105; pp. 539–548, Feb. 1923 (about Marcus Garvey and his movement).
60. "The Hosts of Black Labor," *Nation,* Vol. 116; pp. 539–541, May 9, 1923.
61. "The Negro as a National Asset," *Homiletic Review,* Vol. 86; pp. 52–58, 1923.
62. "Diuturni Silenti," *Fisk Herald,* Vol. 33, No. 1; pp. 1–11, 1924. (Address delivered to the alumni of Fisk University at Fisk Memorial Chapel, June 2, 1924.)
63. "Georgia: Invisible Empire State," *Nation,* Vol. 120; pp. 63–67, Jan. 21, 1925.
64. "What Is Civilization?—Africa Answer," *Forum,* Vol. 73; pp. 178–88, Feb. 1925.
65. "The Black Man Brings His Gifts," *Survey Graphic,* Vol. 6; pp. 655–657, 710, Mar. 1925.
66. "The Negro Mind Reaches Out," *Foreign Affairs,* Vol. 3, No. 3; about 30 pp., July 1925. Reprinted in *The New Negro,* 1925.
67. "France's Black Citizens in West Africa," *Current History,* Vol. 22; pp. 559–564, July 1925.
68. "Judging Russia," *The Crisis,* Vol. 33; pp. 189–90, Feb. 1927.
69. "Race Relations in the United States" (in *The American Negro* number), *The Annals of the American Academy of Political and Social Science,* Vol. 140; pp. 6–10, Nov. 1928.
70. "Education and Work" (commencement address delivered at Howard University, Washington, D.C., June 6, 1930). *Howard University Bulletin,* Vol. 9; 22 pp., Jan. 1931. *Journal of Negro Education,* Vol. 1; pp. 60–74, Apr. 1932.
71. "Will the Church Remove the Color Line?" *Christian Century,* Vol. 48; pp. 1554–1556, Dec. 9, 1931.
72. "Where Do We Go From Here?" (U.S. will come to Communism; big business does nothing to the Negro except exploit him) (address at Rosenwald Economic Conference, May 1933, Washington, D.C.) *Afro-American,* May 20, 1933.
73. "Liberia, The League, and the United States," *Foreign Affairs,* Vol. 12; pp. 682–695, July 1933.
74. "A Negro Nation within the Nation," *Current History,* Vol. 32; pp. 265–270, June 1935.

75. "Inter-racial Implications of the Ethiopian Crisis," *Foreign Affairs,* Vol. 14; pp. 582–92? Oct. 1935.
76. "Social Planning for the Negro, Past and Present," *Journal of Negro Education,* Vol. 5, pp. 110–125, Jan. 1936.
77. "Black Africa Tomorrow," *Foreign Affairs,* Vol. 17; pp. 100–110, Jan.? 1938.
78. "The Negro Scientist," *American Scholar,* Vol. 8; pp. 309–320, Summer 1939.
79. "The Position of the Negro in the American Social Order: Where Do We Go From Here?" *Journal of Negro Education,* Vol. 8; pp. 551–570, July 1939.
80. "Pushkin," *Phylon,* Vol. 1; pp. 265–269, Third Quarter 1940.
81. "Moton of Hampton and Tuskegee," *Phylon,* Vol. 1; pp. 344–351, Fourth Quarter 1940.
82. "The Cultural Missions of Atlanta University," *Phylon,* Vol. 3; pp. 105–115, Second Quarter 1942.
83. "Postscript: Looking Seventy-Five Years Backward," *Phylon,* Vol. 3; pp. 238–248, Second Quarter 1942.
84. "Reconstruction: Seventy-Five Years After," *Phylon,* Vol. 4; pp. 205–212, Third Quarter 1943.
85. "The Realities in Africa: European Profit or Negro Development?" *Foreign Affairs,* Vol. 21; pp. 721–732, July 1943.
86. "The Negro Soldier in Service Abroad During the First World War," *Journal of Negro Education,* Vol. 12; pp. 324–334, Summer 1943.
87. "Prospect of a World Without Race Conflict," *American Journal of Sociology,* Vol. 49; pp. 450–456, Mar. 1944.
88. "Bound by the Color Line," *New Masses,* Vol. 58; p. 8, Feb. 12, 1946.
89. "Georgia: Torment of a State," *New Masses,* Vol. 59?; pp. 3–7, 19–22, Sept. 10, 17, 1946. (Reprint of "Georgia: Invisible Empire State.")
90. "Pioneers in the Struggle Against Segregation," *Survey Graphic,* Vol. 36, p. 90, Jan. 1947.
91. "Behold the Land," *New Masses,* Vol. 59?; pp. 18–20, Jan. 14, 1947. *Masses and Mainstream,* Vol. 3; pp. 42–46, Feb. 1950. *Freedomways,* Vol. 4; pp. 8–15, Winter 1964. Published as a pamphlet by Southern Negro Youth Congress in 1947. (Speech at Southern Youth Legislature, Columbia, S.C., Oct. 20, 1946.)
92. "Three Centuries of Discrimination," *The Crisis,* Vol. 54; pp. 362–364, 379–380, Mar.? 1947.

93. "The Schomburg Collection," *New York Herald Tribune,* Mar. 7, 1948. (Letter about upkeep of Collection after L. D. Reddick resigned as curator.)
94. "From McKinley to Wallace: My Fifty Years as a Political Independent," *Masses and Mainstream,* Vol. 1; pp. 3–13, Aug. 1948.
95. "Race Relations in the United States: 1917–1947," *Phylon,* Vol. 9; pp. 234–247, Third Quarter 1948.
96. "The Talented Tenth Memorial Address" (at the 19th Grand Boulé Conclave of Sigma Pi Phi). *Boule Journal,* Vol. 15; pp. 3–13, Oct. 1948.
97. "The Negro Since 1900: A Progress Report," *New York Times Magazine,* pp. 54–57, 59, Nov. 21, 1948. (Summarized in *Common Ground,* Vol. 9; pp. 95–96, Spring 1949. Reprinted in *Negro Digest,* Vol. 7; pp. 19–26, May 1949.)
98. "The Thirteenth, Fourteenth, and Fifteenth Amendments," *Lawyers Guild Review,* Vol. 9; pp. 92–95, Spring 1949.
99. "Colonial Peoples and the Fight for Peace," *New Africa,* Vol. 8; Apr. 1949.
100. "No More War," *Jewish Life,* Vol. 3; pp. 23–24, May 1949. (Speech about the Cultural and Scientific Conference for World Peace, New York City, Mar. 25–27, 1949.)
101. "Dr. Du Bois on Negro America," *Sunday Compass,* pp. 4, 6, July 10, 1949.
102. "20th Century: 'The Century of the Color Line,'" *Pittsburgh Courier* (newspaper), Pittsburgh, Pa., Jan. 14, 1950, p. 8. (In *50 Years of Progress* series). (Reprinted from newspaper as a 7-page pamphlet.)
103. "Paul Robeson—Right" (part of a debate), *Negro Digest,* Vol. 8; pp. 8, 10–14, Mar. 1950.
104. "Government and Freedom," *Harlem Quarterly,* Vol. 1; pp. 29–31, Spring 1950.
105. "A Portrait of Carter G. Woodson," *Masses and Mainstream,* Vol. 3; pp. 19–25, June 1950 (Just after Woodson's death April 3, 1950).
106. "I Bury My Wife," *Negro Digest,* Vol. 8; pp. 37–39, Oct. 1950.
107. "Most Sinister Evil of the Day" (that war is inevitable), *Daily Worker,* 2 pp., Mar. 11, 1951.
108. "I Take My Stand (for Peace)," *Masses and Mainstream,* Vol. 4; pp. 10–16, Apr. 1951 (also a 15-page pamphlet).
109. "There Must Come a Vast Social Change in the United States," *National Guardian,* Vol. 3; p. 5, July 11, 1951.

110. "Between Birthdays: A Personal Narrative," *Masses and Mainstream,* Vol. 5; pp. 8–14, Feb. 1952.
111. "The Negro and the Warsaw Ghetto," *Jewish Life,* Vol. 6; pp. 14–15, Apr. 1952.
112. "One Hundred Years in the Struggle for Negro Freedom," *Freedom,* Vol. 3; pp. 6–7, January 1953.
113. "Comet's Tail," a short story in three parts. *Afro-American* (newspaper) *Magazine Section,* p. 4, Jan. 24, 1953.
114. "Passing of the First Born," *Masses and Mainstream,* Vol. 6; pp. 26–30, Feb. 1953 (from *The Souls of Black Folk*).
115. "Negroes and the Crisis of Capitalism in the United States," *Monthly Review,* Vol. 4; pp. 478–485, Apr. 1953.
116. "The American Negro in My Time," *United Asia,* Vol. 5; pp. 155–59, June 1953.
117. "The Rosenbergs" (poem), *Masses and Mainstream,* Vol. 6; pp. 10–12, July 1953. (Also in *The Rosenbergs—Poems of the United States* edited by Martha Millet, 1955?)
118. "1876 and After: Democracy and American Negroes," *National Guardian,* Vol. 9; pp. 4–5, Feb. 15, 1954.
119. "This Man I Know" (Benjamin J. Davis, Jr.). (Excerpt from an address.) *Masses and Mainstream,* Vol. 7; p. 43, Feb. 1954.
120. "American Negroes and Africa," *National Guardian,* Vol. 10; Feb. 14, 1955.
121. "Pan-Africanism: A Mission in My Life," *United Asia,* Vol. 7; pp. 23–28, Apr. 1955 (in *Africa in the Modern World* number).
122. "What Is Wrong with the United States?" *National Guardian,* Vol. 10; p. 6, May 9, 1955.
123. "The Wealth of the West vs. a Chance for Exploited Mankind," *National Guardian,* Vol. 10; p. 3, Nov. 28, 1955.
124. "Africa and the American Negro Intelligentsia," *Presence Africaine,* No. 5 (new series), pp. 34–51, Dec. 1955–Jan. 1956.
125. "The Rape of Africa–The Fundamental Question Facing the World," *The American Negro,* Vol. 1; pp. 6–13, Feb. 1956 (speech).
126. "The American Negro in My Time," *Masses and Mainstream,* Vol. 9; pp. 1–9, Mar. 1956.
127. "I Won't Vote," *Nation,* Vol. 183; pp. 324–325, Oct. 20, 1956.
128. "Suez" (poem), *Mainstream,* Vol. 9; pp. 42–43, Dec. 1956.
129. "The Stalin Era—Two Views: I; World Changer," *Mainstream,* Vol. 10; pp. 1–5, Jan. 1957 (part of a discussion).

130. "Negro History Centenaries," *National Guardian,* Vol. 11; p. 8, Jan. 14, 1957.
131. "A Future for Pan-Africa: Freedom, Peace, Socialism," *National Guardian,* Vol. 11; p. 7, Mar. 11, 1957.
132. "Negroes and Socialism," *National Guardian,* Vol. 11; p. 12, Apr. 29, 1957.
133. "La Foi des Ancêstres," *Presence Africaine,* Vol. 13; pp. 31+, April–May 1957.
134. "The American Negro and the Darker World," *Allen University Bulletin,* Vol. 21; pp. 9–15, May 1957. Reprinted in *Freedomways,* Vol. 8; No. 3, pp. 245–51, Summer 1968. (Address delivered at Allen University, Feb. 11, 1957, during Negro History Week Observance and on April 30, 1957, celebrating The Bandung Conference of 1955 and the rebirth of Ghana.)
135. "A Vista of Ninety Fruitful Years," *National Guardian,* Vol. 10; p. 7, Feb. 17, 1958. (Excerpts in *The Crisis,* Vol. 65; pp. 220, 222, April 1958.)
136. "The Future of All Africa Lies in Socialism," *National Guardian,* Vol. 11; p. 7, Dec. 22, 1958.
137. "Probleme de L'integration des Races aux États-Unis," *Presence Africaine,* Vol. 16?; pp. 73–80, Dec. 1958–Jan. 1959.
138. "The Africans and the Colonialist Tactic," *New Times,* No. 7, Feb. 1959.
139. "China and Africa," *New World Review,* Vol. 27; pp. 28–31, Apr. 1959. (Also *Peking Review,* Vol. 2, March 3, 1959.)
140. "The Vast Miracle of China Today," *National Guardian,* Vol. 11; p. 6, June 8, 1959.
141. "Forty Years of the USSR," *National Guardian,* Vol. 11; p. 8, Sept. 7, 1959.
142. "The Dream of Socialism," *New World Review,* Vol. 27; pp. 14–17, Nov. 1959.
143. "The Lie of History as It Is Taught Today," *National Guardian,* Vol. 12; pp. 5, 8, Feb. 15, 1960.
144. "A Negro Student at Harvard at the End of the 19th Century," *The Massachusetts Review,* Vol. 1; pp. 439–458, May 1960. (A re-working and extension of a section of his earlier book *Dusk of Dawn* [1940]; see his recorded autobiography [1961?].) Also in *Black and White in American Culture* (1969), edited by J. Chametzky and S. Kaplan.
145. "On the Vast and Wreckless Waste of Human Life," *National Guardian,* Vol. 12; p. 5, June 20, 1960.

146. "Whither Now and Why" (address delivered before the 25th Conference of the Association of Social Science Teachers, Johnson C. Smith University, Charlotte, N.C., April 1–2, 1960). *Quarterly Review of Higher Education Among Negroes,* Vol. 28; pp. 135–141, July 1960.
147. "I Never Dreamed I Would See This Miracle" (some African history traced), *National Guardian,* Vol. 12; p. 7, Sept. 19, 1960.
148. "American Negroes and Africa's Rise to Freedom," *National Guardian,* Vol. 13; p. 5, Feb. 13, 1961.
149. "Dr. Du Bois, 93, Writes Daughter's Obituary" (Mrs. Nina Yolande Du Bois Williams; she died Mar. 14, 1961). *Afro-American* (newspaper), Mar. 18, 1961.
150. "Comment on Rockwell Kent's Gift" (to the Soviet people of a collection of 80 paintings, over 800 drawings and other graphic art works, books and manuscripts by an American artist—himself). *Mainstream,* Vol. 14; p. 41, April 1961.
151. "The Negro People and the United States," *Freedomways,* Vol. 1; pp. 11–19, Spring 1961.
152. "Africa and the French Revolution," *Freedomways,* Vol. 1; pp. 136–151, Summer 1961.
153. "Letter of Application for Admission to Membership in the Communist Party of the United States," *Political Affairs,* Vol. 40; pp. 9–10, Dec. 1961.
154. "The Negro and the Civil War," *Science and Society,* Vol. 25; pp. 347–352, Dec. 1961.
155. "Ghana Calls—A Poem," *Freedomways,* Vol. 2; pp. 71–74, Winter 1962.
156. "Conference of *Encyclopedia Africana*" (opening speech delivered at the University of Ghana, Dec. 15, 1962). *Freedomways,* Vol. 3; pp. 28–30, Winter 1963.
157. "His Last Message to the World" (written June 26, 1957; released when he died August 27, 1963). *Journal of Negro History,* Vol. 49; p. 145, Apr. 1964.

BOOK REVIEWS

1. Taylor, A. A.: *The Negro in Tennessee, 1865–1880. Phylon,* Vol. 3; pp. 93–94, First Quarter 1942.
2. Smith, Edwin W.: *Events in African History. Phylon,* Vol. 3; pp. 435–437, Fourth Quarter 1942.

3. Nehru, Jawaharlal: *Toward Freedom. Phylon,* Vol. 4; pp. 89–91, First Quarter 1943.
4. Myrdal, Gunnar: *An American Dilemma: The Negro Problem and Modern Democracy. Phylon,* Vol. 5; pp. 118–124, Second Quarter 1944.
5. Linton, Ralph: *Most of the World: The Peoples of Africa, Latin America and the East Today. Science and Society,* Vol. 13; pp. 365–368, Fall 1949.
6. Foner, Philip S. (editor): *The Life and Writings of Frederick Douglass* (Vols. I and II). *Science and Society,* Vol. 15, pp. 351–354, Fall 1951.
7. Sachs, E. S.: *The Choice Before South Africa. Science and Society,* Vol. 17, pp. 269–270, Summer 1953.
8. Rubenstein, Annette T.: *The Great Tradition in English Literature from Shakespeare to Shaw. National Guardian,* Vol. 9?; p. 7, Mar. 8, 1954.
9. Gunther, John: *Inside Africa. Jewish Life,* Vol. 10; pp. 15–18, 35, Feb. 1956.
10. Spencer, Samuel R.: *Booker T. Washington and the Negro's Place in American Life. Science and Society,* Vol. 20; pp. 183–185, Spring 1956.
11. Nkrumah, Kwame: *Ghana: The Autobiography of Kwame Nkrumah. Mainstream,* Vol. 10; pp. 11–16, May 1957.
12. Harris, Abram L.: *Economics and Social Reform. The Crisis,* Vol. 65; pp. 314–315, May 1958.
13. Reddick, L. D.: *Crusader Without Violence. National Guardian,* Vol. 12; p. 8, Nov. 9, 1959 (Biography of Martin Luther King, Jr.).
14. Davidson, Basil: *The Lost Cities of Africa. National Guardian,* Vol. 12; p. 8, Nov. 16, 1959.
15. Nelson, Truman: *The Surveyor* (John Brown's Battle for Kansas). *National Guardian,* Vol. 12; p. 9, June 6, 1960.
16. Nkrumah, Kwame: *I Speak of Freedom: A Statement of African Ideology. Freedomways,* Vol. 1; pp. 340–344, Fall 1961.

Notes on contributors

KWAME NKRUMAH, former president of the Republic of Ghana, is the author of such outstanding books as *Ghana, Africa Must Unite, The Challenge of the Congo,* and *Neo-Colonialism, the Last Stage of Imperialism.*

NNAMDI AZIKIWE, former president of the Republic of Nigeria and one of the early agitators for African independence, is the author of *Renaissant Africa* and other books.

SHIRLEY GRAHAM, first editor of *Freedomways,* widow of W. E. B. Du Bois, is the author of a number of books, the best known of which is *There Was Once a Slave,* the story of Frederick Douglass.

ROY WILKINS is executive secretary of the National Association for the Advancement of Colored People.

LANGSTON HUGHES, late poet laureate of Harlem, was one of the most prolific Black writers of this century, the author of more than forty books.

RUBY DEE, actress, was last seen on Broadway in *Purlie Victorious,* written by her husband Ossie Davis. She is well-known to movie and television audiences and is active in community affairs.

DR. HORACE MANN BOND was formerly dean of the School of Education, Atlanta University. He is now with the Bureau of Educational and Social Research, Atlanta University.

DR. HENRY A. CALLIS is one of the founders of the Alpha Phi Alpha Fraternity. He is a physician in Washington, D.C.

DR. IRENE DIGGS was secretary to Dr. Du Bois when he was Director of Special Research for the NAACP. She is now a member of the faculty at Morgan State Teachers College, Baltimore.

LORRAINE HANSBERRY is the author of the plays *A Raisin in the Sun* and *The Sign in Sidney Brustein's Window.* Her play *To Be Young, Gifted and Black* has been posthumously performed. Her death at the age of 34 was an incalculable loss to the freedom movement in America.

JAMES E. JACKSON, former editor of the *Worker,* first met Dr. Du Bois as a boy in Richmond, Virginia. The association continued during the years of the Southern Negro Youth Congress

(1937–47) until Du Bois' move to Ghana. A leading Communist, he frequently lectures on Marxism and Afro-American history.

C. L. R. JAMES, born in Trinidad, is the author of *The Black Jacobins* and *A History of Negro Revolt.* He now lectures in the Department of Sociology, Federal City College, Washington, D.C.

DR. LEE LORCH now teaches in the Mathematics Department, York University, Toronto, Canada. He was actively involved in integration struggles in Nashville and at Central High School in Little Rock.

GEORGE B. MURPHY, JR., of the *Afro-American Newspaper* has been associated with civil rights and civil liberties for years. He is a contributing editor of *Freedomways.*

PAUL ROBESON is internationally acclaimed as concert artist, actor, and as a pioneering leader in the cause of World Peace and anticolonialism.

ELMA STUCKEY is active in civic affairs in Chicago and is the mother of the well-known Black educator Sterling Stuckey.

RICHARD G. HATCHER, mayor of Gary, Indiana, has emerged as one of the leading Black political leaders in the country.

SAUNDERS REDDING is an editor, author, and former book review editor for the *Afro-American* newspapers. Among his books are *To Make a Poet Black* and *On Being Negro in America.*

VINCENT HARDING is the director of the Institute of the Black World, founded in 1969 in Atlanta, Georgia. He was formerly head of the History Department at Spelman College, Atlanta.

ERNEST KAISER, a staff member of the Schomburg Collection of the New York Public Library and an associate editor of *Freedomways,* is one of ten writers contributing to *William Styron's Nat Turner: Ten Black Writers Respond,* edited by John Henrik Clarke.

EUGENE C. HOLMES, head of the Department of Philosophy, Howard University, was associated with Alain Locke for more than twenty years. He is presently completing a book on the life and works of Alain Locke.

CHARLES H. WESLEY, former president of Central State College, Wilberforce, Ohio, is the director of research and publications for the Association for the Study of Negro Life and History.

WILLIAM LEO HANSBERRY taught African and world history for more than thirty years at Howard University. One of the foremost scholars and researchers in African history, he died in November 1965.

MOZELL C. HILL, sociologist, former editor of *Phylon,* was at the time of his death in March 1969 professor of sociology at New York University.

RICHARD B. MOORE, proprietor of the Frederick Douglass Book Center in Harlem, is a pioneer fighter for both Afro-American studies and civil rights.

W. ALPHAEUS HUNTON, former professor at Howard University and late head of the National Council on African Affairs, was invited to Ghana in 1961 to assist Dr. Du Bois in compiling the *Encyclopaedia Africana.* He died in Zambia, East Africa, in February 1970.

TRUMAN NELSON, novelist and pamphleteer, is an active fighter for civil rights. Among his works are *The Sin of the Prophet* and *The Torture of Mothers.*

J. H. O'DELL is a staff consultant to the Southern Christian Leadership Conference and an associate editor of *Freedomways.*

ELINOR DESVERNEY SINNETTE, former district librarian for the New York Board of Education in central and East Harlem, has for the last four years been living in Nigeria with her family where she trains library personnel.

MARTIN LUTHER KING, JR., founder and first president of the Southern Christian Leadership Conference, is one of the best-known and most beloved civil rights activists of this century.

BERNARD FONLON, educator, former editor of the magazine *Abbia,* Cameroon Cultural Review, is a member of the government of the Federal Republic of Cameroon.